UN-AMERICAN WOMANHOOD

UN-AMERICAN WOMANHOOD

Antiradicalism, Antifeminism, and the First Red Scare

KIM E. NIELSEN

The Ohio State University Press
Columbus

Library of Congress Cataloging-in-Publication Data

Nielsen, Kim E.
    Un-American womanhood : antiradicalism, antifeminism,
and the first Red Scare / Kim E. Nielsen.
        p. cm.
Includes bibliographical references and index.
    ISBN 0-8142-0882-7 (cloth : alk. paper)—
    ISBN 0-8142-5080-7 (pbk. : alk. paper)
    1. Anti-feminism—United States—History—20th century.
2. Anti-communist movements—United States—History—20th century.
I. Title.
    HQ1420.N54   2001
    305.42′0973—dc21

                                        2001002345

Text and cover design by Dan O'Dair.
Type set in Adobe Caslon by BN Typographics West.
Printed by Thomson Shore, Inc.

9 8 7 6 5 4 3 2 1

*To Dagny Nielsen—who, I expect, might have
agreed with Margaret C. Robinson on a few things but
who, I know, would have been proud of me.*

*To Morgan and Maya, for providing pleasurable
diversion after diversion after diversion after
diversion after diversion.*

Contents

Acknowledgments

I did not get here on my own. I owe thanks to the University of Iowa for providing me with teaching and learning opportunities, as well as the Ada Louisa Ballard Dissertation-Year Fellowship. In addition I am thankful to the American Historical Association and for the financial assistance its members provided through the Albert J. Beveridge Research Grant. Librarians at the University of Iowa Main Library, the New York Public Library, the Schlesinger Library, the General Federation of Women's Clubs, the National Archives, the University of Chicago Main Library, the University of Oregon, and the Hoover Presidential Library provided needed assistance. The staff of the Interlibrary Loan Department at the University of Iowa Libraries made it possible to combine the time and financial realities of my life with research; they were always cheerful, diligent, and largely successful at finding widely divergent materials. The Interlibrary Loan Department at the University of Wisconsin–Green Bay assisted once I found myself in Green Bay.

My colleagues and friends have made this journey a joy. Rebecca Dale, Eric Fure-Slocum, Charles Hawley, Marjorie Levine-Clark, Kimberly Jensen (who first pointed me to the *Woman Patriot*), Francesca Morgan, Kathy Penningroth, Anthony Quiroz, Catherine Rymph, Ragna Urberg, and Paul Young provided friendship, encouragement, criticism, and listening ears at various points in the project. Eric and Paul have read more than their fair share of this manuscript in its various drafts and provided me with vigorous appraisals and friendship in the process. At the University of Wisconsin–Green Bay my colleagues in Social Change and Development provided a friendly, intellectual, and supportive atmosphere.

Commentators and audiences at meetings of the Organization of American Historians and the Social Science History Association, as well as anonymous reviewers from various journals, helped to point out weaknesses and forced me to clarify what I often didn't want to. Jane DeHart, Andrew Kersten, Elizabeth Faue, and Kathleen Kennedy helped at critical points, as did anonymous reviewers for Ohio State University Press.

I have learned much about mentoring, professionalism, and history from the faculty around me. Peter Rachleff taught me to love history and to combine it with a passion for the present. Jim Stewart kept me on my toes. While this project grew as a dissertation, Ken Cmiel and Shel Stromquist provided much-needed academic, research, and personal guidance at critical points in my graduate school experience. Colin Gordon offered crucial insight during the transformation from dissertation to book, and help with titles. Throughout everything Linda Kerber has been invigorating and caring, continuing to share with me her wisdom and energy about history, research, writing, and the profession. She has been a constant and dependable presence through crises—personal and professional—and the mundane. Only as I look at myself as a professor do I begin to comprehend the work she has invested in me. And only as I begin to look forward to my second book do I realize the naïveté with which I began my dissertation and the patience that naïveté must have demanded from her.

Iowa was a wonderful place for this project to grow. More than she will ever know, I am grateful to Doris Jacobs, who provided loving day care, leaving me time and energy for work and one less thing to worry about. The people of First Lutheran Church provided acceptance and child care whenever I was frantic. Ron and Kathie Nielsen sustained me with unconditional pride and love, and never asked that terrible question, "When will you be done?" Their joy in my progress and acceptance of my weaknesses have been constant. David and Florence Tuff provided child care during research trips, always conveyed support, and never questioned the life their son and I adopted. Most of all, I thank Nathan Tuff, who shared in my panics, successes, and failures; who continues to add friendship, intelligence, excitement, and fun to my life; and who insists we go out to eat to celebrate each and every minor success.

Rockford College, the League of Women Voters of the United States, the Manuscripts and Archives Division of the New York Public Library, and Williams College Archives and Special Collections gave permission to quote from archived materials.

Abbreviations

AAUW   American Association of University Women
BAF   Better America Federation
BI   Bureau of Information
DAR   Daughters of the American Revolution
GFWC   General Federation of Women's Clubs
IDA   Industrial Defense Association
ICW   International Council of Women
ISNS   Illinois State Normal School
IVA   Independent Voters Association
IWW   Industrial Workers of the World
LWV   League of Women Voters
MID   Military Intelligence Division
MPIL   Massachusetts Public Interests League
NAM   National Association of Manufacturers
NAOWS   National Association Opposed to Woman Suffrage
NCL   National Consumer's League
NCLC   National Child Labor Committee
NCMPTA   National Council of Mothers and Parent-Teacher Associations
NCPW   National Council for the Prevention of War
NCW   National Council of Women
NPC   National Patriotic Council
NPL   Nonpartisan League
NWP   National Woman's Party
NWTUL   National Women's Trade Union League
WILPF   Women's International League for Peace and Freedom
WJCC   Women's Joint Congressional Committee

Introduction

In 1926, Michigan resident Mrs. Schatz queried the Military Intelligence Division (MID) of the War Department, a precursor to the Federal Bureau of Investigation, about the loyalty and radicalism of a local branch of the Women's International League for Peace and Freedom. Regulations prohibited the MID from disclosing the results of its investigations, but Department officials recommended that Mrs. Schatz and others interested query women's organizations such as the Daughters of the American Revolution or the Massachusetts Public Interests League.[1] These women's organizations were only two of many that devoted themselves to Red Scare antifeminism, an ideology that embraced antiradicalism and antistatism as well as gender, sexual, and family conservatism. Gaining political experience in the antisuffrage movement, and mobilizing the energy and sentiment of the post–World War I Red Scare, these organizations and their members went on throughout the 1920s to fiercely oppose the female activists promoting the expansion of the federal welfare state and the legislation developed to accomplish this progressive state building.

Un-American Womanhood focuses upon antifeminism and its female adherents who flourished in the 1920s. These ideological conservatives feared that feminist influence upon the newly enfranchised woman citizen would cause her to support, in ways never possible before, dangerously radical state-expanding measures that they considered detrimental to patriarchy. In a domino-like theoretical framework of politics, antifeminists also argued that women's rights activists were politically radical because they opposed the patriarchal family, which antifeminists believed was the cornerstone of the liberal democratic state. If the patriarchal family was

I

weakened, they argued, the nation would be weakened as well. And if the weakening of the patriarchal family was due also to the expansion of the federal state, the nation would be brought even closer to collapse. Thus, antiradicalism and antistatism were integral to the rhetorical, organizational, and ideological strength of the antifeminism of the 1920s.

Antifeminists linked antiradicalism and antistatism to antifeminism further by arguing that the socialist abolition of private property subverted the proprietary and patriarchal relationship of men to wives and children. Like some on the left, Red Scare antifeminists believed that sexual and familial power arrangements had political implications. Unlike some on the left, however, they were unable to imagine or comprehend the feminist claim that women could be self-governing or individually autonomous; thus, they charged that the subversion of this proprietary relationship would make women physically and metaphorically the collective sexual property of the state. Antifeminists realized that men had been unable to uphold the patriarchal order consistently and thoroughly. Their antifeminism derided men for failing to protect and provide. Yet because of the political importance they ascribed to the patriarchal family and antistatism, they sought to maintain the proprietary right of men over women and children rather than turn it over to the state.

Antifeminists of this period also argued that men and women (with the usually unstated assumption that these were white men and women) had wholly different and gendered relationships to the state. Men were to be self-governing and family-governing citizens directly responsible to the state. Women and children were to be male governed, relating to the state only through the intermediary of the male family leader. The ideals of liberalism—that a person be self-governing, self-autonomous, self-determined—applied only to men because of their uniquely male relationship to the state. Antifeminists feared that an expansive social welfare state would remove men as the intermediaries of women's citizenship and leave women vulnerable to the state or to unscrupulous men. Then women, though unable to live up to the ideals of liberalism as a group, would attempt to do so and threaten the nation in the process.

The entanglement of antiradicalism and antifeminism is not unique to the post–World War I Red Scare or to the United States. Antiradicals have often linked a belief in patriarchal gender roles, fears of sexual chaos, and a derision for feminism. Attacks upon French revolutionaries and Mary Wollstonecraft intertwined charges of sexual, political, and gender chaos. In 1775, English commentators denigrated the political efforts of female American colonists by portraying those women as either aggressively sexual or mannishly ugly. Labor activists, anarchists, and sometimes temperance militants were susceptible to similar attacks. In examining the last half of the twentieth century in the United States, historians Amy Swerdlow and Kate Weigand argue that the relationship between demure femininity and patriotism protected women from accusations of radicalism during the height of the Cold War when they adhered to, or appeared to adhere to, such femininity. And as Elaine Tyler May argues, the containment of communism abroad and the containment of feminism at home were part of the same ideological and political trend.[2] As with these examples, the strength of antifeminism during the 1920s Red Scare appears directly related to the level of antiradicalism.

What makes this historical moment unique is the convergence of the post–World War I Red Scare and the rethinking of women's citizenship caused by the Nineteenth Amendment guaranteeing female suffrage. The vote women gained in 1920 changed women's relationship to the state in a profound way. Antifeminists feared that feminist—and thus, they believed, radical—ideas might cause female voters to support the expansion of the federal government. Progressive women, emboldened by the success of the Suffrage Amendment, had an ambitious vision of what they wanted to accomplish with their newly gained ballots. But antiradicals, conservatives, militarists, and business interests used Red Scare rhetoric and images to launch an organized and concentrated assault upon progressive women because they feared the possibly transformative—and according to antiradicals, potentially subversive—consequences of female suffrage. Although feminism was not defeated in the 1920s, attacks upon progressive women and progressive women's organizations narrowed its definition and limited its appeal. Red Scare antifeminism helps to explain the hesitation of many progressive women to become active figures, their reluctance to take on the feminist label, and the defeat of progressive legislation advocated by many women.[3]

During the Red Scare, in the aftermath of World War I and the Russian Revolution, American politics became conservative and reactionary, haunted by the specter of radicalism. Having defeated their enemies abroad, many U.S. citizens believed that the nation now faced the danger of domestic subversion. The Red radical replaced the German Hun as the primary enemy. Government and private bureaucratic tools designed for wartime were turned to peacetime repression. Strikes, bombings, race riots, and government raids on allegedly subversive organizations reportedly evidenced a radical threat. Reds, many contended, lurked around every corner. Defense of the home front required men and women to secure the country, just as male soldiers had done abroad.

The Red Scare—as this period of antiradicalism is called by historians— generally has been understood to be a political event in which gender played no relevant role.[4] Historians have interpreted the period as one in which the majority of U.S. citizens, exhausted by World War I or simply following cyclical patterns of extreme nativism or antiradicalism, perceived a false threat to the security of the United States and reacted in ways contrary to the ideals of democracy and freedom but came to their senses by mid-1920.[5] Political cycles alone, however, provide an unsatisfactory interpretation of the Red Scare. The tenacity and breadth with which anti-radicalism continued after the scare was assumed to be over suggest that something more was involved. In other words, the Red Scare's relation-ship to American conservatism, particularly antifeminism, warrants fur-ther examination.

Antifeminists embraced the Red Scare, and their political fervor helped to carry and sustain Red Scare antiradicalism throughout the 1920s. From this vantage point, the Red Scare did not end in 1920, as many historians have argued. Instead, it continued throughout the decade as politically conservative women attacked the work of progressives. Antifeminists limited the reshaping and effectiveness of women's political participa-tion in the postsuffrage decade. Red Scare antifeminism also contributed to the development of twentieth-century conservatism, strengthening its embrace of antistatism and imbuing antistatism with gendered overtones. In this analysis, the 1920s appear as a time when antifeminists laid the groundwork for today's conservative political concerns about gender, fam-ily, and centralized government, and when politically conservative and antifeminist women, though few, played a vital role in the development, funding, and staffing of the Red Scare's antiradical organizations.

The majority of the antifeminists of this study are women, many of whom began their political careers as antisuffragists. They defended the patriarchal order via a form of female citizenship that was forceful and pub-lic. Yet they saw no hypocrisy in their actions. Fears of gender disorder, sexual disorder, and political disorder, and a generally unacknowledged delight in politics, propelled them to public lives of activism. Antifeminist women eagerly and proficiently entered the political arena of the Red Scare.

The inclusion of women's politics in an analysis of the Red Scare is im-portant because of the vital role played by politically conservative women

in the political culture of the 1920s. Beginning as antisuffragists but transforming themselves into broad political activists, they used the anxieties
surrounding Bolshevism, expansion of the state, social welfare programs,
and women's peace efforts to foster a political culture hostile to progressive
female activists. Red Scare antifeminists provided organizational strength,
expanded networks, and cultural legitimacy to the larger conservative
movement. These activities helped to weaken the women's peace movement, defeat the social welfare legislation that progressive women endorsed,
and undermine the reconfiguration of the female citizen as an autonomous
political actor.

The inclusion of gender in an analysis of the Red Scare is important
not only because of the antiradicalism of antifeminist women. Gender
lay at the core of Red Scare understandings of healthy Americanism.
Those accused of radicalism were charged with gender roles corrosive to
the nation just as they were charged with political ideas corrosive to the
nation. Conversely, Red Scare enthusiasts praised male antiradical heroes
for living patriarchal gender roles that upheld national ideals and were
exalted by media, business, and private patriot organizations. During the
Red Scare, antiradicals used adherence to and support of the patriarchal
family as a measuring stick of patriotism.

The patriarchal family wishfully supported by Red Scare antifeminists
was one in which the male household head kindly, wisely, and firmly exercised legal, physical, economic, and cultural power over the other members
of his household. My use of the term *patriarchy* goes beyond the family
household to include all systems of male power, whether manifested in
tradition, law, economics, language, or elsewhere. However, as Red Scare
antifeminists knew, all of these systems of male power were grounded,
learned, and first exercised in (the ideology of) the patriarchal family.
These upper- and middle-class activists endorsed patriarchy and this
model of the patriarchal family. Part of the historical specificity, and one
of the ironies, of their endorsement is that it included broad claims about
an essentialized man and essentialized male power. At the same time, they
often balked at and sometimes vigorously resisted extending such power
to men of all races and classes. The patriarchal power they defended and
relied upon for the development of their political theory was limited to
men of specific racial and economic backgrounds.[6] It was a race- and class-
specific prescriptive ideology of gender and power.

Feminist challenges to patriarchy increased feminists' susceptibility to
accusations of radicalism. Energized by stories of gender chaos in the

Russian Revolution and among domestic radicals, antifeminists argued that feminism and radicalism were inseparable and continued to conflate the two throughout the decade. It is ironic but perhaps not unexpected that antifeminists conflated all variations of progressive female activism and erroneously assumed uniform beliefs among the women they opposed. Red Scare antifeminists called all progressive women feminists.[7] Such characterization was erroneous, for neither progressive women nor feminist women were of one mind, instead holding a wide array of disparate views about race, politics, the economy, gender roles, and social welfare legislation. Some targets of antifeminism—the leaders of the Children's Bureau and the Women's Joint Congressional Committee, for example— shunned the feminist label and lobbied against the equal rights feminism of the National Woman's Party.[8] A belief in government's potential to do good, and a consequent effort to harness that potential via legislation and government programs, united those attacked as feminists by Red Scare antifeminists. It is these women, some of whom identified themselves as part of the Progressive movement, as well as women who simply had a liberal social agenda, whom I refer to as progressives.

The antistatism of Red Scare antifeminism severely limited the ability of progressive women to promote social welfare legislation throughout the 1920s. Red Scare antifeminists, however, inconsistently applied antistatism and tended to apply it in a gendered fashion. For example, they opposed the expansion of federal social welfare programs and protective labor legislation, all endorsed by the largest women's organizations, but they did not harbor hostility toward issues not on the agendas of the large women's organizations, such as the growth of the military and domestic spy networks, public highways, or mail delivery. Red Scare antifeminists argued that the expansion of the federal government via female-sponsored social welfare programs was part of a larger effort to reconfigure society in a Bolshevist, socialist, bureaucratic, and feminist fashion. Such feminist radicalism, antifeminists argued, would be made worse by the many women who would inevitably staff such a government expansion.

Red Scare antifeminists further gendered antistatism by arguing that social welfare measures *feminized* liberalism by promoting a political culture characterized by *dependency*. Explicit in their arguments was the belief that the liberalism promoted by progressive women created feminist women, weak men, and a federal government that impinged upon male domains of power. Simultaneously, Red Scare antifeminists referred to antistatism as a masculinist political orientation. Antistatism, in the view of Red Scare antifeminists, was a political ideology that bolstered patriarchal masculinity. The subversive and feminized tinge that Red Scare antifeminists gave to the expansion of the federal government may have been part of the process by which contemporary conservatism claimed antistatism and antifeminism.

Red Scare antifeminism is only one element of a wide spectrum of disparate, but not unrelated, conservative and reactionary sentiments in the 1920s. While the popular image of the period may be one of joyful ragtime and bobbed hair, it also was a time of political, cultural, and social conservatism. The Ku Klux Klan of the 1920s vastly outnumbered the post–Civil War Klan. Eugenics and nativism converged in the 1920s, frequently directed against immigrants, people with disabilities, Jews, Catholics, Mexican Americans, and African Americans, as well as those considered morally deviant. Aided by growing urbanization, industrialization, and the presidencies of Herbert Hoover and Calvin Coolidge, corporate power grew quickly and in a largely unregulated fashion during the 1920s. Moral conservatism and anti-immigrant sentiment advanced the legal prohibition of alcohol.[9]

Though part of this conservative spectrum, Red Scare antifeminists kept their energies focused upon progressive and feminist women seeking to use the state to improve society and the lives of individuals. Though they shared some of the racial, eugenic, economic, and social beliefs of others in this spectrum, they targeted feminism. Feminism, they believed, threatened because it struck at the very core of the nation—patriarchy—and would result in the political radicalism opposed by others. And as women, Red Scare antifeminists believed they had a special responsibility to scrutinize and curtail what was being done in the name of womanhood. By the 1920s, the most publicly visible birth control advocates used increasingly conservative arguments on behalf of birth control instead of appeals for women's sexual freedom, and antifeminists paid birth control advocates little attention. Nor did the women of this study discuss Prohibition. Though they left little evidence as to why, my conjecture is that they considered the Prohibition activists, as they considered the Women of the Ku Klux Klan, a class—economically, politically, and socially—below them. Anti-Prohibition sentiments, which easily could have been considered a logical extension of their antistatism, may have been avoided for similar reasons. They considered it a social issue of concern to women of a lower class, rather than a political issue, and thus as not worthy of their consideration.

The omission of African American women and their organizations from the attacks of Red Scare antifeminists is striking. There are several likely reasons for this omission. First, owing to their own racism, the women's organizations accused by antifeminists of subversiveness had few black members. The Women's Joint Congressional Committee, at the core of a supposedly interlocking directorate of radical U.S. women, had no African American women's organizations as members. Those coalitions that did, like the National Council of Women, were segregated and offered little opportunity for leadership to black women. Second, while black women's organizations such as the National Association of Colored Women were active, vital organizations, racist blinders on the part of Red Scare antifeminist groups may have led them not to see African American women's organizations or to assume them incapable of addressing national issues. Third, Red Scare antifeminist groups kept themselves focused upon legislative and electoral politics. African American women were generally excluded from these formal structures of power.

Most important, the political involvement of black women's organizations was not the same as that of progressive white women's organizations in the years following the Nineteenth Amendment. White women could vote. Violence and discrimination frequently kept black women from the polls. Goals contrasted as well. While many white women sought to outlaw the violence of international war, many African American women sought to outlaw the violence of lynching in their own communities.[10] While many white women sought to prohibit child labor, many African American women sought subsistence for their own communities. African American women, like progressive white women, had a complex vision of social change that included personal, family, community, gender, and racial uplift. However, most black women and women's organizations were caught up in meeting the day-to-day demands of these issues, which required all their personal and political energies. Few had the political access to pursue the expansive and governmentally grounded social transformation envisioned by their white counterparts, who often excluded them and ignored their issues. Many, with substantial historical reason, distrusted the government to which many white women were turning. It is ironic, however, that antifeminists who feared the legislative potential of organized U.S. women ignored African American women, whose vision of social change, while centering on racial uplift, included a more radical transformation of U.S. culture and society than ever envisioned by progressive white women.[11]

Despite the omission of African American women and their organizations, as well as organized groups of other women of color, from accusations of subversion, race was an issue. Red Scare antifeminists argued that a healthy nation required adherence to social order and that in a liberal democratic state a patriarchal division of labor and male governance of individual families were essential to that social order. Sometimes unstated, sometimes explicit, was the belief that racial hierarchies were part of that social order. Also sometimes unstated, sometimes explicit, was the racialized belief that white households should be protected from federal incursion but that individual whites and the white-dominated federal government should be left free to intervene in the household governance of families of color. All three elements of Red Scare antifeminism—antifeminism, antiradicalism, and antistatism—integrated race into their analysis of the radical politics of gender.

Practitioners of women's history, as well as contemporary feminists, can learn from this story of antifeminism and the gendering of politics. We have paid little attention to the political contexts in which antifeminism has thrived and have thus limited our ability to respond effectively to contemporary antifeminism. In the 1920s, progressive women and their political interests suffered a vigorous assault while antifeminism flourished. Understanding how and why this happened, paying attention to the sophisticated use of organization and media by Red Scare antifeminists, recognizing that conservative women played a pivotal role in the development and promotion of antifeminism, and including the broad range of political issues on which progressive women were attacked strengthen the claim of historians of women that the study of gender transforms the study of history. And while unpacking the gendered content of contemporary politics is difficult, this can be made easier by asking historical questions about gender, the legislative process, and conservatism.

Moreover, to understand conservatism it is necessary to unmask the role gender has played in the development of conservatism and conservative politics. The gendering of conservatism—the ideological conflation of states' rights, patriarchy in both family and society, and a noninterventionist government—contributed to the defeat of the proposed Child Labor Amendment and other social welfare legislation. The conservative political environment of the 1920s was inherently shaped by gendered political ideas about male power both within and outside of families, the limited right of government to influence familial politics and other realms of male power, and the security of the nation. When the conservative antistatism of the 1920s is viewed through an analysis of gender, the era appears pivotal in setting patterns for twentieth-century conservative political concerns about gender, family, and centralized government.

Finally, the exploration of conservative and antifeminist women as active and thinking historical figures complements, complicates, and enriches our understanding of both women's history and conservatism. While the historiography is expanding, historians of women have been slow, sometimes reluctant, to acknowledge antifeminist women as political and historical actors. Historians of conservatism have been blind to the actions and influence of antifeminist women in the development of American conservatism. Both fields could benefit from further research on antifeminist women. The women of Red Scare antifeminism often had backgrounds similar to those of their political opponents, and these similarities raise questions about how political interests are formed and influenced.

We cannot understand the Red Scare, conservatism in the 1920s, the fate of progressive legislation ("political history" topics), antifeminism, antifeminist women, or the history of progressive women's organizations ("women's history" topics) without examining their relationship to each other. As many historians are beginning to show, the boundaries between the fields of women's history and political history are permeable and often arbitrary.[12] Though there are no easy answers, as we historians seek to define what history is, to synthesize and to teach effectively, we must continually remind ourselves that the boundaries between our fields are constructions that, when strictly adhered to, hinder our historical understandings. By telling this story, I have tried to redefine what is political by including gender as an integral element of analysis. I do not contend that gender is always the only or primary point for analysis, but I argue that gender was a primary component of Red Scare antiradicalism. Red Scare antifeminists understood radicalism to be an entangled web of economic, gender, sexual, and racial chaos, and they successfully imbued much of Red Scare sentiment with this belief. Scholars—arguing about the prioritization of class, race, or gender analyses—should not disregard the complicated worldviews of our historical subjects. The world, as the antiradicals of the post–World War I United States understood it, was a precarious place in which political security was ever dependent upon economic, gender, sexual, and racial order. Broadening the organizational, analytical, and ideological boundaries of the "political" can give a clearer sense of politics' scope, actors, audience, and consequences in the contentious landscape of the postwar, and post–Suffrage Amendment, decade.

CHAPTER I

Patriotic Heroism and the Red Scare of 1919–1920

Some thought the revolution had arrived in Seattle. In February 1919 more than 100,000 local laborers joined a citywide general strike, expressing sympathy for an additional 35,000 already striking shipyard workers seeking higher wages. As strike activist and journalist Anna Louise Strong described it: "Business men took out riot insurance and purchased guns. Citizens laid in supplies as for a long siege; kerosene lamps were dragged from storage. . . . Some of the wealthy families took trips to Portland to be out of the upheaval. The press appealed to strikers not to ruin their home city."[1] Gun sellers ran short; many families spent nights behind locked doors while women and teenagers were taught gun use. Newspapers and politicians around the country declared that the strike was a sign of the large-scale infiltration of Bolsheviks into the United States, attempting revolution first in Seattle. The *Chicago Tribune* cautioned, "it is only a middling step from Petrograd to Seattle."[2] Minnesota senator Knute Nelson warned that the Seattle strike posed a greater threat to the nation than had the war.[3]

Seattle's mayor Ole Hanson responded decisively against the strike. At his request, federal troops from nearby Camp Lewis spread throughout the city. Hanson warned the Strike Committee that unless they called off the strike by the next morning he would use the federal troops. Hanson reassured residents of the city, "The time has come for every person in Seattle to show his Americanism. Go about your daily duties without fear." Surrounded by troops, pressured by their international unions to halt the strike, and facing hostile public opinion, the local strike leaders issued orders for the general strike to cease.[4]

Mayor Ole Hanson received, and cultivated, credit for single-handedly halting the first Bolshevik incursion into the United States. In Seattle the newspapers proclaimed relief: "Today this Bolshevik-sired nightmare is at an end." In a wire to the *New York Times,* placed prominently on the front page, Hanson told the nation that "this was an attempted revolution which they expected to spread all over the United States. It never got to first base."[5] Almost instantly Hanson became a national hero. Sacks of telegrams flooded his office. Reporters followed him everywhere, waiting for "Oleisms"—colorful quotes from the enthusiastic and voluble mayor. Newspapers and magazines across the country described Hanson in terms that emphasized his patriotism and manliness. The *Washington Post* described him as "considerable of a man," who "stood firmly" and "set his face with unswerving determination." Others described him as a "red-blooded patriot" and as a man "with a backbone that would serve as a girder in a railroad bridge." The popular magazine *Current Opinion* described Hanson as a "two-fisted, square-jawed man" and echoed newspaper writers "in scores of cities" who named Hanson as a candidate "for any thing he wants." Pictures of the mayor featured him either as an ideal family man, with his wife and eight children, or as a hardworking American laborer, pitching in with his wrench wherever needed. The *Woman Patriot* offered Hanson's Seattle as an example of "government in the hands of real men."[6]

Asked to explain his decisive and highly publicized stand against radicalism, Hanson said, "A patient man will endure almost any oppression until you begin to interfere with his family affairs."[7] A Seattle paper explained Hanson's actions by running a front-page picture of Hanson, his wife, and their eight children labeled "Mayor Hanson and his nine reasons why he insisted that Seattle remain an American city."[8] According to Hanson, radicalism threatened the American family as well as the American nation; and when the American family was threatened, true American men responded.

This chapter begins with the traditional story of the Red Scare panic of 1919 and early 1920. Building on this traditional story, however, it also explores the masculine subtext of the postwar moment in which antiradicalism and the lingering urgency of wartime converged and the nation once again turned to and exalted male American heroes. Seattle mayor Ole Hanson, the returning servicemen of the American Legion, and the wistfully imagined laborers of the open shop movement embody three models of masculine heroism cultivated by Americans caught up in fears of domestic subversion. These male heroes reassured the nation of the vitality, strength, and faithfulness of its male citizenry. Building on

This photograph of Ole Hanson and his family appeared in the *Town Crier*, a weekly Seattle-based publication, on February 15, 1919. The caption reads: "Mayor Hanson and his nine reasons why he insisted that Seattle remain an American city." Courtesy Special Collections Division, University of Washington Libraries, negative no. UW18671.

wartime sentiment but excluding women and large numbers of American men (some of whom happened to be veterans), these heroes were a pleasant reminder in a time of crisis that American men were the victors of war. They illustrate the centrality of gender in Red Scare patriotism and how Red Scare patriotism's exclusionary nature limited prospects for women's citizenship.

THE STORY OF 1919–1920

On January 18, 1919, the Allied leaders of World War I met at Versailles to begin the negotiation of the treaty that would formally end what was the most devastating and deadly cross-continental military conflict up to that point in history. Though hopes rose for long-delayed reunions and the end of violence, Americans did not relax into their peace. As the Russian civil

war grew more violent, reports of widespread Bolshevik brutality reinforced the growing anti-Bolshevism, as did the seeming failure of the
short-term U.S. military intervention. Most of the Wilson administration
and much of the American public soon rejected the "onerous responsibility of saving Russia," but that did not result in a dismissal of Bolshevism
as harmless.[9] Congressional investigators, wartime domestic defense
groups, and federal intelligence agencies warned of Bolshevik incursions
into the heart of U.S. society. It was not yet safe for Americans to let down
their wartime guard.

For at least the next year or two, large numbers of Americans believed
their nation was in peril. They feared that government, schools, clubs,
cities, and families were threatened with an imminent Bolshevik takeover,
not by a large-scale military attack but by the more insidious brainwash-
ing and infiltration of institutions such as organized labor, political and
racial reform groups, religion, women's clubs, and the family. Civil liberties and other legalities were often thrown aside, and, as historian David
Bennett points out, for the first time in U.S. history, "federal and state government officials became the leaders of the [antiradical] movement, [and]
national and state policies the instruments of repression."[10] The Espionage
and Sedition Acts, measures designed for wartime security, were continued into the so-called peace.

Though the decisive heroism of Ole Hanson was reassuring, and
though the nation seemed to breathe a sigh of relief at the collapse of
Seattle's general strike, for many the strike accentuated the crisis posed
by domestic radicalism. As Red Scare historian Robert Murray concludes,
"For the first time, public attention was focused sharply and solely on the
issue of domestic radicalism to the virtual exclusion of all other factors."[11]
European incidents increased domestic foreboding. In February the
French Premier reportedly was wounded by a "Bolshevik agent." Communist governments came to power in Bavaria and Hungary in March; U.S.
newspapers also reported growing radicalism among the French and Ital-
ian populations. The formation of the Third International in March gave
added legitimacy to the warnings of increased communist activity.[12] The
Red Scare had begun.

Legislators responded. The day after the Seattle general strike began,
the Senate expanded the powers of the Overman committee to include the
investigation of Bolshevism and "all other forms of anti-American radicalism." Headed by Lee Overman of North Carolina, the committee easily
transformed its mission of wartime investigation of German propaganda

to peacetime anti-Bolshevism. Over the next month, it heard two dozen witnesses tell stories of the horrors of Russian Bolshevism. Mass murder, the abolition of private ownership, the nationalization of industries, and the establishment of "free love bureaus" filled the nation's headlines. Though the committee's 1,200-page final report contained little information on the actual extent of radicalism in the United States, its highly publicized hearings reinforced fears that foreign agitators and domestic radicals threatened the security of the nation.[13] The Overman committee served in staff, purpose, and sentiment as a forerunner of the more well-known New York State Lusk Investigation charged with inquiring into "the scope, tendencies, and ramifications of . . . seditious activities."[14] With the Justice Department, the Lusk committee raided suspected subversive organizations. The committee's four-volume final report warned that radicals had subverted the nation's press, educational system, reform organizations, and religious institutions. In great detail, U.S. citizens again heard that radicals posed immediate danger to the nation.[15]

As 1919 continued, accumulating evidence seemed to point to rising domestic radicalism. From April through June a series of bombs exploded across the United States, the first at the home of Ole Hanson. After the deaths of two women in a second bomb, the nighttime bombing of his own home, and the discovery of thirty-six additional bombs in the mail, Attorney General A. Mitchell Palmer declared the bombings "another attempt on the part of radical elements to rule the country."[16] When riots broke out between white and black residents of Washington, D.C., Chicago, and elsewhere, the New York Times blamed Bolshevik agitation: "[There is] no use shutting our eyes to facts. . . . Bolshevist agitation has been extended among the Negroes." When three major strikes—a police strike in Boston, a nationwide steel strike, and a nationwide coal strike—were blamed on Bolsheviks and captured national attention in the fall of 1919, in historian Murray's words, "The last remaining barrier to hysteria disappeared."[17]

Attorney General Palmer, convinced that the best solution to domestic radicalism was to arrest and/or deport all radicals, intensified the fray in January 1920. In twenty-three states across the country, Palmer raided the homes, businesses, and clubs of suspected radicals, taking more than 6,000 people into the custody of the Bureau of Investigation and Department of Justice, often without benefit of a warrant or legal counsel. Officials turned native-born citizens over to state officials for prosecution under syndicalist laws. "Big Bill" Haywood of the Industrial Workers of the World and Rose Pastor Stokes, a socialist and communist leader, were charged with criminal anarchy. Legal immigrants—including Emma Goldman and Alexander Berkman—charged during World War I were slated for deportation hearings.[18] Justifying the raids a month later, Palmer insisted that "the blaze of revolution was sweeping over every American institution of law and order." The raids, he claimed, had successfully "halted the advance of 'red radicalism' in the United States."[19]

Almost as quickly as it had begun, the frenzy of the Red Scare appeared to be over by the spring of 1920, when the riots and chaos of May Day, confidently predicted by Attorney General Palmer, failed to occur. The Red Scare, however, was not over but continued in an altered fashion. The scare's paradigms of good and evil and its positioning of powerful men and the patriarchal family as a bulwark against radicalism lingered to shape politics, legislation, and women's political experiences throughout the 1920s. The characterization of feminism as politically subversive would strengthen Red Scare sentiments.

The Heroes of 1919–1920

When Ole Hanson found himself basking in national praise as a heroic savior, he resigned as Seattle's mayor and did what any contemporary politician would do. He began a national speaking tour and wrote a book, *Americanism versus Bolshevism,* on the dangers of domestic radicalism. In seven months of speaking, Hanson netted over $38,000, a large jump from his mayoral salary of $7,500. In the summer of 1920 he sat on the platform at the Republican National Convention.[20] Hanson's gruff, impetuous, and friendly manner charmed the national press, which interpreted him as uniquely American. An oft-repeated story told of an audience Hanson had with President Wilson, in which Hanson brusquely asked, "Say, Wilson, mind if I take off my coat?" and then continued his discussion with the president in his shirtsleeves.[21] News and magazine articles repeatedly told of his rise to success. Ole Hanson was, his fame argued, what all immigrants could and should become.

Born in 1874 on a homestead in Wisconsin, the fifth child of Norwegian immigrants, Hanson had a limited formal education. After graduating from the eighth grade he received a teaching certificate, and at seventeen he started studying law. At twenty-one he married a Wisconsin woman, Nellie Rose. In 1902, after a train wreck severely injured Hanson's leg and killed one of his children, Hanson and his family set out for Seattle, with a wagon and horse team, in search of a cure for his leg. Though doctors told him he might be permanently paralyzed, he followed the example of his hero Theodore Roosevelt. As he later told a friend, "I had the feeling that if I could get out there in the open, with the prairie for a pillow and nothing but the sky above my head, I could beat the doctors and bring back my health." Upon arrival in Seattle he was "fit as a fiddle." Overlooking the city lights while camping on Beacon Hill the night of their arrival, as his version of his life went, he decided that he would one day become mayor. He bought a grocery store and then quickly moved into real estate.[22]

Hanson was elected to the state legislature in 1909, where he championed the eight-hour workday, female suffrage, an industrial insurance act, and the prohibition of horse racing. He supported Theodore Roosevelt in the 1912 election and, like Roosevelt, emphasized action, masculinity, and strength in his political life. In March 1918 Hanson was elected mayor. Much of Hanson's political philosophy and development can be learned from the names of some of his children: William Howard Taft, Theodore Roosevelt, Robert La Follette, Lloyd George, and Eugene Field. None of his daughters were graced by the names of contemporary figures, despite his support for female suffrage.[23]

In *Americanism versus Bolshevism* Hanson offered his version of the Seattle general strike, provided a history of Bolshevism, contrasted "Americanism" and "Bolshevism," and explained his antidote to domestic radicalism. Hanson believed that misdirected economic discontent caused innocent individuals to turn to "the Hell-inspired doctrines of Lenin and Trotsky." Radicalism thus could be averted by decent educational opportunities, patriotic employers who treated and paid their employees well, and fair consumer prices. Though the child of immigrants, Hanson believed immigrants potentially dangerous. He suggested limiting their numbers, spreading them equally throughout the nation, and requiring a vigorous background check and interview process for naturalization. Hanson thought that single men should not to be allowed to immigrate, for they were more likely to lean toward radicalism. Marriage and families stabilized married men; thus married men were more likely to become "real Americans."[24]

When Hanson compared Bolshevism and Americanism, gender and family were an integral part of his political analysis. Inherent in Hanson's patriotism was faithfulness to family and wife. A real American male cherished family and violated neither the trust of his wife nor that of his nation. "Americanism," he wrote, "is founded on family love and family life; Bolshevism is against family life." Going further, Hanson connected heterosexual, married monogamy to patriotic fervor: "Americanism stands for one wife and one country; Bolshevism stands for free love and no country." Americans, he proclaimed, were "strong" and "loyal." Bolshevists, on the other hand, "believe in destruction of nationalism, loyalty and patriotism. . . . Loving no country, they excuse themselves by saying they love all countries alike." Issuing what he apparently viewed as a decisive insult, Hanson wrote, "Polygamous men have ever used the same excuse."[25]

Though Hanson's single-issue politics and the lack of a political organization limited the further development of his political career, he was, for the year following the Seattle general strike, a nationally known figure widely praised for his decisive and exemplary actions. Hanson cultivated, and the media embraced, the image of a gruff, loyal patriot who blended loyalty to family and wife with loyalty to nation, and leadership of family with leadership of nation. He embodied, his supporters argued, the type of man needed by the United States in its time of Red Scare crisis.[26] However, though the decisive heroism of Ole Hanson was reassuring, and though much of the nation breathed a sigh of relief at the collapse of Seattle's general strike, for many the strike accentuated the crisis posed by domestic radicalism. More heroes were needed.

The heroes of the Red Scare also included, in a slightly different fashion, the men of the American Legion. Returning World War I servicemen, including Theodore Roosevelt, Jr., formed the American Legion in 1919. With the same vigor they had shown in battle, members opposed the pardoning of conscientious objectors and sought to eliminate the presence of all those they thought radical. They used the authority given them by wartime service and sacrifice to claim the mantle of Red Scare heroism, attempting to prevent or reverse what historian Eric Leed calls the postwar "demotion from 'heroes' to eminently superfluous men used up by an industrialized war."[27] Those who attended the first convention in 1919 resolved that all local American Legion posts "be urged to organize immediately for the purpose of meeting the insidious propaganda of Bolshevism, I.W.W.-ism, radicalism and all other anti-Americanisms."[28]

The American Legion's primary adversaries were the National Nonpartisan League, a populist farmers' organization centered in the Great Plains states, and the Industrial Workers of the World (IWW, or Wobblies), a radical workers' organization. Members of both organizations had questioned the wartime financial gain of industrialists and had opposed military enlistment. Adding to its crimes, from the perspective of the American Legion, the IWW had figured prominently in the Seattle general strike. Legion posts actively attempted to bar the two organizations from their neighborhoods and frequently used violence and threats of violence to do so. Though legal threats forced the Legion's national headquarters to express disapproval of such violence, no local posts were ever punished.[29]

The IWW and the American Legion battled most fiercely in the Pacific Northwest, and the lawlessness and violence of these conflicts are exemplified by the 1919 death of five men in Centralia, Washington. When the local American Legion post and that of nearby Chehalis passed the local IWW hall while parading in celebration of the November Armistice, local tensions were high, for the Wobblies were successfully organizing local loggers. Gunfire erupted, the origin of which is still debated, and soon four Legionnaires were dead and many more wounded. Armed vigilantes rounded up IWW members. Local police detained twenty-two men in cells designed to hold less than ten. That evening the city's lights went out, and when a mob marched to the jail, it entered without resistance. The mob kidnapped and then lynched IWW member—and World War I veteran—Wesley Everest. The story quickly spread that he was castrated— perhaps a symbolic assertion of American manliness over the weakness of radicalism.[30]

Local American Legion members quickly telegrammed news of the Legionnaires' deaths in Centralia to the national convention of the American Legion, then taking place in Minneapolis. Convening the morning session, the chair of the convention introduced Legion member and Washington state attorney general Mr. Thompson, who warned the men that he was to tell them of "an outrage that is almost beyond comprehension." The news stunned Legion members. They blamed radicalism, the insidiousness of the IWW, and general un-Americanism for the deaths of the four Legion members. Within a day the Centralia post received over a thousand telegrams of support. Many posts pledged money to counter the IWW defense fund.[31]

American Legion members and their supporters positioned the Legion in direct contrast with un-American radicals. One Legionnaire wrote, "The American Legion is all that the I.W.W., the Anarchist, the Communist, the Bolshevist is not."[32] Papers across the country wrote that the Legion was "an inspiration and reassurance to every patriot," performing "a great service . . . at a time when widespread danger lurks in the country." Reporters indicated that the Legion's first convention included no tentative "pussyfooting" but instead exuded a "spirit of pure Americanism and law and order." The *Portland Telegram* lauded the Legion and included a cartoon showing the Legion playing the manly and American game of baseball while in military uniform, using 100 percent Americanism to bat Bolshevism (or "ball-shevism") out of the United States.[33]

Members of the American Legion generally conflated all radicals—whether Bolsheviks, communists, socialists, or IWW and Nonpartisan League members—into one subversive menace. The radical was "opposed to all of the institutions of civilization," vile, weak, and dishonorable. He betrayed the United States. He also was, as Legion cartoons showed, a dirty unshaven man who deserved hanging.[34]

This hero of the American Legion used his bat of "100 per cent Americanism" to hit "ball-shevism" out of the U.S.A. The cartoon appeared first in the *Portland Telegram* and was then reproduced in *Literary Digest*, the seventh largest circulating periodical of 1920.

U.S. women and many U.S. men were ineligible for the heroism of the American Legion and the masculine patriotism its members sought to attain. It was a heroism and patriotism dependent upon male strength, military service, and the forging experience of battle and frequently excluded men based upon their race, ethnicity, or politics. The American

Suggestion No. 100,002 for Stimulating Attendance at Local Post Meetings: Hang a few of these birds.

The *American Legion Weekly* represented the "alien slacker" and the "bolshevist" as worthy of being hanged, October 24, 1919. "Canned Willie" refers to a food that soldiers ate frequently.

Legion's vision of male patriotism and antiradicalism lacked the linkage between family and national loyalty that Ole Hanson had articulated. The inspiration and company of other men, rather than the family of nine that inspired Hanson, fostered American Legion heroism. Both forms of heroism, however, placed the masculinity of strong American men at the center of the solution to the Red Scare and, by their emphatic masculinity, emphasized the exclusion of women from Red Scare patriotism.

An alternative Red Scare hero was the honest, sincere, and antiunion laborer wistfully imagined by manufacturing organizations seeking to limit the rise of unionism. In the immediate postwar years the United States witnessed a level of labor unrest never seen before or since. In 1919 over four million workers participated in strikes and lockouts, an estimated one in five industrial workers.[35] The National Association of Manufacturers (NAM) responded by launching an open-shop offensive called the "American Plan," which accused labor activists of un-Americanism. NAM was anything but subtle: "Unionism is nothing less than Bolshevism." Samuel Gompers of the American Federation of Labor tried to "rescue" the labor movement by purging it of radicals, but in the words of historian Alan Dawley, "It was not the minuscule power of Communists that employers were trying to curb, but the growing power of organized workers."[36] To resist that growing power, manufacturers promoted a Red Scare hero—a laboring man who acted out his patriotic masculinity by resisting the lure of labor unions and their radical backers, used physical strength when necessary, and took the wisdom and material needs of his family or girl into consideration when pondering union activities. He was personally independent but always loyal, and his loyalty to the female object of his affections, his family, his nation, and his employer went hand in hand with his development as a man. For example, the Reo Motor Company of Lansing, Michigan, used its in-house employee magazine, the *Reo Spirit*, to portray a man, in the analysis of historian Lisa Fine, "loyal to company and country," who "demonstrated his masculinity by his service to his two families—his public family, the company, and his private family, the wife and children he supported at home." According to the company, Bolsheviks and Bolshevik sympathizers failed in the masculine task of breadwinning, failed to cooperate with their employers, and were willing to forsake the women in their families. Truly patriotic, masculine, and American laborers, the company insisted, would never act in such a manner, and it asked workers to report any un-American activities.[37]

The *Open Shop Review*,[38] published by the National Founders' Association and the National Metal Trades Association for its members to give to employees, used fiction to explicitly link loyalty to family, employer, and nation with masculinity and antiradicalism. In the magazine, unionism and socialism were synonymous: both were treasonous and led to the dissolution of the family. In "How the Union Slugger Broke Up the Family," unionism destroys the happy Laboski family, led by Jacob Laboski, who was "big, gentle, and could look any man in the eye." While crossing a picket line, desiring only to feed his family, Mr. Laboski is beaten to death. Within months, Mrs. Laboski dies of exhaustion and the six children are separated. Such were the lessons of unionism.[39]

In another story, "Ma Becomes a Socialist," the wise women of the neighborhood take the lessons of socialism supposedly literally and show misguided men the folly of their ways. Wise "Ma," exhausted from eking out sustenance for her family during repeated and often unnecessary strikes, takes the abolition of private property to heart by transforming the elder son's silk shirt into a dress for her daughter and taking the car without notifying her husband. (Note the presumption that laboring families had silk shirts and cars.) The women of the block strike, refusing to cook or clean, as their daughters cooperate by calling a "sympathetic strike" until one man agrees to mend the chicken fence for his wife. When the foolish men of the household argue, "But, Ma, that's not fair to the rest of us. Why should we have to suffer for Sam Tyler's meanness?" Ma proves to them the absurdity of sympathy strikes and socialism. Thereafter, the laboring men of the neighborhood meet, calling off their own strike that has caused their families so much deprivation, and advise that "the rights of the public, as well as their own rights, should be considered." And, of course, socialism never again succeeds in that town—the lesson being that good men neither strike nor adopt socialism because they would harm their families by doing so.[40]

Finally, in a serialized story that ran for three months in the *Open Shop Review*, a young industrial hero named John made the strongest argument for a family-centered, antiunion, masculine patriotism. In "I Wanted to Know," the young machine hand falls in love with the company nurse, Frances Payne. Fellow laborers, who have foreign names and look at Frances lasciviously, are ungrateful for the company's kind treatment of them. They hand out pamphlets and give soapbox speeches on socialism. The young hero turns to his employer, kind and fatherly Mr. Whitney, for advice. Whitney rightly assumes that there's "a woman back of all this," but after giving young John a lengthy lecture on the workings of capitalism, asks that John ponder the lecture and make up his own mind. So he may be better educated, John and Frances attend a socialist meeting (their first date). There John finds a pamphlet about radical marriages, the torrid nature of which is left to the reader's imagination: "an insult to all womankind. And when I thought of such principles in the same breath with Miss Payne, and my mother and sister, I can tell you I commenced to get sore." After the speaker insults U.S. soldiers and the U.S. flag, John is enraged. He grabs the speaker but is hit from behind and falls unconscious.[41]

When John awakes he finds that a socialist revolution has taken place. People were killed and homes burned as individuals fought over the distribution of property. No one is working and nothing is being produced. Running to Frances's house, he finds her imprisoned in the arms of one of his fellow laborers, a foreign man, who had expressed interest in socialism and in Frances. Again John is beaten unconscious. When he awakes for the second time he discovers that the previous events were only a dream. Instead, the police broke into the socialist meeting, and he has spent ten days in the hospital (which was kindly paid for by his employer). As John disavows socialism, Frances kisses him on the lips.

The wise and patriotic men of these stories and others like them are family oriented, decidedly heterosexual, loyal to their employers, anti-union, and adamantly against all forms of radicalism. In a patriarchal fashion they value the women around them and work for women's material advancement. Manufacturers exalted such loyalty to nation, employer, and family and would have benefited if all their laborers had behaved in such a fashion. Resistance was common, however, and many workers rejected the notion that union activities signified unmanly and unpatriotic behavior. Despite or perhaps because of such resistance, the goal manufacturers had for these stories was to model appropriate and patriotic behavior for working-class men.

The three Red Scare heroes discussed here—Ole Hanson, the men of the American Legion, and the ideal laborer of manufacturing organizations—were all valorized as male patriots. The heroes of the American Legion differed from Ole Hanson and the ideal manufacturing laborer because of the absence of an emphasis upon family in their reworking of male patriotism; their patriotism and masculinity, however, had been forged on the exclusively male battlefield. For Ole Hanson and the mythical worker, patriotism and masculinity were learned and acted out through benevolent but strong faithfulness to wife and children. The widespread postwar Red Scare praise of male heroes underscored the notion that the nation needed patriarchal power—properly exercised both publicly and privately—to withstand domestic subversion and to sustain a healthy nation.

The story of 1919 and 1920, in which the remaining tensions of wartime and postwar antiradicalism converged, conveys the urgency with which Americans once again turned to male heroes to strengthen and protect the nation. Americans were accustomed to male heroism with patriotic, politicized, and frequently racialized overtones. Male "tamers" of the West, such as Daniel Boone or George Custer, were valorized as heroes motivated by national loyalty. Their heroism applauded westward expansion and the destruction of American Indian cultures. For many white Americans, heroism and the maintenance of white male supremacy went hand in hand as they cheered white boxer Jim Jeffries in his losing round against African American world heavyweight champion Jack Johnson in 1910. Wartime also had produced a series of local and national heroes whose patriotism was an essential part of their heroism. Their heroism glorified the rightness of the Allies in World War I.[42] With the war over, wartime opportunities for heroism and excitement no longer existed; with the Red Scare crisis facing domestic America, however, new opportunities for male heroism emerged. It is not surprising that as many citizens thought themselves facing a national crisis once more, they sought male heroes to redeem the nation.

It is important to consider the Red Scare discussions of masculinity in their postwar context for several reasons. World War I propaganda had promised that the experience of war would "effect 'Americanization'" and that the experience of war would create masculine and patriotic Americans out of all men. While the war did provide an opportunity for some non-upper-class men to become national heroes, opportunities were not democratic. Troops were frequently racially and ethnically segregated; non-English-speaking and African American troops were assigned menial tasks or hard labor. Many native-born whites used the results of Army intelligence tests, which revealed high illiteracy rates, to reinforce denigrating stereotypes of new immigrant groups and African Americans. The outbreak of racism and nativism that accompanied the Red Scare may have expressed the frustration many Anglo-Americans felt over the inclusion of black and immigrant men in the wartime process of manly development. Grounded in wartime experiences and larger U.S. culture, the patriotism of heroic Red Scare masculinity was not an honorable characteristic that all men could claim, for wartime "slackers," radicals, unassimilated immigrant men, and men of color were ineligible. The Red Scare presented a postwar opportunity for those already uneasy about a loyal citizenry to prove patriotic manliness—and thus good citizenship—in a way that excluded, even more than World War I, large numbers of American men.[43]

Second, as historian Kathleen Kennedy has shown, the political repression of wartime also had gendered aspects. The trials of antiwar activists such as Rose Pastor Stokes and Kate Richards O'Hare included charges that they threatened patriotic motherhood with gender and sexual subversion and that because of their lack of patriotism they would produce sons of weak political and moral character. This use of gender disorder as a key trope to explain the dangerous nature of Bolshevism was repeated during the Red Scare.[44]

Finally, it is important to consider the Red Scare discussions of masculinity in the postwar context because the adulation of male heroes also was part of a postwar reassertion of male power. As historians attuned to gender have shown, central to the social and physical reconstruction of postwar Europe was an assertion of essentialist gender roles. Returning soldiers often directed their anger about cultural and economic changes or the destruction of war against female targets. Women and their wartime service were denigrated; social commentators emphasized differences between men and women, arguing that separate spheres for men and women were both natural and essential for national well-being. Feminist movements in both Britain and France, for example, suffered because of postwar assertions of essentialized gender roles.[45] Like the other combatant nations of World War I, the postwar United States experienced a period of gender reconstruction. But in the United States, unlike postwar European countries, discussions of gender's role in postwar national well-being became intense only when Red Scare hysteria took hold. When U.S. citizens, fresh from praising the male heroism of U.S. soldiers, perceived themselves to be threatened by the domestic crisis of radicalism and in need of national salvation, they emphasized distinctions between men and women by again praising the patriotism of male heroes.

With the war over, wartime opportunities for heroism and excitement no longer existed; with the Red Scare crisis facing domestic America, however, new opportunities for male heroism emerged. A select portion of U.S. men could now claim or regain wartime importance. Seattle mayor Ole Hanson, the men of the American Legion, and the wistfully imagined laborers of the open shop movement embody the patriotism exalted by Americans caught up in fears of domestic subversion and illustrate the types of men who were eligible for that patriotism. Their success as heroes depended upon a combination of antiradicalism, physical strength, male leadership, and loyalty to family, wife, and nation, as well as their white, native-born status.

It is ironic that although family played such a vital role in the cultivation of male Red Scare heroes, few women were proposed as heroines. Though many women worked in war industries, managed farms, did hospital work in military service, and altered their homemaking practices in support of the war, the war did not provide women the opportunities for patriotic expression that were available to men. During wartime, gender roles blurred somewhat as women moved into jobs previously held only by men, but the fact remained that U.S. men could serve as heroic soldiers and women could not. This distinction between men's and women's capacities for patriotic heroism carried through to the Red Scare. The attractive Frances and the wily "Ma" serve as heroines, but their heroism is in the motivation of men. Through their actions, and sometimes through their attractiveness, they teach, manipulate, and provide *reasons* for men to exercise patriotic masculinity. Rarely do the women of these stories exercise heroism themselves. Throughout discussions of the Red Scare crisis, women are most visible in the articulation of what Bolshevism was, illustrating how it would victimize innocents and providing the reasons why truly masculine men, men loyal to nation, women, and family, should resist radicalism.[46]

CHAPTER 2

Bolshevik in
the Shape of a Woman

Gender and American
Antiradicalism

"Dreamed last night I was to be hanged on a charge of 'Red' activities," chronicled Alice Stone Blackwell in a diary entry of April 1920. Blackwell was a gentle but spirited woman of sixty-three years in 1920, a seasoned political activist of wide-ranging interests and a revered pioneer in the suffrage movement, who only four months later would see the successful passage of the Nineteenth Amendment. Yet she awoke one morning with the lingering memories of a dream in which she was to be hanged as a Red. Why?[1]

To many Americans, the true nightmare was Russian Bolshevism, for reportedly it went beyond politics and economics to gender and sexual disorder. During the post–World War I Red Scare, in congressional testimony and newspaper reports on the Russian Revolution, legislators and their constituents heard, and many became convinced, that integral to Bolshevism were unnatural gender roles, immoral sexual values, victimized feminine women, and power-hungry masculine women. While many Americans praised male heroes for reinforcing the nation against Bolshevism, they worried that women remained a weak point where foreign radicals could infiltrate. Many Americans saw proof of Bolshevized gender disorder in the proliferation of female "parlor Bolsheviks," in the alarming radicalism of professors at women's colleges, and in the female activism in possibly radical political groups such as the National Nonpartisan League. Antiradicals charged that nontraditional gender roles were "proof" of un-American politics. Simultaneously, the passage of the Nineteenth Amendment guaranteeing female suffrage signified a rethinking of civic gender roles. The convergence of Red Scare antiradicalism with the postsuffrage reshaping of the civic female created a political and cultural environment in which Alice Stone Blackwell could have a nightmare in which charges of radicalism led to her hanging.

The Red Scare fears of 1919 and 1920 laid the groundwork for a Red Scare antifeminism that went on to damage the progressive women's movement and carry the Red Scare through the 1920s. During the Red Scare, antisuffragists tried but failed to link radicalism with suffrage. Of greater consequence, the attempt to link radicalism and feminism succeeded. The renewal of attempts to link these movements in 1923 and 1924, and the adaptability, effectiveness, and vehemence of these arguments when applied to progressive U.S. women, are testimony to the power and versatility of gender and antiradicalism as weapons of U.S. politics.

WOMEN AND BOLSHEVISM

After the Russian Revolution of 1917 and the Bolshevik rise to power in 1919, the U.S. press and government investigated the new state to which the United States was so opposed. Initially few people in the United States understood Russian Bolshevism, although most agreed that it was an unhealthy form of governing made worse by the abolition of private property. In September 1919, President Wilson warned that Bolshevism was "government by terror, government by force, not government by vote. It is the negation of everything that is American."[2] The final report of the Senate's Overman committee read, "The activities of the Bolsheviki constitute a complete repudiation of modern civilization." The *World Outlook* called it the same as "Czarism . . . the opposite of Democracy." A pamphlet of the American Defense Society called Bolshevism "a direct appeal to Greed and Lust through Ignorance and Brute Force. Show me a Bolshevist and I will show you a potential robber and free-lover."[3]

The ways in which the new Russian government and its leaders mistreated and encouraged the mistreatment of women and children were highly publicized in press and government investigations as the most serious examples of Bolshevik political and moral depravity. The source of these abuses, it was commonly argued, was the abolition of private property. As each man lost exclusive rights to his property to the Bolshevik government, so did he lose exclusive claim to his woman and children. That left women and children without male protection, and like dominoes, all the bulwarks of social order subsequently were falling. The new Bolshevik government, investigators argued, nationalized the bodies of innocent women just like other industries and resources, for the good of the Bolshevik state and the lust of the Bolshevik male. Easy divorce laws encouraged promiscuity and female prostitution. Red Guards forced refined and delicate women to do the harsh physical labor ordinarily reserved for men. They tore children from their mothers and placed them under the control of the state. They raped as routine official policy. Utah's senator William King asked one witness before the Overman committee, "Do the Red Guards rape, ravish and despoil women at will?" "They certainly do," the man replied.[4]

The most sensationalized and often repeated story of Russian Bolshevism concerned the nationalization of women—the mandatory registration of all unmarried women eighteen and over at a government "Bureau of Free Love" where men came to choose wives and where women were forced into sexual and marital relationships. When the Overman committee began its hearings on Bolshevism in February 1919, these stories became front-page news. Questioned by senators, witnesses shared lurid stories of the Bolshevik victimization of women and of the valiant but ineffective efforts of moral women to resist. Robert E. Simmons, a Department of Commerce trade commissioner who had worked in Russia, and the U.S. ambassador to Russia David R. Francis both testified that nationalization policies were spreading throughout Russia. The *New York Times* interviewed a refugee from Moscow who warned that some local soviets had gone further than nationalization and had begun conscription of women for "immoral purposes"—brothels. A Russian noblewoman used the *New York Times Magazine* to appeal to U.S. women to help defend "everything that is sacred to a woman's heart . . . honor, family, home," claiming that Bolsheviks murdered many of the nationalized women once men were finished with them.[5]

Though the nationalization stories were new, the charge that radicals promoted sexual arrangements antithetical to the patriarchal family and marriage was not new. A long line of domestic radicals had critiqued society by questioning sexual conventions, insisting that women be free to make their own sexual decisions. As recently as the 1910s, female activists based in Greenwich Village had insisted that opponents of political and economic oppression target sexual oppression as well. Anarchist Emma Goldman argued that women's sexual freedom could come only when capitalism and monogamy were overthrown. Both before and after World War I, antiradicals used the advocacy of women's sexual freedom by some on the left to charge that leftists advocated the degradation of women.

In 1915, for example, conservative Benjamin Hubbard charged that social-ism, feminism, and suffragism were "terrible triplets" whose goal was to "revolutionize society, to destroy the home, break up the unity of the fam-ily, bring discord where harmony now prevails and annihilate the church."[6] Hubbard was not alone in his views, and when nationalization stories appeared, they weren't a far stretch from what already circulated.

[margin annotation: destroy the family]

Americans widely believed the stories of the nationalization of women. In June 1919, Ole Hanson referred to "the common use of women" as a widely known extension of the abolition of private property. The *New York Times* issued two editorials on the subject, concluding with roundabout logic that while evidence to support the stories was meager, more disproof was required, for "the nationalization of women is just about what the Bolsheviki would be expected seriously to attempt."[7] American journalist Louise Bryant appeared before the Overman committee to deny the nationalization stories after returning from Russia with her husband, John Reed. Bryant insisted that the nationalization decrees came from a small anarchist club rather than a regional or national soviet. Enduring two days of hostile grilling, she emphasized that strong female leadership in Russia would not have allowed such decrees: "I never have been in a country where women were as free as they are in Russia and where they are treated not as females but as human beings."[8] Bryant sought to use the feminism of Russian women to deny the stories of nationalization. For much of the U.S. public and Congress, however, Russian feminism and the sexual dis-order they assumed to accompany feminism only reinforced stories of nationalization.

The involvement of Bolshevik women in leadership and lawmaking dis-turbed many Americans. After the Revolution, Russian women had equal political rights and guaranteed equal access to civil service jobs, teaching positions, and the legal profession. Women had equal rights to hold land, had full membership in rural communes, and could act as heads of house-holds. Civil registration of marriage, which replaced ecclesiastical regis-tration and may have been the source of free love bureau rumors, was designed to give equal authority to men and women and remove divorce restrictions. Bolshevik feminists such as Aleksandra Kollontai participated actively and visibly in the Revolution and pursued the implementation of feminist ideas.[9]

The U.S. press described female Bolshevik bureaucrats, from Kollontai on down, as unnatural and unfeminine. For example, the *Ladies Home Journal* characterized the women of the Bolshevik government as young and short-haired, with "a cynical sense of power" that "strikes at the root of fine womanhood."[10] The active participation of women in the Red Army shocked many Americans and was used, by those who saw female military service as antithetical to proper womanhood and social order, as further proof of the unhealthy and unnatural gender roles adopted by Bolsheviks. In October 1918, the Associated Press issued a story entitled "Women Cruelest of Red Terrorists," which told of "short-haired, leather-jacketed women" devoid of "all the better instincts expected of their sex." Women Bolsheviks, the story concluded, were "harsher" than men, cruel to children, and callously indifferent to death.[11]

By the beginning of 1920, there were two popular U.S. images of Russian women. Female Bolsheviks were thought to be feminists who used government to promote sexual libertinism and to take women and children away from men—manly, unattractive women, possibly lesbian, who chose power and cruelty over kindness and femininity. Russian women who rejected Bolshevism were feared to be the victims of brutal and indiscriminate attacks—feminine women who were forced to do hard physical labor and who were the likely victims of sexual assault. Public discussions of Bolshevism linked it with feminism, the sexual assault of women, and gender inversion—the denial of women's "natural" gentleness, respectability, and political reticence.[12]

While considerable confusion existed in the United States over what constituted Russian Bolshevism, even greater confusion existed over domestic Bolshevism. By late 1919, as historian Robert Murray claims, all questionable isms "were lumped together as being the same. . . . There was no endeavor to separate liberals from radicals, progressives from revolutionists, or legitimate reformers from irresponsible crackpots. . . . Even those who advocated the mildest reforms were dumped into the 'Red' classification."[13] Yet most Americans felt confident that they could identify "Reds." *The Lying Lure of Bolshevism,* a pamphlet of the American Defense Society, claimed that "when Socialist and Bolshevik travel together and sleep in the same bed, we are justified in calling them all by the universal name, Bolsheviki."[14] One author blamed the female leaders of the settlement movement for spreading Bolshevism. Other authors placed A. Philip Randolph and anyone affiliated with the African American newspaper the *Messenger* in lists of domestic Bolsheviks. Another argued that New York Jewish immigrants promoted Bolshevism. Going further, one journalist blamed Bolshevism on all immigrants. Bolshevism, a writer in the *Forum* claimed, "is an excrescence of the political melting pot—the social refuse, or slag, that will not fuse—the impure or foreign substance in our population that would otherwise Americanize."[15] Theodore Roosevelt wrote that American Bolshevists ranged from "the Germanized Socialists, the leaders of the Non-Partisan League, the professional pacifists and so-called internationalists, to the I.W.W. and anarchists and bomb-throwers and dynamiters and 'direct action' men generally."[16] Finally, in a phrase that best portrays the versatility of accusations of radicalism, one journalist simply called Bolshevism "a state of mind—a most unhealthy state of mind."[17]

Despite these vague understandings of the ideology and constituency of domestic Bolshevism, public discussions repeatedly expressed fears that women were a primary target of radical propaganda owing to their natural and political weaknesses. Women purportedly lacked the knowledge and skills necessary to repudiate radicalism. This susceptibility manifested itself in the growing visibility of radicals in women's colleges, in women's large representation among the "parlor" Bolsheviki, and in women's activism in suspect political groups.

A discomfort with the consequences of large-scale women's education may have combined with Red Scare fears to initiate an attack on women's colleges. In 1920, the percentage of women in college enrollments peaked at 47.3 percent; educators, many women, and much of the general public lacked certainty about what a college education was to mean in women's lives. The Massachusetts Public Interests League, an antisuffrage organization led by Margaret C. Robinson, launched an investigation to discover whether Bolsheviks had gained a "foothold" in "girls colleges." Because these women would become the nation's teachers, Robinson argued, it was "a crime" to teach them "the doctrines which have made Russia a shambles." She insisted that parents had a right to know if "these immature girls are to be drilled in the doctrines of Lenine and Trotzky [*sic*]." In February 1920, the *Iowa Magazine* followed with a lengthy article reporting that women's colleges had been infiltrated by socialists desiring to indoctrinate young women. While the circulation of the *Iowa Magazine* was small, the article was to be of great consequence.[18] That this was a concern of such a small magazine illustrates the widespread cultural concern about women's political maturity.

In June 1921, then vice-president Calvin Coolidge wrote a three-part essay series in the *Delineator*, a sewing and literary magazine that was one of the five largest women's magazines of the time. In this series Coolidge issued a thinly veiled warning against educational trends in women's colleges and linked them to radicalism. His first article, "Are the Reds Stalking Our College Women?" used the *Iowa Magazine* article as its main source. Coolidge warned that women's colleges "are the object of adroit attacks by radical propagandists." He cautioned women away from radicalism, arguing that it meant "the ultimate breaking down of the old sturdy virtues of manhood and womanhood . . . the destruction of the foundations of civilization." In subsequent issues Coolidge went on to tell women of their special role in championing patriotism and dispelling radicalism. He argued that because women created the nation's homes, and because "to make a home is to be a capitalist," those who advocated socialism would certainly be defeated by "the mothers of the land." After Coolidge's articles, the Daughters of the American Revolution voiced similar concerns about women's education and its connection to radicalism.[19]

The growing presence of American women in the ranks of those called "parlor Bolsheviks" also upset many Americans. It signified that intelligent, native-born white women of middle- or upper-class backgrounds, many who had come from women's colleges, might support radicals with their money and invite radicals into their parlors to speak. The U.S. press derided parlor Bolsheviks as stupidly misguided Americans who had nothing better to do with their time than waste it supporting radicals—"after-tea philosophers whose social secretaries do most of their thinking for them," people "who like to think of themselves as bold 'intellectuals' in their efforts to stir up forces they in no wise comprehend."[20] The parlor Bolsheviks were accused of being the weak followers of the ideological fad of the moment and were disdainfully called "pinks" because they supposedly lacked the courage to become full "Reds."

Despite the parlor Bolsheviks' supposed reluctance to do anything other than talk, many considered them a threat. *Current Opinion* called them "as great a menace as the I.W.W. type" because of their ability "to drive home the pernicious propaganda of Bolshevism in circles where the I.W.W. type cannot enter." A federal court judge told the Harvard Liberal Club the same: the "prating pseudo patriots" were more dangerous than "real Reds" because of their access to new groups of people.[21] Parlor Bolshevik men supposedly were weak and had been pacifists or draft evaders during World War I. Theodore Roosevelt derided the masculinity of these men and warned that the "dilettante sentimentalism" of "the parlor or pink-tea or sissy Bolshevism dear to the hearts of so many of our people who like to think of themselves as intellectuals" would encourage immigrants to become Bolsheviks.[22]

Women constituted the majority of those called parlor Bolsheviks, but this made parlor Bolsheviks no less threatening. Women's money could support the cause, their respectability could shelter the cause, their political inexperience could blind them, and their naive sincerity could be compelling. In the words of one woman, "As amateur spreaders women are even more dangerous than men; for, whether more skilful or not, they are infinitely more daring."[23] In a cartoon in the *Saturday Evening Post* (the most widely circulated U.S. periodical in 1920), the American Pink is represented by a woman cheerfully waving the Bolshevik Reds in to help widen the crack in the Liberty Bell and weaken American institutions.[24]

Many ridiculed the intelligence and mental stability of middle- and upper-class women sympathetic to radicalism. Such women, the argument went, had to be motivated by personal defects, for an interest in radical politics could never be the result of an educated, well-reasoned political decision. Attorney General A. Mitchell Palmer called them "hysterical neurasthenic women."[25] One writer in the *New York Times* argued that

In this *Saturday Evening Post* cartoon of June 24, 1922, the female "American Pink" is among those waving "Reds" in to help widen the crack in the Liberty Bell. The caption reads, "Keep an eye on those inside, too."

parlor Bolsheviks were spoiled rich women who supported radicals in pathetic attempts to gain publicity. He told of one woman who complained to him at a dinner party that she couldn't get herself arrested and that, despite the loveliness of her thumbs, could not get them fingerprinted. She complained to him, he wrote, of her many preparations done in vain. "I had an expensive gown specially made to be arrested in. I had another for my trial. I had a hat especially for the newspaper photographers, another for the movie man. I had seven interviews prepared, all made by my poets, musicians, and special writers."[26] John Spargo, who had left the U.S. Socialist Party at the beginning of World War I and reconfigured himself as an expert on radicalism in the 1920s, similarly refused to acknowledge political knowledge or decision making on the part of women interested in radicalism. Spargo claimed that all such women were "victims of nervous derangements, emotional excess, unfruitful marriage, and religious mania" and suffered from variations of "hysterical hyperesthesia." Some were "rich, idle women who have nothing else to do." Others were "unemotional, creatures of pure intellect," whose "sexual life has either been arrested or is abnormal. . . . They have been thwarted in love and remain unmarried, their normal desires having starved, or if married they are sterile." Others were "disappointed idealists," dissatisfied by settlement-house work.[27] Spargo's language echoed earlier arguments against women's participation in higher education.

Parlor Bolsheviks were not working-class radicals. They would pose no general strike, they were unlikely to initiate violence or the wholesale abolition of their private property, and their numbers were small. However, the animosity toward those called parlor Bolsheviks, particularly women, was fierce and continued, combined with other antiradical sentiments, throughout the 1920s. Parlor Bolsheviks were purported class traitors who, if eager to disregard and endanger the orderliness of class relations, could be expected to disregard and endanger other systems of social order. And reportedly parlor Bolsheviks were women who refused to accept happily their "natural" femininity. Women's presence among the feared horde of domestic Bolsheviks aggravated the hysteria of the Red Scare and accentuated the role of gender in U.S. antiradicalism.

Un-American Gender Roles, Un-American Politics

To those who believed in the strength and immediacy of the threat of radicalism, the identification of domestic radicals was imperative if the

United States was to purge itself of danger. Gender roles became a litmus test. Since Bolsheviks promoted unhealthy gender roles, the argument went, all those who lived or encouraged such gender roles must be radicals. Un-American gender roles and un-American politics went hand in hand. The successful red-baiting of the National Nonpartisan League (NPL) as well as the less successful red-baiting of American suffragists illustrate this point well. Opponents of these organizations used the conviction that radicals lived perverted gender roles to discredit political movements and discourage women's political involvement.

The NPL, a populist farmers' organization primarily in the northern Great Plains states, sought to influence state legislation through the election of representatives committed to NPL objectives. The NPL platform emphasized state-run programs designed to guarantee farm families greater economic influence: a state-owned bank with rural credit opportunities, state ownership of grain mills and elevators, a regulated grain-grading system, and state-funded crop and farm insurance. When the NPL's membership peaked at over 208,800 people in thirteen states in 1919, it controlled the North Dakota state government and was well entrenched in Minnesota.[28]

The NPL had faced fierce opposition since its inception in 1915. This intensified when the Red Scare began, and the NPL and its public ownership programs were condemned nationwide as socialist, Bolshevist, and dangerous. Several NPL leaders were socialists, including Arthur and Marian LeSueur, and this gave credibility to the attacks. The Minnesota Public Safety Commission, a wartime agency with broad police and regulatory powers, included the NPL in its investigation of "agitators of disloyalty." The arrest of well-known socialist speaker and pacifist Kate Richards O'Hare while she was staying with prominent Minnesota NPL members, and the arrest of NPL president A. C. Townley on charges of encouraging draft evasion, gave credibility to the attacks. This was, in the words of NPL historian Robert Morlan, "a made-to-order method for 'smearing' the Nonpartisan League, and the opposition was not slow to utilize it."[29]

Opponents of the NPL insisted upon the organization's disloyalty and radicalism, warning that the fight went beyond politics. It was a fight between good and evil, "between civilization and Christianity on the one hand, and Socialism and atheism, masquerading under the guise of a 'farmer's program,' on the other."[30] The NPL was "Socialism disguised as a farmer's movement . . . in close sympathy with un-Americanism, with

I.W.W.ism and with Bolshevism."[31] Minnesota representative Clarence Miller testified in Congress that the NPL was disloyal to the United States and had German sympathies: "All pro-German elements within the state are either in the Non-Partisan League or affiliated with it."[32] *American Industries,* the journal of the National Association of Manufacturers, called the NPL "the most radical and revolutionary farmers' movement ever organized in America" and claimed that it had ties to the IWW.[33] A pamphlet for farmers warned that the NPL was "the latest scheme of the astute Socialist politicians . . . the most radical and most bitterly class-partisan agrarian movement in our history."[34] Fred Marvin, a journalist from Colorado who figures prominently in later chapters of this study, claimed to have proof of "the close relationship" between "the Socialists, Communists, I.W.W. and Nonpartisan League . . . and all other radical organizations of this country."[35]

Integral to the attacks upon the NPL, at the core of their success and viciousness, was gender. Opponents accused the NPL not only of political subversiveness but of destroying marriage, family, public education, and Christianity. In the context of Russian Bolshevism and its reported gender upheaval, these accusations and the evidence of unconventional gender roles among NPL members gave weight to charges of radicalism. The *Red Flame,* a vehemently anti-NPL periodical, equated the NPL with socialism and argued that "socialism strikes at home, at marriage and at family life." It charged that the NPL would abolish marriage, pass laws forcing women to comply with any man's sexual demands (drawing upon the stories of Russian free love bureaus), and institute state control of children (drawing upon the stories of the Russian nationalization of children).[36]

A *Red Flame* story, "When the Revolution Came to North Dakota," portrayed the lives of Jim Thorpe and "his little, blue-eyed, flaxen-haired wife," whose name was never given. Supposedly a "logical application of Bolshevist chronology in Russia," the story exemplified what would happen if the NPL took over in North Dakota. One evening Jim arrived and found:

> The living room was in a wreck; tables and chairs were overturned and splintered; curtains and hangings had been torn down, and in a corner, still feebly struggling in the grasp of a villainous Tartar in the uniform of the Red Army, was "Muvver" [Mother], while a wide-eyed, frantic Jimmy Junior alternately clung to her skirts or beat with unavailing little fists against the boots of her captor. In the middle of the room, looking on with a gratified grin, were two other soldiers of the Red Army.

When Jim protested, "You leave my woman alone," the obviously foreign
soldiers ridiculed him and said, "She so mooch our woman as yours." The
message was clear that this was the NPL future of North Dakota—women
would be raped and traded as nationalized state property, and real men
would be defenseless to stop it. Feminine virtue would be destroyed and
masculine strength usurped. Political radicalism would bring familial and
sexual upheaval to the United States, just as it had in Russia.[37]

The Independent Voters Association of North Dakota (IVA) also
attempted to discredit the NPL and tie it to Russian Bolshevism by claiming that NPL measures would leave women vulnerable to the sexual whims
of any male. The IVA distributed a "free love bill" as though it were an NPL
legislative proposal. Women frantically contacted Gov. Frazier to discover
if they really were compelled legally to submit sexually to any returning
soldier who approached them. The Nonpartisan Women's Club protested
that "in some localities women actually believed that it was not safe to go

scared women from going out into public.

A supposed result of Nonpartisan League electoral success in North Dakota. *Red
Flame,* February 1920.

to town."[38] The believability of these rumors is testimony to the widespread belief that sexual and gender upheaval were an integral part of radicalism. A cartoon from the *Red Flame* emphasized the message that women would be sexually vulnerable if the NPL got its way—burly men attack seemingly helpless women while George Washington looks on disapprovingly.

NPL members, it was claimed, not only practiced free love but would teach it in the schools once the NPL took over public education. In the schools, another *Red Flame* cartoon showed, provocatively dressed young women would teach free love rather than history. Much was made of literature in North Dakota's traveling libraries advocating "atheism, free love, anarchy, and contempt for government." Authors of these works included Upton Sinclair, Ellen Key, Trotsky, and Charles Beard.[39] The *Red Flame* reported that higher education in North Dakota had already been infiltrated, for the state university taught free love and the "glorification of

A representation of what would happen if the Nonpartisan League directed public schools. *Red Flame*, January 1920.

indiscriminate prostitution." Even more extreme, it reported that "Our country, tis of thee; Sweet land of love made free" was the new opening stanza sung at the university.[40]

The false rumors of the nationalization of women within the NPL, and the strong conflicts between the NPL and IVA, had implications for organizing the newly enfranchised women. While the national League of Women Voters (LWV) attempted to organize in Montana, the leader of the Butte LWV organization declared that women and children would be nationalized if the NPL candidates won. Local women sympathetic to the NPL then left the LWV. When LWV organizers went to North Dakota in 1922, they found IVA and NPL women still unwilling to work together on any political project.[41] Alice Stone Blackwell, the famed suffragist whose dream of being hanged began this chapter, was one of few to point out the link between the rumors of the NPL's endorsement of women's nationalization and stories of the Bolshevik nationalization of women. Both, she wrote in the *Woman Citizen*, were "new forms of political camouflage . . . being invented for the special purpose of deceiving women."[42] Both tried to damage progressive political movements and women's involvement in them by arguing that radicals lived debauched gender roles.

Female NPL members responded vehemently to charges against the NPL and themselves, for it was claimed that they threatened the nation's welfare. NPL women reasserted their patriotism by emphasizing the physical labor they did for their country and the sacrifice of sending their sons to war. Women used their religious beliefs to explain and justify their NPL action. Finally, and most emphatically, NPL women denied the allegations that they advocated or practiced sexual promiscuity. The North Dakota Auxiliary tried to ease the anxieties of women by reminding them that even Susan B. Anthony had been accused of free love.[43]

Anti-NPL propaganda also derided NPL men. It accused them of being disloyal to their country by discouraging military enlistment and advocating pacifism. The NPL men of one county found their farm cooperative painted an insulting yellow, an accusation of unmanly weakness.[44] Anti-NPL literature hinted that NPL men could not enforce the sexual fidelity of "their women." If NPL men were real and patriotic American men, the inference went, the NPL would not advocate free love.

The gendered red-baiting of the NPL occurred during the same period as the gendered red-baiting of suffragists. In tactics and arguments similar to those of NPL opponents, antisuffragist organizations such as the

National Association Opposed to Woman Suffrage (NAOWS) contended
that those who endorsed suffrage also endorsed Bolshevism, radical feminism, and the consequential weakening of the nation state. NAOWS,
founded in 1911 at the height of antisuffrage activity, had begun to move
further right in 1917. By 1918 the passage of the Nineteenth Amendment
granting female suffrage appeared nearly inevitable, and many antisuffragists had dropped out of the movement. Remaining NAOWS members,
like other Red Scare believers, maintained that radical subversives inside
the United States were numerous and powerful. In April 1918, members
renamed the organization's biweekly journal, originally entitled *Woman's
Protest,* the *Woman Patriot* to signify the organization's desired place in
the politics and culture of the Red Scare. After the Suffrage Amendment
passed, NAOWS members voted to rename their organization the Woman
Patriots.[45]

Antisuffragists had long argued that a civilized democracy (namely, the
United States) and civilized peoples (respectable, white U.S. citizens)
required order. The security of the nation depended upon the faithfulness
of men and women, black and white, immigrant and citizen, to their
ordained places in their families and in the larger social order. Female
suffrage threatened to upset necessary systems of hierarchical order by
forcing women into the civic sphere of the electorate.

Building upon the Red Scare, the NAOWS added another layer and a
sense of crisis to its argument that suffrage endangered the nation. Writers for the new *Woman Patriot* insisted that female suffrage, feminism, and
radicalism were integral and entwined parts of a single subversive menace.
Because of this, the defense of home and nation required during the Red
Scare merged into one effort requiring battle against all of radicalism's
fronts: female suffrage, feminism, Bolshevism, and socialism (pacifism, the
IWW, the NPL, the LWV, and the National Woman's Party also were
thrown in as the situation required). Though the journal rarely called all
suffragists disloyal, it continuously made the reverse argument: "Practically
every person indicted for a disloyal or treasonable attitude toward the
United States since the beginning of the war is an advocate of votes for
women!"[46] Domestic radicals, the argument went, endorsed female
suffrage because their women, disreputable and brazen, would vote while
respectable women stayed at home. Domestic suffrage would enable radicals to win in the electoral process, and thus radicals would take over the
nation. The NPL of North Dakota served as proof. According to the
Woman Patriot, female suffrage there had brought the state to a point

where it was "now cultivating its own Bolsheviki."[47] Domestic radicals and the feminists among them, the argument also went, endorsed female suffrage because it would weaken the individual and structural patriarchy necessary for a healthy nation.

The *Woman Patriot* insisted that the ideal female patriot was one who centered her life on her family. Making her home a "sweeter, happier and better place for her family" was "the highest patriotic service" she could offer. Though not glamorous, this work was "none the less important."[48] Separate male and female spheres, writers for the *Woman Patriot* argued, were necessary and were based on natural sexual differences: "Men and women were created and ordained to fill different stations." Women were to be subordinate members of families led by strong and able men. This division of power was in "the best interests of the family and state," for male leadership in both the family and the nation was "divine and democratic."[49] The feminist disavowal of this ideal served as proof of feminists' subversiveness.

Such an ideal, however, did not exclude women's activism. For example, Woman Patriots encouraged New York antisuffrage women to "take up the political responsibilities that have been forced upon you" and vote against socialists and suffragists. Throughout the 1920s, the *Woman Patriot* encouraged political participation by women they considered patriotic in order to counter radical women and their polluting influence on women's politics and organizations.[50] Women's citizenship was vital, but different from male citizenship. Individual liberty and self-government lay at the base of male citizenship. Female citizenship was secondary and dependent upon male liberty. Female citizens were to question male liberty only when it went awry, posing dangers that had managed to slip past responsible male leadership. Though the *Woman Patriot* emphasized the womanly responsibilities of the home and family sphere, it allowed that female activism was right and patriotic in times of national need.

Writers for the *Woman Patriot* feared that suffrage would enable weak, unmanly men, men incapable of patriotic heroism and military service, to flourish. One article proclaimed that it was the male "slacker and the coward" who advocated suffrage in hopes that "women will vote for peace-at-any-price, so that he may not be obliged to fight for his country."[51] The journal ridiculed "the Feminist Husband" who allowed his wife to be economically independent but then, out of cowardice, claimed to be the sole economic supporter of his family in an effort to avoid military service.[52] Even men who opposed suffrage would be doomed to emasculation if

suffrage succeeded, the journal proclaimed; for if female suffrage succeeded, so would socialism. Women would be nationalized, unruly men
would have unfettered sexual access to them, and respectable manhood
(previously bolstered by the exclusive sexual ownership of one woman)
would be destroyed. Again, combining all evils into one, the *Woman
Patriot* explained that "no nation can adopt Woman Suffrage, Feminism
and Socialism without reaching the ultimate goal of radicalism—the so-
called 'socialization' of womanhood and the degeneration of manhood."[53]

Writers for the *Woman Patriot* argued that with American men weakened by radicalism and suffrage, the supremacy of white, native-born men
and the delicacy of southern white women would be threatened. Racial
upheaval would accompany the gender and political disorder of radicalism.
Suffrage advocates supposedly included "the sworn, implacable enemies of
the South" who desired "that the White Woman of the South shall be subordinated to the black woman of the South." (Note capitalization.) Journal writers predicted that black women would outnumber and outvote
southern white women. One writer warned that as a result of female
suffrage, white women would be subordinate to their black maids and
cooks and that disgruntled Northerners intent upon finishing "the program for reconstruction projected by intemperate fanatics at the close of
the civil war" would be triumphant.[54]

When racial violence broke out in Chicago and other parts of the country in 1919, *Woman Patriot* writers denied the existence of legitimate racial
tensions and, in a contradictory fashion, blamed radicalism and female
suffrage for inciting previously contented African Americans to violence.
"I.W.W. and Bolshevist agents," the paper insisted, were "capitalizing
[upon] the bewildered and embittered Negro residents . . . to carry their
point."[55] Female suffragists were blamed for racial tensions because they
used the language of social equality adopted by African Americans.[56]

The *Woman Patriot* also drew upon its own version of Native American
history to bolster the argument for a racialized and gendered patriotism
that excluded female suffrage. Feminism, one article began, was the
antithesis of civilization. Native American women had exercised feminist
"squaw rights," the argument went; thus they (and not European immigrants) were at fault for the destruction of their culture. "Feminism among
the American Indian," which the journal described as "hard labor and civil
responsibility imposed upon the Indian woman," caused physical damage
to women. As a direct result, the Native American woman "FAILED TO
REPRODUCE HER RACE, and the Indian LOST A CONTINENT

by imposing on women the SQUAW RIGHTS that modern feminists demand!"[57] If suffrage was unnaturally forced upon U.S. women, the journal concluded in an echo of the eugenics movement, the United States would meet the same tragic end. Responsible women voters would fail to reproduce because of their civic involvements, and irresponsible women would breed numerous inferior children. The United States would weaken, radicals would take over, and feminists would be at fault. For these antisuffragists, white supremacy—and the gender roles they thought properly accompanied it—were an essential part of the battle against radicalism.[58]

These arguments against suffrage failed to enter mainstream Red Scare hysteria. By 1919, most people did not believe that female suffrage was part of Bolshevism or dangerous to politics, social order, or family. Suffragists had argued successfully that suffrage would serve as a stabilizing, perhaps even conservative, force. As the suffrage movement increasingly used what historian Aileen Kraditor calls the "expediency argument," the argument that voting women would improve and strengthen society, it identified more closely with the class, ethnic, and racial prejudices of the white middle class. The moderate nature of female suffrage, believed by some and used as strategy by others, rendered the antisuffrage claims of suffrage's subversiveness ineffective.[59]

Antisuffragists' arguments against feminism, however, saturated the Red Scare. While antisuffragists failed to prevent passage of the Nineteenth Amendment, they succeeded in discrediting feminism with the help of testimony before the Overman committee, reports from Russia, and widespread gendered red-baiting against organizations such as the NPL. Antisuffragists won the battle of definition. They succeeded at defining feminism as antifamily, antimale, sexually suspect, sometimes racially deviant, and politically subversive. The transformed arguments of antisuffragists went on to disrupt progressive women's politics and limit the re-formation of women's citizenship and political activism throughout the entire postsuffrage decade.

The disconnection of feminism from female suffrage cannot be blamed on antisuffragists alone. The suffragists themselves—a disparate collection of men and women drawn together only by their interest in suffrage—distinguished female suffrage from feminism as a political strategy to preserve unity and to make suffrage palatable. Many progressive women who avoided the feminist label throughout the 1920s continued making this distinction in an effort to distinguish themselves from members of the National Woman's Party and its endorsement of the Equal Rights

Amendment. The labeling of all progressive women as feminists must have been infuriating to them. The reluctance of suffragists to acknowledge the feminist implications of female suffrage may have helped the suffrage cause, and the disavowal of the term *feminism* by many progressive women in the 1920s advanced protective labor legislation for working-class women. But the willingness of many suffrage and progressive women to abandon the term *feminism* allowed antisuffragists to more easily manipulate its meaning, imbuing it with subversive connotations. And because the term was applied to progressive women nonetheless, their reluctance to fight for it helped to discredit their own political causes.

As part of the Red Scare manipulation of the term *feminism,* antiradicals worked hard to infuse feminism with sexually suspect overtones. Lurid accounts from Russia, stories about parlor Bolsheviks, and attacks on the NPL and other radical organizations frequently contained accusations of sexual perversion. Although the connection between suspect politics and suspect sexualities was not new, during the post–World War I Red Scare the linkage between suspect politics and suspect sexualities was particularly strong. Why was this so? Why was the potential combination of radical politics and radical sexuality so explosive?

For many caught up in the Red Scare, an inherent part of political radicalism was the infusion of sex—explicit and "unhealthy" sex—into the civic realm. The separation of sex from the civic, antiradicals argued, was part of what made the United States strong. As the glorifying of Ole Hanson and other Red Scare heroes shows, the containment of sex within monogamous heterosexuality was used to reassure the nation of its strength.[60] Sexuality may have been prominent in music, dating practices, and advertising during the 1920s, but it was not thought part of the civic world. During the Red Scare, antiradicals feared that subversives were bringing explicit sex into the civic arena. Bolsheviks supposedly did so in Russia by nationalizing women, and antiradicals feared that radicals were about to do so in the United States.

The lack of concern among antiradicals about birth control supports this contention. Though antiradicals were seemingly obsessed about sex, birth control was not an issue for them. By the time of the Red Scare, Margaret Sanger and other birth control activists had dropped class analysis and appeals for women's sexual freedom from birth control arguments. Instead, they argued for birth control on the basis of protecting maternal and child welfare, limiting family size, and controlling the nation's ethnic

birth control

populations. The post-1916 omission of sex from birth control arguments helped to guarantee that antiradicals paid it little attention.[61]

Antiradicals, particularly antisuffragists, considered a sexualized civic world a consequence of feminism. Yet the sexualized civic world they envisioned was not proposed by feminists—indeed, it is antithetical to feminism and is a further illustration of the antiradical distortion of feminism. Antiradicals assumed that as sex became part of the civic realm, as radical politics became radical sexualities, women would become more and more sexually vulnerable. Women's bodies, eligible for nationalization just as other physical resources were, would become the property of all men via the state. Antiradicals feared that in a sexualized civic world, decisions about women's bodies would be made, not by women themselves, but by a lecherous radical state. Red Scare antifeminists voiced fears that women would lose male support and protection, and in doing so they illustrated not only their deep distrust of radicalism but also their deep distrust of men.

This obsession with a sexualized civic world was certainly related to concrete changes in sexual and gender mores that began even before the war. Divorce rates were increasing while marriage rates were falling, there was wider acceptance of premarital sex, courtship patterns were reflecting decreased parental control, and there was greater knowledge of birth control. Miscegenation, prostitution, and "white slavery" legislation continued in public discussion. Gay and lesbian subcultures emerged in urban areas. Legislators, police, social workers, and reformers devoted immense energy to female adolescent sexuality. Women's increased education and wage employment were forcing family changes as well as bringing women into public places that respectable women had not previously frequented. Sexuality and women's bodies *were* increasingly visible in the civic world. The Red Scare added fears of radicalism to a changing social situation that for many was already threatening.[62]

Neither the Red Scare's sense of crisis nor its connection of feminism and radicalism ended in 1920. The rhetoric, imagery, urgency, and fears of the Red Scare firmly grounded themselves in U.S. political culture. During the 1919–22 strike wave, antiradicals found their primary opponents among organized labor, which sought to use strength garnered during wartime to transform industrial systems to better benefit laborers. Public authorities used wartime regulatory agencies, criminal syndicalism laws, and local and federal "red squads" to squelch the wave of strikes. By the

— woman were going to new places.

mid-1920s, however, according to historian David Montgomery, "The designs of corporate management had clearly prevailed over those of its rivals."[63] Repression, unemployment, and economic depression caused many workers to avoid radical labor organizations and strike activities. With the threat of insurgency among organized labor seemingly put to rest, the Red Scare antifeminism that first emerged in 1919 renewed itself in 1923 and 1924 as part of an effort to limit the scope of women's political activities and visions throughout the 1920s. Antiradicals believed they had doused the fires of radicalism among organized labor and began to look for red flames elsewhere. They shifted their concerns from working-class men to middle-class progressive women.

There are two primary, though not completely distinct, reasons for the resurgence and reuse of Red Scare antifeminism between 1923 and 1924. Many conservatives, manufacturers, and antiradicals were apprehensive about the still unknown consequences of female suffrage. Antiradicals feared the active female participation in and support of the Progressive Party of Robert La Follette and its potentially radical platform.[64] Republicans in Congress and manufacturers feared women's support for governmental regulation of business, labor relations, and the economy. Business interests, antiradicals, and antiregulatory politicians used and encouraged the identification of progressive women's politics with radicalism to discredit further progressive women's political activism.[65] The revival of a military preparedness movement in 1923 and 1924, alongside a growing, broad-based, and effective peace movement and women's visible peace activism, also contributed to the rise of Red Scare antifeminism. Women's effectiveness and visibility in the demobilization campaign threatened military goals. In these years the movement to outlaw war gained legitimacy. With the assistance of Washington lobbyist Dorothy Detzer, the Women's International League for Peace and Freedom (WILPF) became an influential organization with legislative clout. Women reluctant to join the WILPF joined Carrie Chapman Catt, who took up the peace cause in the winter of 1923–24. Forced to accept cuts in its appropriations and staff from 1920 to 1923, and reluctant to anger the president or Congress with criticism, the War Department attacked the women's peace movement as subversive and un-American. Civilian organizations such as the American Legion and the American Defense Society assisted the War Department in its campaign against the electoral agenda of progressive women.[66]

The pragmatic strategies of military and industrial interests combined with genuine Red Scare antifeminism to sustain the Red Scare. Embedded in the highly sexualized charges of gender and political subversion made in 1919 and 1920, the Red Scare continued throughout the postwar decade in a transformed fashion. This political environment encouraged the growth of right-wing women's organizations, helped to defeat legislation endorsed by progressive women and women's organizations, and made possible viable and widespread attacks upon progressive women and women's organizations.

Women becoming more radical
destroyed family.
— birth control —
— broke barrier b/n public
+ private sphere. seen more
often now. —

CHAPTER 3

Women Attacking Women

Gender and Subversion
among Women

In April 1923, the *Springfield Union* praised the Massachusetts Public
Interests League as "one of the few women's organizations in the country
whose objects are to defend the Constitution and oppose paternalistic,
bureaucratic and socialistic legislation." How encouraging it was, the newspaper claimed, when so many women were "misled," to find a woman's
organization "displaying a different attitude . . . and endeavoring, so far as
they are able, to hold State and national legislators to a safe and sane
course."[1]

The Massachusetts Public Interests League (MPIL) was one of a network of politically conservative women's organizations whose embrace of
Red Scare antifeminism helped to carry the Red Scare into the 1920s.
Claiming the protection of the Constitution, the family, and the nation as
their foremost goal, this network of political organizations with roots in
the antisuffrage movement played a vital role in the development, funding,
and staffing of antiradicalism. Though these organizations were not the
first to equate feminism with political radicalism, or to link the well-being
of the patriarchal family to that of the nation, their political ideology is
significant because they articulated it at a time when antiradicalism was
particularly potent. The women of this network promoted an antistatist,
antifeminist political vision, grounded in the gendered antiradicalism of
the post–World War I Red Scare, concerning a wide array of political
issues. After failing to prevent passage of the Suffrage Amendment, these
women helped to create a postwar political culture hostile to the largely
female remnants of the Progressive Era and helped to launch the twentieth-
century conservative movement.

These women also are noteworthy because they used the Red Scare to articulate and model a seemingly contradictory form of female citizenship at a pivotal time: antifeminist female activism. They wanted to be taken seriously as citizens, political actors whose actions were grounded in ideological patriotism. While adamantly antifeminist, they understood women and women's lives to have political implications for the nation-state that went far beyond the home and demanded activism. Their resulting ideology provided them, in the years immediately following the passage of the Nineteenth Amendment, opportunities to create political and organizational lives for themselves as newly enfranchised female citizens in direct opposition to the model posited by former suffragists.

What motivated women's Red Scare antifeminism? Susan Marshall, in her recent study of antisuffragists, has argued that the antifeminism of female antisuffragists made economic sense. Motivated by "gendered class interests," this female urban elite believed that female suffrage would diminish their power, already under siege by increased immigration, labor unrest, progressive social reforms, and the accompanying expansion of the social welfare state. Female antisuffragists rightly feared that the increasing professionalization and employment of women that accompanied suffrage would reduce their access to positions of influence and prestige.[2] Other historians have argued that some female activists of the mid-nineteenth through early twentieth century were motivated by maternalism: political expression driven and justified by a belief in women's unique capacity to mother, and a responsibility to extend those essentialized mothering virtues to the entire world.[3] Maternalism went beyond the left. Scholars Sonya Michel and Robyn Rosen call maternalism a "bridge across left-to-right differences within the pre-war years" and identified the wide variations within maternalism that developed in the interwar years, particularly as exercised by conservative Elizabeth Lowell Putnam.[4]

It is my contention, however, that while politically conservative women certainly cared about economics and maternalist politics, neither maternalism nor class interests adequately explain the majority of women discussed in this chapter and the organizations to which they belonged. Nor does the social conservatism of many antisuffragists. Female antiradicals fought radicalism because they believed that it threatened all of the social and economic relationships on which they—*and society*—depended. Though they believed that radicalism posed an economic threat (to them), and though their class interests are quite apparent, ideology mattered. They occasionally used maternalism but seemed to find it too internationalistic and essentialist. Morals mattered, but because of the effects of immoral behavior on social order. Their primary interest was the ideological and political task of protecting U.S. civilization. They believed that their nation—and all of its economic and social relationships—was built upon and relied on a complex network of public and private patriarchal structures. Red Scare radicals threatened this network. To protect it, Red Scare antifeminist women positioned themselves to act as final guardians of the nation, whose task it was to step forward with ideological certainty and public activism when men let the network weaken. The paradoxical task of their skillful public activism was to strengthen male power. The historical coincidence of the Red Scare and the remaking of female citizenship after the passage of female suffrage made their activism, in their analysis, vital and compulsory. The activism of Red Scare antifeminist women was part of the intellectual lineage of eighteenth-century republican motherhood and a continuation of the patriotic sentiments that led to wartime bandage rolling. It was unique, however, because of its insistently antifeminist stance, its aggressive and public insistence that all of society was threatened by the Red Scare crisis, and its immersion in the postsuffrage rethinking of women's citizenship.

The politically conservative women of this decade did not see a paradox in their public and forceful antifeminist stance. Feminists, they argued, did not monopolize strong female characters. And in the Red Scare moment of crisis, the nation direly needed strong female characters who were antiradicals and antifeminists. As patriotic female citizens, it was thus their duty to do whatever was necessary to rescue the nation—regardless of the discomfort or distaste for activism that they might feel. The generally silent, but sometimes explicit, statement that men were failing to hold a firm line against female suffrage, radicalism, and other challenges to American civilization lay embedded in their activism. Also unacknowledged was the delight that many women seemed to derive from their activism.

Although antifeminist women had backgrounds similar to those of progressive maternalist activists, they actively sought to differentiate themselves from the women they opposed. The activism of Red Scare antifeminists emphasized women's duties but did not build upon women's identity as mothers. The antifeminists were extremely skittish about relying upon the essentialist views of womanhood implied by maternalist arguments, for undermining any claim of female essentialism was the fact that their primary political opponents were women. Angry that progressive women were claiming to speak for all women, they constantly argued that differences among women existed and, furthermore, that some women were dangerous subversives.

This network of politically conservative women has not, to put it mildly, figured prominently in the history of U.S. conservatism. Histories of U.S. conservatism often begin in the post–World War II period. Surveys of U.S. conservatism that do include this time period focus upon male electoral success and characterize the entire period from the Civil War to the New Deal as the "nadir for conservative thought." When one places gender and women's activities in the historical narrative, or when one seeks an understanding of the social history of conservatism, the picture of U.S. conservatism that emerges is quite different. The decade of the 1920s appears as a time when, energized by the Red Scare, antiradicals laid the groundwork for contemporary conservative political concerns about gender, family, and centralized government, and when conservative women, though few, were well organized, vocal, and ideologically sophisticated.[5]

Neither does this network of politically conservative women fit tidily into the general narrative of women's history.[6] The organizations of antiradical women were part of the nineteenth-century women's club movement, yet they evolved in a markedly different direction than the larger club movement. They were antistatists who felt that the ongoing "domestication of politics," to borrow Paula Baker's phrase, the process of early twentieth-century state formation in which the federal government took over much of the moral authority and responsibility for social welfare from middle-class white women, undermined democracy.[7] And even though these were women's organizations, they never presumed a shared sisterhood, interests, or moral sentiments among women. Furthermore, though it is correct to call these women conservative or right-wing, there are marked differences between them and those who advocated evolutionism around the Scopes trial, or social conservatives complaining about the short skirts and hair of flappers.

Comparing Red Scare antifeminists and the Women of the Ku Klux Klan (WKKK) may be helpful. As recent historians have shown, female Klan leaders were politically active and astute, they sought to reassert and strengthen repressive racial and ethnic hierarchies in order to create the social order they felt necessary for the success of the nation, and they crafted one of the largest women's organizations of the 1920s. Certainly the two groups shared an ideology of white (racially and ethnically defined) supremacy, antifeminism, and antiradicalism and a wide array of political interests. As pointed out elsewhere in this book, both groups endorsed antifeminist, antiradical literature such as Samuel Solomon's *The Red War on the Family* (1922). Both also walked the fine line of advocating an active, educated, and reactive female citizenry while supporting the patriarchal family and a patriarchal society. Class, however, distinguishes the two groups dramatically. My conjecture is that Red Scare antifeminists considered WKKK members a class—economically, politically, and socially—below them; while they may have agreed with much of what the WKKK said, and with the ideology that illegal Klan actions tried to impose, Red Scare antifeminists considered the actions and methods of the WKKK unrespectable and lower class. The two groups, however, shared an ideological spectrum.[8]

Many details about Red Scare antifeminists are difficult to track down. The organizations of this network—for example, the Woman Patriots, the Daughters of the American Revolution (DAR), the Woman's Patriotic Conference, and the MPIL—apparently amassed huge libraries of documents attempting to prove the breadth of domestic radicalism. However, very little material about their organizations remains, and most of it is in the collections of those whom they attacked.[9] In addition, these organizations often centered on the energies of one individual who stored organizational materials in her own home, and many individuals were members in several or nearly all of the organizations discussed here. Assessing the impact of these organizations is thus easier than analyzing constituencies or discerning the realistic nature of membership claims.

A New Brand of Women's Organizations

According to Red Scare antifeminists, the threat of radicalism, combined with new voting rights for women that radical women would be especially likely to exercise, had created a national crisis. Antiradical, antifeminist women needed to address that crisis by creating and strengthening effective organizations for women to exercise good citizenship. While many similarities existed among these organizations, each was unique. What drew women together was their joint effort to redefine female citizenship and civic agency in a politically conservative but publicly assertive framework. They sought to create an organizational space, in the world of women's politics, for politically conservative women.

Most conservative women's organizations of the 1920s had roots in the antisuffrage movement. The roots of the Woman Patriots, the renamed National Association Opposed to Woman Suffrage, were the most direct.

Giving up on stopping female suffrage, in the 1920s the Woman Patriots directed Red Scare antifeminism against a wide variety of social welfare legislation. Using the ideological base they had built in antisuffrage debates, they argued against feminism, the proposed Child Labor Amendment, a national education department, and the Sheppard-Towner Act, and in support of the Wadsworth-Garrett Amendment (a proposed constitutional amendment to limit further constitutional amendments). These legislative stands grew from a distrust of centralized government and a fear that such programs were part of a larger socialist effort to use bureaucracy to nationalize women and children.

Leaders of the Woman Patriots fostered ties to other like-minded organizations that saw them and their journal, the *Woman Patriot*, as important partners in the national fight against radicalism. For example, in 1923 the National Association of Manufacturers worked with the Woman Patriots to seek prosecution of American communists.[10] Richard M. Whitney, author of *Reds in America* and director of the American Defense Society, was a favorite of *Woman Patriot* readers. He often submitted articles and sold his book through the paper.[11] Despite these connections, however, the Woman Patriots adamantly maintained their autonomous female activism. When a shortage of finances forced a discussion of a possible takeover of the *Woman Patriot* by the like-minded organization the Sentinels of the Republic, with the stipulation that the name be changed, the women resisted. Mary Kilbreth, president of the Woman Patriots, wrote, "Being men in active politics they will undoubtedly make us stop some of our attacks and become innocuous (and impersonal) like other periodicals. It's hard just as we are establishing ourselves!"[12]

Though the Sentinels of the Republic was not a women's organization, many politically conservative and antiradical women belonged to and were welcomed in the umbrella organization—"a clearing house for patriots"—founded in 1922.[13] The Sentinels, whose first president was Boston lawyer and manufacturer Louis A. Coolidge, modeled themselves on Samuel Adams as guardians of the republic. Members vowed that, as other patriots had supported the nation through its first two major crises, the Revolutionary and Civil Wars, it was their responsibility to take the nation through its present crisis—unfettered government expansion. As one pamphlet urged, "The third [crisis] is now at hand, with Federal paternalism and other forms of Communism threatening the bulwarks of the national structure that the patriots of 1776 and 1861 built and cemented with their blood."[14]

As with the other organizations discussed here, it is hard to find exact membership figures, but the Sentinels claimed to have 600 members in 1923 and 8,000 by 1927. Letterhead from 1925 claims members in forty-eight states. In 1929, the director of the Children's Bureau, Grace Abbott, claimed that the organization had a "very small membership" but felt that it shouldn't be ignored. Its membership included prominent men and women in leading business, legal, and political positions and included women of the MPIL, the Women's Constitutional League of Maryland, the Women's Constitutional League of Virginia, the Woman Patriots, and the DAR.[15]

Also claiming defense of the Constitution, the Sentinels opposed the Equal Rights Amendment, uniform marriage and divorce laws, and a proposed department of education, and they favored abolishing "useless governmental bureaus" such as the Home Economics Bureau, the Children's Bureau, the Bureau of Labor Statistics, the Bureau of Agricultural Economics, and the Women's Bureau.[16] The Sentinels actively worked against the Sheppard-Towner Act and the Child Labor Amendment, arguing that these measures were socialist, threatened the sanctity of the home, and took legitimate household governing power away from fathers.

The Sentinels attacked feminism but encouraged women's political involvement. Members recognized that the organizations backing the measures they opposed, particularly the Women's Joint Congressional Committee and its member organizations, were "practically all feminist organizations," and this was used as proof of the radicalism of social welfare legislation.[17] Women, however, composed an integral part of what the Sentinels called the "campaign in defense of the Constitution, the Courts, and the *rights of the People* against dangerous Federal amendments and *radical legislation.*" Eleven of the twenty speakers at the Sentinels' first convention, including Margaret C. Robinson of the MPIL, spoke on the importance of "organizing women in defense of the constitution."[18]

Many female Sentinels members were activists in the MPIL. The MPIL began its work in 1915 with antisuffrage activities but, directed by its president Margaret Robinson, quickly expanded its interests to include a wide array of Red Scare antifeminist concerns. Woman suffrage, the organization claimed, went "hand in hand" with socialism and was pro-German.[19] There are no membership records, but a 1925 newspaper story claimed that the MPIL had members in 118 cities, 20 states, and the District of Columbia. The organization, the article proclaimed, included "many, many mothers" among its members who "possess[ed] the full feminine quota of instincts, creative, protective, maternal and the rest."[20] Though reassuringly feminine, the MPIL was formed "to defend the Constitution, to oppose destructive legislation, and to further objects for the public interest."[21] In the 1920s, this organization centered on Robinson. The organization dissolved only a month before her death in 1932.[22]

The involvement of the DAR in Red Scare antifeminism is unique, for before the 1920s the DAR would not have fit into this organizational list. Women founded the DAR in 1890 as a patriotic society dedicated to the preservation and teaching of American history, whose membership—which by 1926 was 156,850—was limited to women who could prove themselves descendants of a Revolutionary War veteran. The DAR initially endorsed most of the progressive legislation supported by other women's organizations. Beginning in 1923, however, the DAR figured prominently in campaigns against progressive women's organizations, disarmament, pacifism, social welfare legislation, and individuals feared to be subversive, and it developed relationships with the U.S. military as well as other Red Scare antifeminist organizations.[23]

The transformation of the DAR undoubtedly was influenced by the same outside factors that enabled the resurgence of the antiradicalism of 1919 and 1920—debates on military preparedness, the rise of conservative Republicans, uneasiness over the impact of female suffrage, and the increasing level of women's pacifist activities. President-General Lora Haines Cook led this transformation, and it was continued by the leadership team of Grace Brosseau, who succeeded Cook as president-general, and Flora A. Walker (both Brosseau and Walker were in Cook's cabinet). Cook, Brosseau, and Walker had long records of DAR service as well as the financial resources to fund their travel and volunteer work.[24]

When Cook became president-general in 1923 she echoed the concerns of the previous president-general, Anne Rogers Minor, about the level of radicalism within U.S. higher education but amplified and combined them with warnings about a larger radical and pacifist menace. For example, in her presidential message of September 1924 she cautioned members about the "steady persistent effort . . . to impose dangerous doctrines" in educational settings and the "'peace at any price' wave of hysteria" spreading across the country. Cook read Richard M. Whitney's *Reds in America*, already a favorite of the Woman Patriots, and distributed it to all state regents. By the end of her term, speakers on pacifism and industrial reform deemed undesirable by DAR members had been "silenced" in Connecticut, New Jersey, West Vermont, and Georgia. The 1924 Continental

Congress resolved to "withstand and expose all pacifist efforts" and reaffirmed "unqualified opposition to all forms of sovietism, socialism, communism, and bolshevism." In 1925 those attending the Continental Congress recommended the organization of "an intensive campaign" in every state to combat "the plan for destruction revolution . . . by 'Red' Internationalists." While Cook was a less public figure than Brosseau was to be, both Flora Walker and DAR historian Margaret Gibbs credit her with initiating the DAR's antiradical crusades.[25]

Grace Brosseau, president-general from 1926 to 1929, took the changes initiated by Cook and made the DAR and its politics highly public and controversial. Once in office, she immediately authorized the creation of a DAR National Defense Committee and brought the society into the Women's Patriotic Conference for National Defense. Under Brosseau the national DAR and various chapters issued statements against the radicalism of the Child Labor Amendment, the Children's Bureau, and the Sheppard-Towner Act, but they focused primarily on military preparedness.[26]

Brosseau drew a distinction between unwomanly militarism and maternal support for preparedness. "Normal, human mothers and wives," she insisted, "do not believe in war." Mothers, however, needed to promote "the instincts of courage and self-preservation" in male children. If such instincts did not exist, "the net result will be in lack of virility, initiative and productivity. . . . It is a dangerous business to juggle with the potentialities of the future."[27] At another point she claimed that U.S. citizens, women apparently included, had no choice but to support militarism: "There is no longer any middle ground. . . . Either [a citizen] is for his country, defended and protected, or he is for his country, defenseless and unprotected."[28]

Brosseau's friend Flora A. Walker chaired the newly created National Defense Committee. This post gave Walker a great deal of influence, for hers was the only DAR committee to receive a monthly column in the society's magazine, and she had frequent opportunities for public speaking. Walker's interests and consequently those of the National Defense Committee resembled those of similar organizations. She actively participated in the Women's Patriotic Conference, was a member of Fred Marvin's Key Men of America, and took over the leadership of the American Coalition of Patriotic Societies after Marvin died in 1930.[29] In its first year the committee claimed to have amassed "comprehensive files" on subjects deemed subversive, displayed this information at various conferences, supplied information to those who desired it, and developed correspondence with like-minded individuals and groups. Walker rallied against atheism in education and blamed it on Russian Bolsheviks. Walker also cautioned against government centralization and bureaucracies, claiming that they were part of a radical plan to destroy family autonomy and male power in order to undermine Americanism. Referring to both Sheppard-Towner and the Child Labor Amendment, she warned of "a centralized bureaucratic despotism over American women and children."[30] In reference again to the Sheppard-Towner Act and Child Labor Amendment, she wrote: "Collectivity and bureaucracy would snatch the child from the nursery and make of it an un-American citizen."[31] Like Brosseau, however, Walker's passion was military preparedness. Throughout her tenure in the National Defense Committee she enthusiastically supported the National Defense Act of 1920, which proposed universal military training of young men in high schools and colleges and an expanded navy and army. Walker also urged continuation of the 1922 Limitation of Arms Conference, which established U.S. naval superiority.[32]

The hostility of the DAR leadership toward progressive women centered on the strength and activism of women in the peace movement. Cook, Brosseau, and Walker believed that the advocacy of peace by U.S. women—largely women they believed to be feminists—contradicted the ideals of female citizenship, for women were to support the military and physical strength of men. They believed that female peace activists were radicals and feminists who sought to destroy the patriarchal family along with the nation. DAR members and other militarists built upon the antagonism to peace activists remaining from World War I.[33]

Women concerned about women's advocacy of peace also could join the Women's Patriotic Conference on National Defense as Peace Insurance. This coalition of organizations, which met once a year in highly publicized meetings in Washington, D.C., positioned itself in direct contrast to women's peace organizations. The DAR and American Legion Auxiliary dominated the group. Female citizenship, as expressed by those attending the conference, included active female endorsement of a strong military and the exposure and defeat of U.S. subversives.[34]

According to Adalin Wright Macauley, national president of the American Legion Auxiliary and chair of the 1927 Women's Patriotic Conference, the conference "was our answer to the pacifists." She and others had attended the 1924 National Conference on the Cause and Cure of War led by Carrie Chapman Catt but had come away frustrated.[35] "Well, we were so fed up with idealism, and the Gold Star mother who sat next to me was so wrought up, that we decided we would call a conference and we went to the Daughters of the American Revolution and asked them to join with us, and we had a wonderful conference. . . . We picked up the gauntlet the pacifist women had thrown down, the women who had told Congress that the American women did not believe in adequate national defense."[36]

The 1925 Women's Patriotic Conference included a reception by President and Mrs. Coolidge at the White House; speeches by numerous military officials, including Secretary of War Weeks; and a closing speech entitled "Propaganda" by professional antiradical Fred Marvin. The *Washington Post* reported that fifteen or twenty "members of pacifist organizations" attended as "observers."[37] In 1927, the delegates adopted resolutions urging construction of additional navy cruisers, urged expansion of the army and navy air service, and expressed support for Amos Fries's Chemical Warfare Division (see chapter 4). They pledged their opposition to "pacifist, defeatist and radical individuals." They "decried" attempts to replace wartime heroes with "civilian and scientific heroes" in public school textbooks. Flora Walker of the DAR's National Defense Committee chaired the Resolution Committee. Margaret Robinson of the MPIL spoke against pacifism and the susceptibility of women to radical sentiments.[38]

Calvin Coolidge and members of the Women's National Defense Committee, February 1925. Reproduced from the Collections of the Library of Congress, 210105.

In 1928, presidential candidate Senator James Reed of Missouri received great support (he had alienated progressive women by his anti-Bolshevik rhetoric in the Child Labor Amendment campaign; see chapter 5) when he warned of "internationalists and near-internationalists, socialists and near-socialists." Grace Brosseau of the DAR led the conference, Lucia Ramsey Maxwell of the War Department was secretary, and Secretary of War Dwight Davis thanked the women for their interest in defense policy.[39] (Ramsey is better known for her involvement with the spider web chart; see chapter 4.) Military officials always were the most numerous speakers.

The Women's Patriotic Conference on National Defense claimed a large membership. The combined membership of the DAR and the American Legion Auxiliary numbered over 356,000 in the late 1920s, and the conference claimed an additional thirty-six women's organizations as members. In 1927 the delegates claimed to represent over two million women. And each year the Women's Patriotic Conference received the attention of prominent government officials when its members were in Washington. Despite these strengths, it did not garner the legislative clout of liberal women's organizations. Individual members rarely involved themselves, on a large scale, in the day-to-day lobbying and participatory political work done by activist progressive women. Yet this group, as well as many others, actively participated in the attacks of the 1920s upon progressive women's organizations.[40]

The MPIL, the Woman Patriots, the Sentinels of the Republic, the DAR, and the Women's Patriotic Conference drew and expanded upon Red Scare antifeminism. Fearing a radical threat to the complex web of U.S. civilization, they carried their political philosophy into the political realm, using a variety of forms of activism. They opposed feminism, government expansion, the development of bureaucratic social welfare measures, and the advocacy of peace as part of a larger effort to Bolshevize the nation. Attempting to mold the outcome of female suffrage, they used continuing Red Scare sentiment to model a form of female citizenship simultaneously politically conservative and antifeminist, but dynamic and strong-willed.

Margaret C. Robinson

The individual women active in the continuance and transformation of Red Scare antifeminism demanded to be taken seriously as political and ideological actors. They generally were educated, from upper- or upper-middle-class backgrounds, and focused on legislative and electoral politics. Their tenacity promoted their brand of politically conservative but active female citizenship and helped to sustain the Red Scare atmosphere of crisis. Their fervor for documenting radicalism, however, was not accompanied by a commitment to leaving behind their historical records. Because of the elusive character of these organizations and the absence of helpful membership lists, this chapter examines the life of activist Margaret C. Robinson in the hope that through one individual we can understand others. The example of the MPIL's Robinson is useful because she is representative of many of the leading women in right-wing women's organizations of the 1920s. She was highly educated, developed her political acumen in the antisuffrage campaigns, involved herself in a wide variety of political and social issues, and actively participated in a complex network of antiradical organizations.[41]

Robinson understood women to be politically independent creatures, for she always appealed directly to women and assumed that women could and would act on their own initiative. She believed that the primary citizenship role of women was to be guardians who protected home, nation, and civilization from subversive influences. Because of women's

Margaret C. Robinson.
Zion's Herald, October 20, 1915.

vital importance as guardians, their political world included but extended far beyond the home. Their duties had political ramifications that were connected to and were part of what was understood to be the political world of men. In Robinson's early career, she believed that women's citizenship was best exercised outside suffrage. Once the Suffrage Amendment passed, however, she believed that voting was a burden that responsible women, as political creatures, needed to shoulder.

Though Robinson was an active public woman, she was not a feminist. Like the feminists she opposed, however, Robinson understood women, women's lives, and the home to be inherently political. Also like the feminists she opposed, she believed in progress and believed that the United States was the international leader. And like them, she argued that women had political responsibilities that were based on women's unique abilities and interests. However, if we use Nancy Cott's definition of feminism as an ideology that (1) is opposed to sex hierarchy, (2) understands women's condition to be socially constructed, and (3) understands women to be a social grouping with a shared identity, Robinson clearly does not fit. She felt that sex hierarchy was vital to an orderly nation, understood women's subordination to be part of the natural order, and, though she was active in some single-sex organizations, felt that alliances of women promoted "sex wars."[42] Robinson believed that all women promoting the expansion of social welfare programs were feminists and that feminism was a backward movement that undermined the civilizing progress made by citizens of the United States. Robinson also differed from the feminists and female reformers of the Progressive Era because she believed that government regulatory efforts to reshape people, politics, and industry were insidious to individuals, society, and democracy.[43]

Margaret Robinson and her colleagues saw no paradox in their political activism. They believed in the rightness of patriarchy but did not believe that it implied invisibility on the part of women. Women, they believed, had the ironic civic duty of guarding patriarchy, and when patriarchy was threatened, women were to respond strenuously and visibly in the political sphere. The political influence they sought was to strengthen rather than challenge patriarchy. In essence, Robinson argued that patriarchy benefited women by solidifying and clarifying a strong social and political order.

Robinson was born Margaret Louise Casson in Hennepin, Illinois, in 1864. Hennepin, the county seat of Putnam County, was a small trading town established in 1831 along the Illinois River. Her father clerked for the circuit court and then had his own law practice. The Casson family emphasized music, literature, and education, even the education of women. Robinson received her education in the Hennepin public schools and at Illinois State Normal School (ISNS), where she may have met her future husband.[44] When Robinson attended ISNS, she most likely studied a variety of subjects. The 1874 curriculum included teachers' training courses as well as advanced mathematics, astronomy, geography, history, and a variety of science classes. The study of music was optional, but since Robinson later taught music in Illinois, she probably took this optional course.[45]

Robinson's early life is striking in its similarities with the experiences of social reformers and Hull House activists Jane Addams and Julia Lathrop. All three women grew up in small Illinois villages and were born in approximately the same decade. Each came from a family prominent in her locale. Robinson, Addams, and Lathrop were all highly educated compared to most women of their time and were educated amid a general debate regarding the purpose and safety of women's education. All three agreed that women's activities were intensely political and that women had political responsibilities. At some point, however, the similarities stop. Robinson took a dramatically different political and life path from Addams and Lathrop, and the two eventually became favorite targets of Robinson's antiradicalism.[46]

On June 29, 1887, sometime after her teacher's training, Casson married recent Harvard graduate Benjamin Lincoln Robinson. Benjamin, born in 1864, was from a well-established family. His father, president of the First National Bank in Bloomington, had an extensive library, and his mother encouraged Benjamin's education. The couple's early years of marriage were spent in Germany, where Benjamin earned his Ph.D. in botany from the University of Strasbourg. Benjamin's older brother, James Harvey Robinson, future progressive historian and cofounder with Charles Beard of the New School for Social Research, studied with Benjamin both at Harvard and in Strasbourg.[47]

In 1890 the couple moved to Cambridge, Massachusetts, where Benjamin began work at Harvard in the Gray Herbarium. The Robinsons' only child, a daughter, died in 1896. At Harvard, Benjamin established himself as a botanist of national reputation, but there is no evidence that he was interested in the social and political issues to which Margaret was dedicated. In Cambridge, Margaret studied piano with the internationally known pianist and composer William Sherwood but shortly left the study of music to devote herself to political and social action.[48] Margaret "weakened" in 1929 and died on May 9, 1932. Benjamin died in 1935.[49]

During her husband's tenure at Harvard, Margaret Robinson actively joined the wider Cambridge and Harvard communities. She was vice-president of the Cambridge Hospital League and an executive committee member of the Cambridge Anti-Tuberculosis Society. Robinson also followed activities at Harvard. For example, while it doesn't appear that her husband was involved with Harvard's eugenicists, Robinson spoke highly of prominent psychologist and professor William McDougall. In his controversial and highly publicized 1920 Lowell Lectures at Harvard, McDougall proclaimed the superiority of the "Nordic race" and argued that social class was set by the inheritance of mental ability. Robinson admired McDougall and shared his concerns about U.S. civilization.[50]

Robinson's antisuffrage activities were extensive. She edited the antisuffrage journal *Remonstrance* until its 1912 merger with the *Woman's Protest* (which would later become the *Woman Patriot*) and compiled a weekly column called "Anti-Suffrage Notes." As an antisuffragist, Robinson sat on the executive committee of the National Association Opposed to Woman Suffrage (NAOWS) and was the longtime president of the MPIL.

Two prominent themes repeatedly appear in Robinson's writings against female suffrage. First, she sought to debunk the "expediency argument"—the argument that women's suffrage would bring women's inherent goodness into the political realm and clean up politics. Robinson repeatedly claimed that "woman suffrage . . . does not purify politics." In a 1915 article, using a strategy she frequently employed, she gave examples from states with female suffrage to show that it had not eradicated child labor, alcoholism, or violence. This argument placed Robinson in the same framework as other prominent antisuffragists. Annie Nathan Meyer, for example, also rejected the belief that women would bring morals to politics.[51]

Second, Robinson argued that suffrage led to feminism, which led to disastrous consequences—consequences that varied but all of them threatened the nation. In 1915 Robinson argued that because feminism led women to ignore the family, marriage, morals, and Christianity, suffrage was "a blow at civilization itself." In 1916, when Robinson began to equate socialism and feminism, she characterized feminism as "a backward movement toward conditions many of which have been long outgrown and discredited by civilized nations."[52]

In her antisuffrage arguments and elsewhere, Robinson rejected an essentialist view of womanhood that understood women to be morally superior to men. She was adamant that female suffrage had not brought and would not bring moral improvement. She believed that radical feminist women were irredeemably immoral and feared the consequences of their activities. While Robinson believed most women desired to do good and believed that this was the source of much of women's political strength, she repeatedly cautioned that women's desire to do good also could be a liability. She feared that the desire of many women to help others made them tend toward radicalism while ignoring its full consequences. For example, she argued that radicals targeted women's colleges for potential converts because the women there held high ideals. Robinson solicited help from the readers of the *Woman Patriot* in her efforts to learn the truth about what went on at women's colleges. Robinson also cautioned against women's susceptibility to radicalism in her campaigns against the Sheppard-Towner Act and the proposed Child Labor Amendment.[53] Radicals, she argued, had included "women" and "children" in the titles of subversive legislation in order to attract women's support. Women, she claimed, "have shown themselves very easily influenced . . . if the appeal comes to them in a humanitarian guise."[54]

An orderly civilization was at the center of Robinson's political ideas and worldview. Robinson believed that in a civilized society men gladly shouldered "the responsibility for wife and child." Feminism and radicalism threatened civilization because they endorsed women's economic independence and would deprive men of this "steadying and civilizing influence."[55] Civilization also demanded a monogamous patriarchal family. According to Robinson, feminism and socialism posed a dual threat because they challenged monogamy and the family by promoting women's sexual independence and by nationalizing women and children (the contradictory nature of these claims was never explored). Robinson believed, like nineteenth-century liberals, that civilizing progress was best achieved when government refrained from interfering in family, education, business, or the economy with regulations or assistance. The progressive women who dominated the Children's Bureau and advocated government social welfare programs threatened the nation by advocating government intervention. Feminism, by attempting to remake family and national politics, was a backward movement that undermined civilization and subverted its progress.

Much of Robinson's politics evolved from the antistatist belief that growing government bureaucracy was the enemy of democracy and threatened national security. The bureaucracies she referred to were the governmental regulatory and social service agencies created by political progressives in an effort to improve government, the economy, industry, and the welfare of individuals. Bureaucracies, she felt, substituted political appointees for elected officials and thus undermined and contradicted democracy. Once implemented, bureaucracies were expensive and self-perpetuating, always seeking their own interests rather than the greater good of the nation. Bureaucracies were dangerous because they centralized power in the government and, the Children's Bureau particularly, undermined individual male power in families or business. Bureaucracy not only was antidemocratic but was encouraged by radicals and feminists for their own ends. Radicals, Robinson argued, "encourage every tendency toward centralization, because it will arouse the antagonism of the people. . . . [They] want bureaucracy because it tends to destroy our form of government." Feminists crassly wanted bureaucracy "because it offers jobs for women in politics." Though Robinson acknowledged that these two forces were not always openly allied, "their combination is inevitable and is rapidly approaching." This remark directly pointed at the Women's Bureau, the Children's Bureau, and the many women employed there and included the charge that they were self-interested and dangerous political radicals.[56]

In the 1920s Robinson focused her political attention on the growth of the government bureaucracies she believed to be dangerous: the Children's Bureau, the Women's Bureau, an education department as proposed in the Smith-Towner bill, the regulatory measures in the proposed Child Labor Amendment, and the agencies established by the Sheppard-Towner Act. Robinson's criticisms included broad proclamations of antistatism alongside specific complaints. The Sheppard-Towner Act, which provided health care and education for mothers and children, was supposedly part of "the unannounced campaign of those behind it 'to make motherhood a governmental institution.'" She called the Smith-Towner bill, an educational reform bill that included a proposed federal department of education, "a bill to Prussianize education in this country." Both bills, she claimed, were "in essence Socialism" and were promoted by female lobbyists in search of easy jobs.[57]

Robinson wrote most prolifically about the proposed Child Labor Amendment to the Constitution, intended to give Congress the power to limit the labor of citizens under the age of eighteen. The Amendment, which easily passed Congress, quickly floundered and died when it went to the states in 1924; one of its earliest defeats was in Massachusetts, due to a campaign by the well-organized Citizens' Committee to Protect Our

Homes and Children, of which Robinson was a part. Robinson feared the Child Labor Amendment's general move toward bureaucracy, but her main contention was that the amendment was part of a larger socialist effort to use bureaucracy to destabilize the patriarchal family by nationalizing women and children. Robinson warned, "When American children are fed and clothed by the government, when the government decides whether or not they may work, where and how they shall be educated, they will have been nationalized as completely as the children in Soviet Russia."[58] She claimed that the amendment began in the platform of the Socialist Party and pointed out that the amendment was supported by socialist Florence Kelley, secretary of the National Consumers' League; Owen Lovejoy, president of the National Child Labor Committee; and Victor Berger, former socialist congressman from Wisconsin and mayor of Milwaukee, names she expected people would recognize as socialist.[59] She went on to claim that the amendment would lead others to socialism, particularly the small farmer who would be harmed economically and whose discontent "may lead him to join the Socialist Farmer-Labor Party."[60]

Beginning with her anti–Child Labor Amendment activities, Robinson worked with manufacturers' organizations and supported the open shop (anti–labor union) movement. Manufacturers organizations participated in and provided financial assistance to the Massachusetts anti–Child Labor Amendment campaign, and prominent manufacturers were active in the Sentinels of the Republic. Either of these places may have been where Robinson formed her ideological and personal connections with manufacturers. In *American Industries,* the journal of the National Association of Manufacturers, she wrote that the closed-shop movement was part of a larger tendency toward bureaucratic state "compulsion" and away from "liberty." In a special pamphlet of Cleveland's *Iron Trade Review,* Robinson wrote about attempts to convert U.S. youth to socialism.[61]

Robinson also alleged socialist influence in the Women's Joint Congressional Committee (WJCC), a large coalition of progressive women's organizations whose congressional lobbying activities included support of the Child Labor Amendment. She worried that organized women didn't know what their leaders were doing and had "so long meekly submitted to radical dictatorship."[62] The organizations of the WJCC, she warned, had "interlocking directorates, and a number of them interlock with some of the most radical and subversive organizations in the country."[63] The majority of women's political organizations thus were dangerous organizations, leading the well-intentioned women of America down a socialist path.

Robinson criticized pacifism, tied all peace efforts to it, and equated it with communism and socialism. In a speech to the 1927 Woman's Patriotic Conference on National Defense, in which she defended the U.S. invasion of the Philippines as a kindness toward a "backward" nation, Robinson argued: "In all the shades of destructive propaganda striving to mislead the American people . . . there is none, I believe, more dangerous than the so-called pacifist movement. It is the path, I believe, to all disloyalties, because it is the path to communism, which teaches disloyalty to family, to country and to God." Robinson warned women that while this view might make them unpopular—"you will be laughed at and thought queer"—women needed to be wary because radicals were attempting to manipulate women's well-meaning peace organizations. Though there is no record of Robinson attacking particular peace organizations, she spoke in a political environment in which the loyalty of women's peace organizations such as the Women's International League for Peace and Freedom was widely questioned.[64]

In this speech against pacifism, the common threads of Robinson's political vision are clear. A secure nation depended upon loyalty to family and country. Radicalism, feminism, growing state bureaucracies, and pacifism threatened those loyalties. Government interference in the patriarchal family—via the prohibition of child labor or via maternal health care—threatened patriarchy and unleashed a burgeoning government bureaucracy. An active women's citizenry was vital but dangerously susceptible to manipulation.

It is hard to know what others thought of Robinson and her activities. Feminist and progressive women clearly were aware of her. As early as 1917, National American Woman Suffrage Association president Carrie Chapman Catt used an open letter to ask Robinson, "in the name of our common womanhood," to stop "impugn[ing] my loyalty as an American." As chair of the Press Committee of the Cambridge Anti-Suffrage Association, Robinson apparently had linked Catt to radicalism and antiwar efforts, despite Catt's leadership in the National American Woman Suffrage Association's support of the war. In 1927 Catt still acknowledged Robinson as a political force.[65]

Helen Tufts Bailie, a Massachusetts resident expelled from the DAR in 1928 for criticizing their antiradical measures, disliked Robinson and her politics. (Bailie's dismissal from the DAR is discussed in chapter 6.) Though the two never met, Bailie frequently wrote derisively about Robinson in her diary. Bailie speculated that Robinson, whom she described as "stoutish, homely and commonplace" was "a little off in her head."[66] Once she wrote that Robinson was "well known to have a screw loose since the death of her daughter." Another time Bailie wrote that "the woman [Robinson] nearly went out of her head when the Suffrage Amendment went thro."[67] Bailie reported gossip that after Robinson's daughter, named Brunhilde after the Wagnerian heroine, died in 1896, "at Symphony she [Robinson] would laugh hysterically during a Wagner piece so as to be heard all over the hall."[68] Bailie wanted to have an "alienist" (a psychiatrist) observe Robinson in debate. After a letter from Bailie was printed in a Boston paper, Bailie wrote "Hope Robinson has hysterics when she reads it." Later she wrote, "Mrs. Robinson is a hard nut to crack, but I shall get her if I live."[69] Bailie also tried to enlist Catt's help and described herself as "very desirous of discrediting Mrs. Robinson."[70] The fact that Robinson was the sister-in-law of James Harvey Robinson, a progressive historian closely aligned with social reformer and historian Charles Beard, surprised others as well as Bailie.[71]

Bailie's characterization of Robinson as insane is hard to assess. The death of Brunhilde undoubtedly was tragic for Robinson and her husband. On a political as well as a personal level, Bailie may have perceived the lack of children in Robinson's home as a point of personal vulnerability, particularly since Robinson understood the nuclear family to be essential to successful democracy. Robinson may have been mentally unstable. Accusations of insanity, however, have often been leveled at women in attempts to discredit them. Bailie's accusations may be part of this pattern. Just as Bailie questioned Robinson's sanity and described her as unattractive, antisuffragists questioned the sanity of suffragists and described *them* as unattractive.

While Bailie criticized Robinson and questioned her credibility, others praised her. The *Springfield Union,* for example, applauded Robinson and her political influence. The paper assured its readers that Robinson was "well poised, tactful. . . . She has a dignified presence and displays sure feminine knowledge of an important subject—what to wear and how to wear it." With Robinson's femininity well established, the paper went on to tell of her heroic efforts against the Child Labor Amendment and other radical legislation, the medal given her by the Polish government in recognition of her war relief work, and her long-term dedication to the "ideals of the republic." Robinson could not be accused, like many women could, of "scenting bands of pink wool and tying them over their pretty eyes." Instead, Robinson laid aside women's natural inclination to look only at good things and devoted herself to fighting political subversives.[72]

The Military Intelligence Division (MID) of the War Department, as the next chapter will show, also endorsed the MPIL and similarly minded women's organizations by reinforcing their status as experts on radicalism. When unable to make public judgments on feared radicals, the MID routinely recommended that those with questions speak to Robinson or read pamphlets published by the MPIL or the DAR.

While Margaret Robinson cannot be taken to represent all politically conservative women of the 1920s, her ideological and political battles against political subversiveness illustrate the wide variety of women's political expression. She and other members of conservative women's organizations were by no means feminists, flappers, or the women voters thought to have disappeared in the 1920s. Women such as Margaret Robinson, whom Carrie Chapman Catt appealed to "in the name of our common womanhood," belied the notion of "women's political interests." Robinson and other Red Scare antifeminist women show how historically inaccurate it is to refer to women as a cohesive, interest-sharing group; in Nancy Cott's terms, they are an example of "women's . . . reluctance to say *we*." Indeed, conflicts over understandings of womanhood and the implications of those understandings were at the core of Red Scare antifeminist ideology and the political debates that its adherents entered.[73] The existence and activism of politically conservative women's organizations, actively antifeminist and actively antiradical, make clear that even after the Nineteenth Amendment granting female suffrage passed in August 1920, the content and style of women's participation in the public sphere were still being contested.

Robinson and other members of women's antiradical organizations fought radicalism because they believed that it threatened all of the social and economic relationships upon which society depended. They tapped into and genuinely believed the Red Scare fears and archetypes about feminism first developed between 1919 and 1920 and used them to combat the wide array of political actions they thought subversive. They understood male power in the family and society to be easily endangered and thus saw no paradox in their political activism in defense of male power. These women functioned as defensive guardians of family, nation, and civilization to promote a political vision deeply grounded in Red Scare antifeminism.

Robinson and other female activists of this network also used continuing Red Scare sentiment to model a form of female citizenship that starkly contrasted with that of former suffragists. In the years immediately following female suffrage, progressive female activists remained confident in women's abilities to create a progressive and feminist state. Red Scare antifeminist women encouraged women to use the leverage of their newly gained votes to exercise an active but politically conservative female citizenship.

Finally, Robinson and her compatriots used the Red Scare to foster a political culture hostile to the progressive female activists of the 1920s. The activities of conservative antifeminists helped to weaken the women's peace movement and defeat the social welfare legislation that progressive women endorsed.

CHAPTER 4

The Insidiousness of Peace

*Red Scare Antifeminists and
the War Department*

Stunned by the violence of World War I, many U.S. women hoped that they, in cooperation with European women, could use their newly gained franchise to prevent future bloodshed. Led by the National Council for the Prevention of War (NCPW), the growing but disparate U.S. peace movement—over thirty organizations and a combined constituency in the millions—relied upon women's leadership, involvement, and recruitment efforts. Despite the widespread support for the peace movement and the fact that its opponents were in the minority, there was, to those opponents, something particularly frightening about women's peace activities. Women's exercise of citizenship in support of pacifism and disarmament undermined social conventions about male military knowledge, female adoration of male strength, and female political invisibility.[1]

Women's peace organizations had been attacked as disloyal before and during World War I, but the Red Scare intensified these attacks and provided militarists with a new weapon. Antiradicals charged that radicals within many U.S. women's organizations were trying to weaken the nation's military in order to assist a Russian attack. The endorsement of disarmament proposals by many of the largest and most prominent U.S. women's organizations—for example, the Women's Joint Congressional Committee, the General Federation of Women's Clubs, the National Congress of Mothers and Parent-Teacher Associations, the American Association of University Women, and a myriad of women's peace organizations—convinced antiradicals that the organizations of progressive women were politically, socially, and militarily subversive. The dual crises of World War I and the Red Scare made women's peace efforts, particularly as exemplified by Jane Addams and the Women's International League for Peace and Freedom (WILPF), an immediate and dire threat.[2]

In the cause of national security, antiradical men and women opposed to peace programs formed organizations, shared information, and encouraged and used links with the War Department. While the constituency of these organizations was not large, the activists within it were dedicated men and women who worked hard to spread their political views and benefited from the legitimacy granted them by their affiliations with the War Department. This network included the Sentinels of the Republic, professional antiradical Fred Marvin and the various organizations and publications with which he was involved, Edward Hunter and the American Defense Association, Cornelia Ross Potts and the National Patriotic Council, H. M. Haldeman and the Better America Federation, various members of the military and War Department, the Woman Patriots, the Massachusetts Public Interests League, the Daughters of the American Revolution, and the Women's Patriotic Conference. Imbued with Red Scare antifeminism, these organizations defined women's exercise of citizenship in pursuit of disarmament or peace efforts as treasonous radicalism.

WOMEN AND PEACE

Antiradicals attacked women's advocacy of peace and women's organizations interested in peace. The National Congress of Mothers and Parent-Teacher Associations (NCMPTA) was one of the first women's organizations to distance itself from the peace movement. The NCMPTA listed peace as a primary legislative goal, but in 1923 it withdrew from the NCPW because of fears of communism after Brigadier General Amos Fries of the Army's Chemical Services Division and Secretary of War John Weeks began publicly denouncing peace activists in 1923.[3] Florence Watkins, general secretary of the NCMPTA and a member of the NCPW's executive committee, continued her personal membership in the NCPW. Brigadier General Fries noted this and, criticizing Watkins personally, warned of subversive pacifist influences in the NCMPTA. The 1923 convention of the NCMPTA then centered on the issue of peace. Watkins's opponents claimed that the organization was losing members because of its connection to subversives. Unsuccessful attempts were made to remove peace from the group's "Six P's" legislative plan and to reassure the War Department of the organization's support.[4]

The Socialist-Pacifist Movement in America Is an Absolutely Fundamental and Integral Part of International Socialism (Lusk Report Page 11.)

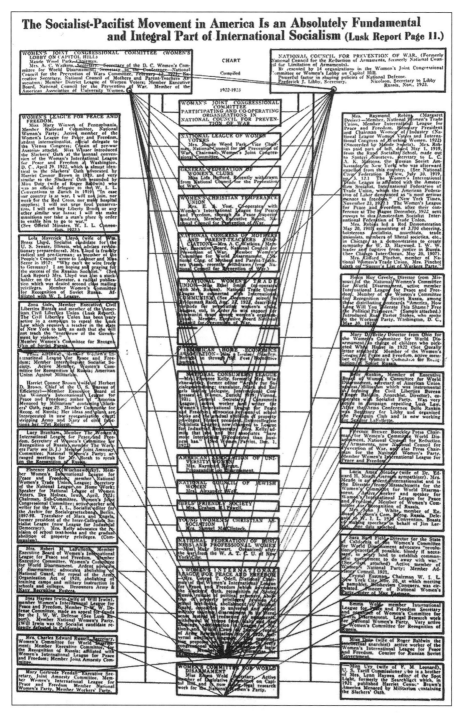

The spider web chart, 1924.

In April 1923, as Fries and Weeks denounced peace activists, allegations of female subversiveness were leaked from Fries's office. With Fries's knowledge, Lucia Ramsey Maxwell, librarian of the Chemical Warfare Service, compiled what has come to be known as the spider web chart.[5] Maxwell, a member of the Patriotic Committee of the League of American Penwomen and future secretary of the Women's Patriotic Conference, distributed the chart from both home and office.[6] The chart, which would be published in several different versions, linked seventeen women's organizations and twenty individual women, claiming them part of an international "socialist-pacifist movement" to bring about international socialism. The WILPF and the Women's Joint Congressional Committee, a lobbying coalition of progressive women's organizations formed after the passage of female suffrage, figured prominently.

At the bottom of the chart was a poem outlining the unique role of women in preparing for a U.S. Bolshevik revolution. While men were busy with violence and mayhem, women were to infiltrate women's organizations, using politics and the newly won vote to disarm and undermine the United States. The poem targeted advocates of disarmament, but the chart included women and women's organizations of wide interests.

> Miss Bolsheviki has come to town
> With a Russian cap and a German gown,
> In women's clubs she's sure to be found,
> For she's come to disarm America.
>
> She sits in judgment on Capitol Hill
> And watches the appropriation bill
> And without her O.K. it passes—Nil
> For she's there to disarm America.
>
> She uses the movies and lyceum, too,
> And alters text-books to suit her view
> She prates propaganda from pulpit and pew
> For she's bound to disarm America.
>
> The male of the species has a different plan
> He uses the bomb and the firebrand
> And incites class hatred wherever he can
> While she's busy disarming America.

His special stunt is arousing the mob
To expropriate and hate and kill and rob
While she's working on her political job
AWAKE! AROUSE!! AMERICA!!![7]

Maxwell and others distributed the spider web chart widely. J. Edgar Hoover at the Department of Justice thanked Maxwell for her "magnificent piece of work," as did Richard M. Whitney of the American Defense Society. In March 1924, Henry Ford's *Dearborn Independent* published the chart, and the paper's half a million readers—subscribers as well as all Ford owners, dealers, and employees—could read the accusations. The chart and parts of the accompanying articles were consequently reprinted and distributed by the Manufacturers Association of Kentucky, the Allied Industries of New York, and Fred Marvin's *New York Commercial.*[8]

In the *Dearborn Independent,* a newspaper also ardently anti-Semitic, the chart was published alongside two articles, "Are Women's Clubs 'Used' by Bolshevists?" and "Why Don't Women Investigate Propaganda?" Written by "An American Citizen," these articles argued that there was an "interlocking directorate" by which "a few key women dominate the legislative program in most of the women's organizations." The key women included Margaret Dreier Robins of the Women's Trade Union League, Mary Anderson of the Department of Labor's Women's Bureau, suffragist Carrie Chapman Catt, activist Florence Kelley, Florence Watkins of the NCMPTA, peace activist Lucia Ames Mead, and Maud Wood Park of the League of Women Voters. Dominated organizations included the League of Women Voters, the WILPF, the Women's Joint Congressional Committee (WJCC), and the National Council of Women.[9]

While innocent women were drawn in "through all sorts of camouflage interests," their radical leaders promoted subversive goals. Through the lobbying coalition of the WJCC, "this 'Women's Bloc' . . . can in co-operation with the radicals in Congress practically dictate our legislation. . . . Women who would quickly resent being called Socialists or Bolsheviki, are blithely passing resolutions and voting for a program that was inaugurated . . . in Russia." The only hope, as far as the author was concerned, was her conviction that "once they are informed, the majority of women do not favor the Radical-Pacifist program despite the cleverly contrived appearances to the contrary."[10]

As Mary Anderson, the director of the Women's Bureau, later characterized it, this was "a wholesale attack on practically every well-known

women's organization in the United States and their leaders."[11] Those
attacked responded quickly and concentrated retaliatory efforts in a Special Committee of the WJCC.[12] Under the leadership of the League of
Women Voters' president Maud Wood Park, the women wrote to Secretary of War Weeks, calling the chart "exceedingly irritating." It disturbed
American women, they wrote, that "a branch of the Government, is
engaged in this contemptible attack on the Women's organizations in the
country." They demanded a correction from Brigadier General Fries and
distribution of Fries's correction. Throughout April and May of 1924,
Weeks and the women exchanged numerous letters and visits. Weeks, who
had been a prominent Massachusetts antisuffragist, most likely did not
enjoy meeting again with many of the same national suffrage leaders who
had provided money and energy to defeat him in his unsuccessful 1918
reelection campaign for the U.S. Senate. He disavowed the chart and
promised to request that all copies be destroyed.[13]

Clearly, however, requests from Weeks that all copies be destroyed were
useless. The chart and its allegations had already been distributed widely
and had done damage. The American Defense League reportedly framed
their copy and hung it on the wall. In June, Lucia Ramsey Maxwell
claimed it to be her property and announced plans for an expanded and
copyrighted version.[14] As an official of the League of Women Voters wrote
to Julia Lathrop, "Some of the more timid sisters seem a bit shaken by the
Independent's attack."[15] The chart had confirmed and reinforced suspi-
cions about the political activities of American women.

The women's peace organization attacked most vociferously and
often—and which was featured in the spider web chart and its accompanying articles—was the WILPF, founded in 1919 by an international coalition of suffragists. The organization's constitution pledged to use suffrage
to support "movements to further peace, internationalism, and the freedom
of women." With prominent U.S. reformer Jane Addams as its international president in 1920, WILPF members renewed their commitment to
work for peace, human rights, the League of Nations, and eventual universal disarmament. U.S. members established an office in Washington,
D.C., to begin effective lobbying under the leadership of Dorothy Detzer.
By 1923, the organization had grown to over 5,000 members. While relatively small, the WILPF was visible and legislatively influential. Two of its
leaders were to win Nobel Prizes for Peace: Jane Addams in 1931 and Emily
Greene Balch in 1946.[16] When speculations about subversive women's
peace organizations increased, the WILPF was a public and likely target.

Its combination of internationalist and feminist perspectives convinced many antiradicals of its subversive nature.

Those seeking further proof about the WILPF turned to a network of professional antiradicals. Richard Merrill Whitney, president of the American Defense Society, was an influential source and allegations of WILPF subversiveness significantly increased with his publication of *Peace at Any Old Price*. (DAR and Woman Patriot members recommended Whitney's *Reds in America* highly.) Whitney charged that the WILPF's national convention of 1923 was "probably the most subversive, certainly the most insidiously and cleverly camouflaged, thoroughly anti-American and un-American public meeting that has been held in this country since the United States entered the European war." The conference was dominated, Whitney insisted, "by the spirit of Russian communism." Leaders boasted of their radicalism while editing "rabidly red sentences and expressions" out of their press releases in order to avoid jail. Whitney warned that inspired by such fiery speeches, delegates returned home "to start agitation in EVERY CONGRESSIONAL DISTRICT." This agitation included "a veritable orgy of letter writing, in which they are past masters and remarkably assiduous."[17]

In Whitney's analysis, there were many dangerous elements to the WILPF agenda. The internationalism of the organization suggested a lack of love for one's own country and an inclination toward communism. The appeals for disarmament were part of an effort to ease the communist takeover. Advocacy of U.S. recognition of the Soviet Union meant endorsement of communism. The WILPF encouraged its members to form coalitions with other organizations, something Whitney called "boring from within."[18] In *Peace at Any Old Price*, Whitney warned that Rosika Schwimmer, "an Austrian Jewish Communist," had been involved in the creation of the WILPF. The 1919 Lusk Report, he reminded his readers, had called Schwimmer "in reality a German agent." By 1923, Schwimmer, who had emigrated to the United States but was denied citizenship later, was well known in the United States. She was variably attacked for being a feminist, a pacifist, and a Jew. Whitney could include affiliation with Schwimmer in his list of WILPF indictments with confidence that, for some, her presence in the WILPF would be adequate evidence of its dangerous nature.[19]

Fred Marvin, one of the most active members of the antiradical network of the 1920s, also included the WILPF in his listings of subversive organizations. Marvin was a lifelong newspaper reporter, publisher, and member of the Republican Party. He edited the *New York Commercial*, which echoed his antiradical sentiments, until the paper was shut down by libel lawsuits brought by Schwimmer, Arthur Garfield Hayes, and others. There he wrote a column entitled "Searchlight," warning of radical inroads.[20] Once the paper closed, Marvin founded the Key Men of America, an organization whose six-dollar membership fee included daily and then weekly "Data Sheets" exposing radical and subversive movements inside the United States. Marvin also was involved in the *National Republic*, a journal semi-affiliated with the Republican Party and endorsed by the DAR, for which he was onetime associate editor and a frequent contributor.[21]

Members of Marvin's Key Men of America, both men and women, came from manufacturing, patriot, and military backgrounds. Hanford MacNider, assistant secretary of war, was a member. Its advisory council was a litany of others involved in antiradicalism in the 1920s: Grace Brosseau, president-general of the DAR; Mrs. Edward Cameron of the Women's Constitutional League of Virginia; Joseph Cashman, a New York lawyer; George Darte of the Military Order of the World War and favored DAR speaker; Harriet Frothingham of the Woman Patriots and Sentinels of the Republic; Lucia Ramsey Maxwell, compiler of the spider web chart; and Margaret Robinson. Officers of the American Legion, the Legion Auxiliary, the Better America Federation, and several employers' organizations also were included.[22]

A less prolific colleague of Marvin's was Edward A. Hunter of the Industrial Defense Association (IDA), which claimed to serve as an informational bureau to more than forty national patriotic organizations. Its membership overlapped with that of the Massachusetts Public Interests League (MPIL), including Margaret Robinson and other unnamed but supposedly prominent Bostonians. The association's beliefs were similar to those of other antiradical organizations. *What's What*, an October 1926 publication, warned in a headline, "Subversive, Radical and Doubtful Societies Spread over America Like a Gigantic Spider Web." The Child Labor Amendment, Hunter believed, was a product of Moscow. Jane Addams, the American Civil Liberties Union, the WJCC, and labor, peace, and educational organizations were subversive.[23]

Drawing on the anti-WILPF and antipacifist resources of these organizations, attacks upon the WILPF spread throughout the country. Michigan representative M. C. McLeod asked the U.S. attorney general to investigate the WILPF and "most heartily recommend[ed]" jail for those affiliated with the organization. He later introduced a bill to the House "to curb the activities of organizations and individuals preaching the doctrines of Bolshevism," which he said was aimed primarily at the WILPF.[24] The New Jersey and New York units of the Women's Overseas Service League and the D.C. Daughters of American Colonists issued resolutions against the WILPF.[25] When local residents of Dayton, Ohio, wrote to the Bureau of Investigation seeking information on the WILPF, Bureau Director W. J. Burns regretfully informed them that Bureau files were confidential but referred them to Whitney's *Peace at Any Old Price.*[26] Other Dayton residents relied upon *Bootlegging Mind Poison,* a pamphlet by Fred Marvin. Marvin warned that slogans like "'brotherly love,' 'internationalism,' 'no more war,' 'peace and freedom,' 'industrial democracy,'" were all beautiful "in the abstract" but actually were quite dangerous: "All of them were manufactured in other lands and sent across the water to this country to destroy the morale of the American people, that we, as a nation, might in the end be destroyed."[27]

In St. Louis, Missouri, rumors circulated that the WILPF endorsed the abolition of private property (this came from Whitney's *Peace at Any Old Price* and referred to the Russian Revolution) and was aided by Russian and German agents.[28] WILPF members in the Boston Armistice Day parade were jeered.[29] Attendees at a D.C. meeting were told that the WILPF was a means for Bolshevik propaganda and that some members believed in "free love."[30] In Detroit, clergymen received letters, the substance of which appeared in the local paper, warning of the unpatriotic nature of the WILPF; WILPF members were characterized as "women under some extraordinary and peculiar internal irritation."[31] At its national headquarters in Washington, D.C., the WILPF had problems renewing its building lease after the landlord received an anonymous copy of the American Legion's attacks on the organization.[32]

Local disputes involving WILPF chapters were a part of the national debate but also reflected local issues and concerns. When Elizabeth Hutton of Sioux City, Iowa, wrote to international WILPF president Jane Addams, she painted a picture of a community-wide dispute. "That we are having a rather hard time of it is putting it mildly," Hutton wrote. "The American Legion and D.A.R. would shoot us at sunrise some glad morning if they had their way. . . . Don't fail us," she implored. "We are about on our last legs." In Sioux City, generational, class, and gender issues became embedded in the ideological conflict. A small group of older, educated, and monied women stood in opposition to the younger, less educated men of the American Legion, most of whom had fewer financial resources than local WILPF members.[33]

The April 1926 newsletter of the Sioux City American Legion Post warned its members that a local chapter of "the notorious Women's International League for Peace and Freedom" had recently been organized in Sioux City. While the women involved were "the outstanding women of Sioux City whose patriotism is unquestioned," they had been "deceived by the 'wolf in sheep's clothing.'" The author of the newsletter confidently predicted that "as soon as they learn what the organization really is and stands for, they will immediately withdraw from membership." According to the local Legion post, the WILPF was "one of the most vicious and unpatriotic organizations in the United States." It was "directly affiliated with the Communist Government of Russia" and financially affiliated with individuals who advocated immoral sexual behavior.[34] Before the dispute died down, the local American Legion, the DAR, and the League of Women Voters became involved. Even Dorothy Detzer, Jane Addams, Emily Greene Balch, and Hannah Clothier Hull of the national WILPF were consulted about the local dispute. Detzer eventually visited Sioux City, met with the local parties involved and local newspaper editors, and tried to bring the *Des Moines Register* into the story.

Jane Addams was cited by both sides in Sioux City. Local WILPF members noted her presidency as proof of the worth of the organization. Local opponents cited her presidency as proof of the WILPF's radical nature. Addams was known internationally as a cofounder of Chicago's Hull House, the center of the U.S. settlement house and social reform movement, a prominent suffragist, and a vocal peace advocate. By the 1920s, however, she was no longer the nearly universally revered woman she once had been. Addams's affiliation with peace organizations, her international presidency of WILPF, and the involvement of Hull House residents in social reform efforts made her a target for attacks.

While Addams was not mentioned in the spider web chart of Maxwell and Fries, she and Hull House were denounced by Fries as "the reddest of the red" and assailed by patriot, veteran, and antireform organizations. The Woman Patriots, in their petitions against the Child Labor Amendment and the extension of the Sheppard-Towner Act, claimed that "practically all the radicalism started among women in the United States centers about Hull-House" and Hull House graduates.[35] The omission of Addams in

Maxwell and Fries's spider web chart was "corrected" by the 1927 chart of Charles Norman Fay of Cambridge, Massachusetts. Fay also attacked Addams in a letter to the *Boston Herald* listing 115 examples of her bolshevism. Fay admitted that Addams was "a lady," but he denounced her wide-ranging political interests: "She is one of those curious *Pacifists* who would disarm every nation, including her own, except the only one that plots violence against all the rest. She is one of those strange economists who would better the conditions of working-folk by thrusting them, bound hand and foot, into the throttling grip of the trade-unionist and the politician."[36] A variety of American Legion members also denounced Addams. Ferre C. Watkins, commander of the Illinois American Legion, claimed that Hull House was "the rallying point of every radical and communistic movement in the country."[37] Prominent Iowa Legion member and Assistant Secretary of War Hanford MacNider called "all forms of 'sob sister' pacifism" dangerous and ridiculed Jane Addams and Carrie Chapman Catt, who as women claimed authority to criticize war.[38] The ROTC Honorary Society called Addams "the most dangerous woman in America."[39]

The DAR also feared Addams's corrupting influence. According to one attack, "All her actions have tended toward the strengthening of the hands of the Communists to make for the success of a Communist civil war in our country." The DAR of Washington, D.C., compiled a nine-page report on Addams, listing her organizational and personal affiliations with what it called reds, pinks, yellows, socialists, and pacifists. Addams's many reform and political interests made her suspect, but it was her affiliation with the WILPF and women's peace activism that made her dangerous.[40]

In their efforts to promote national security and attack Addams, the organizational and individual members of the antiradical network articulated a Red Scare antifeminism seeped in militarism and antistatism. The antistatism of these attacks, however, did not include a hostility to all elements of government, for its adherents promoted domestic and foreign military expansion. Many of the organizational and individual members of this network developed close ties with the War Department and used those ties and their network to survey radicals, relay information, proclaim the legitimacy of antiradicalism, and promote their political beliefs. The involvement of the War Department in this antiradical network caused significant damage to progressive women and the cause of peace.

The War Department

The WILPF interested both the Justice Department's Bureau of Information (BI) and the War Department's Military Intelligence Division (MID). The MID, its staff routinely pointed out, was not supposed to "make investigations of individuals or of organizations in time of peace, nor does this division make adverse criticism of any individual organization."[41] Despite this, BI and MID agents attended local and national WILPF meetings and submitted synopses of speeches and the names of those who figured prominently in meetings. Throughout 1923 and 1924, the MID sent agent reports on the WILPF to J. Edgar Hoover at the Justice Department but filed no charges.[42] When MID officials failed to find the incriminating information on the WILPF that they had sought, they turned to Richard M. Whitney and Fred Marvin.[43]

When citizens wrote in search of information, the MID was not to give it out. Nor was the MID to publish the results of surveillance on U.S. organizations. To circumvent this policy the MID became intricately involved in, used, and promoted an already existing network of private, patriotic organizations involved in combating radicalism. In this way the government and its intelligence networks became a part of Red Scare antifeminism.[44]

The War Department was aware of its uneasy political relationship with organized women, for progressive women's organizations were some of its most powerful opponents in appropriations debates. Anita Phipps, Director of Women's Relations for the U.S. Army, thus sought to ease relations between the military and U.S. women. In January 1924, she warned her superiors that the WJCC was "in a position to do very definite work for or against the Army." To protect preparedness expenditures, Phipps proposed a conscious effort to improve relations between the War Department and the WJCC.[45] That, however, would not happen. Only months later, the War Department released the spider web chart, causing a public relations disaster for the entire U.S. military and placing progressive women in direct and public conflict with the War Department.

In the following months, Phipps argued against extremism on both sides and tried unsuccessfully to bring what she called "ultra-pacifist" and "patriot" organizations into agreement. After visiting the International Congress of the WILPF and the WILPF's U.S. annual meeting, and attending meetings with the American Legion Auxiliary, the Daughters of 1812, the president-general of the DAR, and the Women's Overseas

Service League, Phipps was unimpressed with both sides. Women's peace organizations, she concluded, were "well-financed and highly organized groups of societies" whose composition ranged from "the radicals who know what they are doing, through various stages to the truly patriotic, sincerely peace-loving citizens who are innocent tools of a power of which they are totally ignorant." Opposing them were "ultra-patriotic societies who collect their own unofficial information, make many false statements which often cannot be proven and which discredit their true state-ments . . . groups of zealous, patriotic women who are anxious and eager to do their best to combat vicious propaganda but who have no facts to go on, have not the same kind of sharpened wits as they [*sic*] antagonists and who are attempting to meet the enemy's rapiers with broomsticks." Phipps concluded that the solution was for a "constructive, consistent, wise and definite program of action" to be developed and given to women's organi-zations who sought to combat "dangerous doctrines." The plan should be the responsibility of a committee including someone from the MID, the War Department's General Staff, the Department of Justice, and Phipps.[46]

The MID, however, saw Phipps's suggestion as "incorrect in principle" and "inexpedient." Any plan recommended by the War Department, it feared, would only bring "greater embarrassment" to the department. The MID's Colonel Reeves recommended that the War Department make no direct move but refer inquiring organizations to "civilian agencies inten-sively engaged in anti-pacifist work," such as R. M. Whitney's American Defense Society, the Woman Patriots, or Fred Marvin of the *New York Commercial*. Colonel Barnhardt of the General Staff agreed, and such became the policy.[47] Phipps's hopes for cooperation between the MID, militarist, and peace-minded women were replaced by a War Department policy that endorsed antiradical and Red Scare antifeminist organizations already hostile to peace activists.

Phipps persistently continued her efforts to improve relations between the U.S. military and progressive women's organizations. In 1924 she reminded the assistant chief of staff that pacifists were largely women and that "the women's vote is of the same weight as the men's." She warned that "the serious consideration of every department of the Government and no opportunity should be lost for the education of women on Army matters so that they will not be misled by specious statements." The "sensational and false" information given out by groups such as the Woman Patriots caused the War Department "much harm."[48] In 1926 Phipps unsuccessfully attempted to convince the chief of staff of the Army to appear at the second Women's Conference on the Cause and Cure for War. His presence, she argued, "would be of great educational value for the women delegates."[49] In 1927 she appealed to the secretary of war for increased authority, money, and a board of women to advise the War Department. Phipps warned that voting women could be "a serious menace" and complained that the War Department was creating unnecessary antagonism by failing to use her expertise to correctly distinguish between female patriots and female subversives.[50]

In 1927 Phipps, along with Maude Wetmore of the National Civic Federation, recommended that the War Department appoint an advisory board of women.[51] Despite the opposition of War Department advisers,[52] the secretary of war and his chief of staff decided to appoint a "Civilian Aide for Women's Relations" to help garner women's support.[53] After considerable debate, Secretary of War Dwight Davis called thirteen prominent women to his office in February 1929 to discuss "the growing responsibility of the women of the country."[54] Mrs. John Sippel of the General Federation of Women's Clubs was appointed chief civilian aide, and a March date was set to create an advisory council.[55] Male civilian aides, congressmen, clergymen, and others complained to the secretary of war about the inadvisability of female aides. Despite reassurances in March and October to the women who had met with Davis that plans for the aide position and advisory board were simply postponed, they were soon canceled.[56]

Phipps's efforts mark an interesting middle ground. Phipps believed that women's endorsement of disarmament programs was dangerous, but she never adopted the view that progressive women and progressive women's organizations were radical insurgents. At the same time, Phipps's analyses make clear her very conditional support for, and wholehearted skepticism about, women's patriot organizations. Phipps was concerned enough about the tensions between the War Department (particularly the MID) and organized women to attempt educational and reconciliatory programs with organizations she did not like.

Despite Phipps's hesitations, the MID often used the resources of anti-radicalist organizations and endorsed their views by sending requests for information to their offices. Private citizens as well as MID staff with questions about the WILPF were referred to civilian organizations. For example, Margaret Robinson's MPIL was recommended to the MID by a regional commander, who then arranged for Robinson to meet Lieutenant Colonel Walter Wilson. Robinson, the officer claimed, "has the best library on radicals and radical activities in this Corps Area." Only a month later, when a private citizen sought information on the communist youth movement, MID staff referred her to an MPIL pamphlet.[57] When Mrs. Schatz of Birmingham, Michigan, sought information on whether the WILPF was subversive, an MID officer referred her to the DAR. John Madden of the MID referred queries on the WILPF to R. M. Whitney and the *Woman Patriot.*[58] Apparently, information went both directions. In 1922, Mary Kilbreth of the Woman Patriots claimed to be in "direct communication with the heart of the government. We have access to the most important secret files etc (confidential) and the little Patriot is used or quoted by officials who accept our documentation as reliable and safe to use."[59]

The civilian on whom the War Department appears to have relied most heavily was Fred Marvin. In 1923, Army officer Kerr Riggs recommended Marvin's *New York Commercial* column as "a valuable daily review of the many phases of radical, communist and pacifist activities." In 1926, the MID went to the *New York Commercial* for a list of over 200 organizations "directly or indirectly" connected with socialists and communists. When the Manufacturers Association of Erie, Pennsylvania, wrote to Assistant Secretary of War Hanford MacNider for the War Department's analysis of the WILPF, MacNider sent the standard statement of the War Department's inability to release information but included copies of Marvin's anti-WILPF pamphlet *Ye Shall Know the Truth.*[60] MID officers often sent or recommended Marvin's writings to other MID officers,[61] and from 1923 until at least 1928 the MID subscribed to the various journals for which Marvin wrote.[62] Several prominent War Department officials—MacNider, Fries, Major General Eli Helmick—were members of Marvin's Key Men of America. Fries and Helmick were on the Advisory Council.

Marvin believed that radicalism posed a serious threat to the United States and that women shouldered much of the blame for the successful spread of radicalism. His analysis of the WILPF, the WJCC, and other progressive women's organizations and their members was decidedly unfavorable and damaging. The reliance of the War Department upon his information undoubtedly shaped War Department policy and affected its thinking. Yet it is clear that members of the War Department did not completely agree about the value and suitability of Marvin and other civilian patriots.

Despite this lack of unanimity, the War Department's involvement in this network of Red Scare antifeminist organizations clearly damaged progressive women's organizations. The War Department's involvement signified direct government support of the continuance of Red Scare sentiments, organizations, and networks. The civilian members of this network saw their involvement and connections with the War Department as proof of progressive women's radicalism and as an endorsement of the attacks upon progressive women. As later chapters will show, this network provided rich resources with which to attack as dangerous to the security of the nation progressive women, progressive women's organizations, and the multitude of issues endorsed by progressive women. This surveillance network policed the boundaries and constructions of women's citizenship. It also offered antifeminist women political legitimacy and a space for political expression.

Connected by a belief in the continuing crisis of the Red Scare, the political insidiousness of feminism, the dangers of peace activism, and the antidemocratic nature of federal social programs, the individuals and organizations of this network opposed a series of 1920s bills, including the Child Labor Amendment, the Sheppard-Towner Act, and a bill proposing the establishment of a federal bureau of education, as well as the existence of the Children's Bureau. The organizations working against this legislation often accused progressive women of working at the guidance of an "interlocking directorate" that could be traced to the Soviet Union. Yet they themselves rarely acknowledged the interlocking and overlapping personal and financial relationships between and within their own organizations.

CHAPTER 5

"What Is Home without a Federal Agent?"

Social Welfare Policy in the Postsuffrage Decade

Throughout the 1920s, the convergence of antiradicalism and antifeminism severely limited the ability of progressive women to promote social welfare legislation. Antiradicals and Red Scare antifeminists argued that the state-expanding legislative goals of progressive women were part of a larger subversive effort to reconfigure society in a Bolshevist, bureaucratic, and feminist fashion. Claiming patriotic defense of the nation, these men and women opposed a constitutional amendment restricting child labor, a bill providing health care and education funds for women and children (the Sheppard-Towner Act), a federal department of education, and the Children's Bureau.

These federal measures were continuations of Progressive Era reform. Advocates of these measures believed that government should and could better society, and they used pressure group politics to lobby legislators. The antiradical opponents of these measures correctly understood, however, that these legislative proposals were not the result of a gender-neutral progressivism.

Social welfare reform in the 1920s, to borrow Robyn Muncy's phrase, was a "female dominion."[1] Social welfare legislation was developed by, promoted by, and identified with progressive women who had learned activism in settlement house communities, particularly Chicago's Hull House. Convinced of government's potential to do good, these female activists had successfully lobbied for the 1912 creation of the U.S. Children's Bureau of the Department of Labor, a federal agency dedicated to monitoring and improving the lives of the nation's children. Directed first by Julia Lathrop and then Grace Abbott, economically and organizationally sustained by the lobbying of U.S. women's organizations, the bureau illustrated the increasing female influence and presence in government. With the lobbying help of activists like socialist Florence Kelley and many U.S. women's clubs—the General Federation of Women's Clubs, the National Consumer's League, the National Congress of Mothers, and, after 1920, the League of Women Voters and the Women's Joint Congressional Committee (WJCC)—the women of the Children's Bureau led the effort to expand social welfare programs pertaining to women and children in the United States.

Opponents of these measures argued that the government bureaucracies initiated by the measures threatened already weakened patriarchal prerogatives. In the words of one Nevada legislator, "They have taken our women away from us by constitutional amendments; they have taken our liquor away from us; and now they want to take our children."[2] The opponents of these legislative measures claimed that the expansion of social welfare programs would nationalize women and children and erode both individual and collective patriarchy.

The female proponents of social welfare legislation made reasoned arguments in their own defense to the press, the American public, and Congress. Proponents rarely understood themselves to be radicals, never considered themselves subversives, and assumed that the logic of their well-researched arguments would prevail. The damning figures on the horrors of child labor, the stacks of letters from women praising the Sheppard-Towner Act, and the loud denials of subversiveness did little, however, to change the minds of Red Scare antifeminists convinced that progressive women were part of an overwhelming radical threat.

The debates swirling around the Child Labor Amendment provide an excellent context in which to tell this story, for the Child Labor Amendment was the most dramatic legislative loss that progressive women suffered in the 1920s. Building on that context, I then look at the larger program of social welfare (the Sheppard-Towner Act, a department of education, and the Children's Bureau) believed by Red Scare antifeminists to be subverting government and family.

The Child Labor Amendment

Since the turn of the century, many reformers had believed child labor to be an economic and social problem. Though the numbers were decreasing, over a million children aged ten to fifteen remained in the workforce in

1920: 11.3 percent of boys and 5.6 percent of girls. African American children were four times as likely as white children to be employed.[3] Over 20 percent of all children aged ten to fifteen were employed in the southern states of Alabama, Georgia, Mississippi, and South Carolina. While child labor in the North and West was more limited, young children still labored widely in factory cities and farm industries. For example, in Passaic, New Jersey, over 75 percent of child laborers began working when fourteen years of age or younger. Labor investigators reported seeing children as young as five or six picking berries or shucking oysters.[4] Most children worked long hours, some as many as twelve hours per day, in unsafe working conditions that threatened their health and development, and few had educational opportunities. Employers preferred children to adults because they worked for lower wages, did not unionize, and often were faster and more agile than their already labor-weary parents. Parents argued that their families depended upon the wage earning of children for subsistence. Reformers, appalled at the working conditions of children, argued that children laboring under such conditions would grow up to be unhealthy and uneducated citizens.

Despite the horrors of child labor, by 1924 it was clear that federal legislation restricting child labor would not work. In 1918 the Supreme Court had declared the 1916 Keating-Owen Act, which standardized child labor regulations across the country, unconstitutional (*Hammer v. Dagenhart*) as a usurpation of state police powers. In response, Congress imposed a 10 percent interstate commerce tax on goods created in firms that employed children. In 1922, the Supreme Court also struck down these tariffs (*Bailey v. Drexel Furniture Co.*). Reformers' frustration increased when the director of the Children's Bureau, Grace Abbott, testified in January 1923 that child labor had actually increased after the second Supreme Court decision.

A constitutional amendment seemed the solution to those seeking to end child labor. Pushed forward largely by Florence Kelley and female activists from the Children's Bureau, the resulting Child Labor Amendment was purposefully broad. Section 1 granted Congress "the power to limit, regulate, and prohibit the labor of persons under eighteen years of age." Section 2 left states free to establish more rigorous standards than the national level, which the amendment's proponents assumed would be accomplished following the amendment's passage. The amendment received most of its support from women's organizations, and many in Congress saw it as a woman's issue. The League of Women Voters, the

WJCC, and the General Federation of Women's Clubs made it a top priority.[5] But Julia Lathrop, former director of the Children's Bureau, warned astutely that "much sentiment exists against central control" and cautioned against the timing of the amendment.[6]

Though the national congressional debates and public hearings were not as contentious as the subsequent states' debates, they laid the groundwork for the exploitation of fears in state campaigns. Congressional opponents warned that the amendment would centralize power in Washington, creating a dangerous "new army of officeholders" whose sustenance would depend on the additional bureaucracy and whose job it would be to infiltrate homes. This bureaucracy would be "tyrannous," expensive, and "dangerous to the liberties of the people and to the safety of America."[7] The bureaucracy created by the Child Labor Amendment would become "the big national father in Washington." Parental authority would be transferred from parents to a federal bureaucracy; "Parent would be set against child, and child would be set against parent." Government agents would then become the power brokers in American homes. In the joking fears of one congressman, this meant that the familiar motto "What is home without a mother?" would be replaced by "What is home without a Federal Agent?"[8] However, this was no joking matter. The opponents of the Child Labor Amendment feared a politically radical inversion of the patriarchal family.

The penetration of the home by the federal government, via the Child Labor Amendment, signaled to amendment opponents the increasing expansion of a dangerous and ever more powerful and pervasive government influence in state and personal matters. Senator James Reed of Missouri argued that the amendment was only one of a series of legislative proposals that would ensure that "human beings from the cradle to the grave . . . [would] be a statutory product." The government bureaucracy created by the Sheppard-Towner Act would control the infancy of all children, the Child Labor Amendment would render parental control ineffective, the proposed federal department of education would subject them to congressional dictates, the current attempt to make uniform marriage and divorce laws in all the states would subject their marital relations to federal control, their income would be taxed, and finally, their estates would be taxed.[9]

This slippery slope of government influence and bureaucracy was dangerous by itself. It was even more dangerous, opponents claimed, because it was part of a continuing Bolshevik strategy to destroy democracy and the nation via the gradual takeover of government and the nationalization of children. Virginia representative Joseph Deal warned that the amendment originated in Russian theories: "There is a close alliance between the Russian proletariat and the social workers" behind the amendment. The Children's Bureau, which would enforce the amendment, formed the foundation that radicals would use "to build and extend this socialist scheme and incidentally make the American people pay the bill."[10]

Congressional opponents to the amendment also cited Florence Kelley's influence in the drafting of the amendment to prove its political and social subversiveness. As a member of the Hull House community and New York's Henry Street Settlement and as a factory inspector, Kelley knew the horrors of child labor intimately and was dedicated to its abolition. She also was a socialist, had known Friedrich Engels and translated his work, and was a divorced woman with children. She had been deeply involved in drafting both the legislation creating the Children's Bureau and the Child Labor Amendment and was accused of drafting both in order to train American children in radicalism.[11] In arguments against the amendment, opponents almost always referred to Kelley by the name Wischnewetsky, that of her ex-husband, in an attempt to link her with foreign radicalism, to remind people of her divorced status, and to rudely call her by a name she did not wish to use.[12]

Despite opposition, in April 1924 the House voted favorably on the amendment, 297 to 69. In June the resolution passed the Senate, 61 to 23.[13] The opposition to the amendment entered into the *Congressional Record* and would be used later with the benefit of the *Record*'s authority. The amendment then needed approval by thirty-six states for ratification. Most assumed that the amendment would easily become part of the nation's Constitution; the horrors of child labor would demand its ratification. In the summer of 1924, Arkansas rapidly approved the measure, but then in quick succession Louisiana, Georgia, and North Carolina voted it down by large margins.[14]

By fall, the upcoming Massachusetts statewide advisory referendum was believed to be nationally decisive. Owen Lovejoy, who chaired the National Child Labor Committee (NCLC), warned that losing Massachusetts would "seriously jeopardize the campaign throughout the country." Most expected the Massachusetts battle to be easy: the Massachusetts legislature had previously endorsed the amendment, the state's child labor laws already were among the most restrictive in the nation, and the state's prominent politicians were overwhelmingly in favor. The NCLC often

National Child Labor Committee pamphlet comparing child labor conditions in Georgia and Massachusetts. Lewis Hine, *Why This Double Standard? One New England Corporation Owns Cotton Mills in Georgia and Massachusetts...*, n.d. Silverprint, silver gelatin. 6²/₁₆″ × 4¹⁵/₁₆″. Milwaukee Art Museum, Gift of Robert Mann.

cited Massachusetts in its literature as an example of the positive results of child labor laws.[15]

Massachusetts activists quickly drew battle lines, and women played vital political roles on both sides. The proponents of the amendment joined efforts in the Massachusetts Committee on Ratification of the Child Labor Amendment, chaired by Dorothy Kirchwey Brown. Brown was well qualified for the position: a graduate of Barnard and former agent of the U.S. Commission on Industrial Relations, she also chaired the League of Women Voters' Child Welfare Department.[16] Massachusetts' activists from the General Federation of Women's Clubs, the League of Women Voters, the Women's Trade Union League, the Federation of Churches, and the Republican Council of Women joined Brown. Julia Lathrop, former director of the Children's Bureau, left retirement in Illinois to canvass Massachusetts for the amendment (aware of the sentiment against the amendment, Lathrop wrote to Florence Kelley that she would "rather go to the dentist"), and the American Federation of Labor provided funds for Ethel Smith, legislative secretary of the National Women's Trade Union League (NWTUL), to spend October lobbying in Massachusetts.[17]

People opposing the amendment organized the Citizens Committee to Protect Our Homes and Children. Members of the committee were tied to the Associated Industries of Massachusetts, the state unit of the National Association of Manufacturers; the Massachusetts Public Interests League (MPIL; Margaret C. Robinson's home was given as the committee's mailing address); the Woman Patriots; the Sentinels of the Republic; and the Constitutional Liberty League, an organization with antiprohibition roots.

When Ethel Smith of the NWTUL arrived in Massachusetts, the effectiveness of the opposition surprised her, and she felt that amendment proponents had been "caught unprepared." Those against the amendment, she lamented, had waged "an active campaign, but a quiet one" since April or May. In early October, "it broke out with the most terrible virulence." By the end of October, she wrote, "Don't let the enemy get you upon the defensive as they have got us in Massachusetts. The tragic inactivity of our side during the summer months will cost us."[18]

The Citizens Committee to Protect Our Homes and Children massively outspent and outorganized the proponents of the Child Labor Amendment. Members of the Boston Women's Trade Union League, who visited the committee's headquarters incognito in order to view antiamendment literature, were amazed: "We found them well stocked with tons of it—

piled high on all sides of the place. Six telephones going at once. A room full of workers and desks and complete equipment."[19] With the $16,000 that the committee took in, it employed the Hunt-Luce Advertising Agency, spent nearly $5,000 on newspaper ads, and bought radio time during which Louis Coolidge, who chaired the antiamendment Sentinels of the Republic, and Margaret Robinson spoke.[20] The largest contributors were the MPIL, which donated over $1,300; the Sentinels of the Republic, with $500; and the National Association of Manufacturers, with $150. Dorothy Kirchwey Brown, whose Massachusetts Committee on Ratification of the Child Labor Amendment had only $3,000 to spend, suspected that the Citizens Committee received additional and unreported financial help from manufacturing organizations.[21] The Massachusetts Committee on Ratification was indeed, as Lathrop characterized it, "like little David without a sling."[22]

As the campaign in Massachusetts progressed, amendment opponents increasingly used the argument, both in Massachusetts and nationally, that the amendment was Bolshevik in origin and un-American in its consequences. It would result in "a national calamity." This argument augmented pleas for states' rights and warnings of the dangers of government centralization, for amendment opponents bound the various arguments together with concerns about gender and home. While accusations of political subversiveness were voiced in exaggerated form by groups such as the Woman Patriots, often dismissed as a small group of extremists, the argument also was used by the larger Citizens Committee to Protect Our Homes and Children, popular media, and academics.[23]

All-encompassing arguments against the amendment began with the premise that the proposed amendment had very little to do with regulating child labor. Rather, it was "a determined endeavor to obtain a grant of power from the people un-American and revolutionary in its effect."

> The amendment aims, not at the exploitation of child labor, but at the right of the individual under eighteen to work for a living, for his own advancement, or for service to others,—at the right of parents to direct their children and to receive from them such assistance as may be essential to the maintenance of the family. It seeks to substitute national control, directed from Washington, for local and parental control, to bring about the nationalization of children, and to make the child the ward of the Nation. It is a highly socialistic measure,—an assault against individual liberty.[24]

It was a measure "hatched in Moscow" and fostered in the United States by subversives who sought to weaken the nation. Utah senator William King, in an oft-quoted statement, claimed: "Every Bolshevik, every extreme Communist, and Socialist in the United States is back of this measure."[25] While King could not decide whether the measure was Bolshevist, communist, or socialist and did not care to distinguish between the three, like others he warned that the major culprit behind the amendment was Florence Kelley.

As further proof of the amendment's radicalism, opponents drew on U.S. images of the Russian Revolution and claimed that it would "nationalize" U.S. children. Texas lumberman and Sentinels member John H. Kirby said it was "a step in the direction of the Socialist plan to make the children the chattels of the State instead of the jewels of the home."[26] The amendment meant that parents would lose control of their children. The wisdom and intimacy of parents would be replaced, in the words of Margaret Robinson, by "a Socialist Bureau at Washington, hundreds of thousands of miles away."[27] That Socialist Bureau would attempt to indoctrinate children as part of the plan to subvert the nation.

Opponents of the amendment argued that as children were nationalized, dangerous bureaucracy would enter the most intimate arena of citizens' lives: the home. The Citizens Committee to Protect Our Homes and Children—painting themselves as the defenders of children, parents, and the idyllic home from the polluting influence of government, bureaucracy, and socialism—warned that the amendment would subject "your children and your home to the inspection of a federal agent."[28] Federal inspectors, committee members claimed, would invade homes to ensure that children were not working. Henry L. Shattuck, Boston state representative and member of the Citizens Committee, warned, "If you would defend your hearthstone from centralized bureaucratic control and from the hordes of agents and inspectors sent to enforce bureaucratic rules and regulations, if you believe in local self-government, and if you would preserve the foundation stones of democracy,—*vote 'NO' on Referendum No. 7.*"[29]

Not only would the home be infiltrated by the amendment, but its relationships of power would be upset. Columbia University president Nicholas Murray Butler was only one of many public figures to warn that the amendment would infringe upon the rights of parents and reshape family life.[30] A cartoon from the Columbus (Ohio) *Dispatch*, which echoes earlier congressional jokes about children appealing to Children's

Bureau agents when unwilling to do their chores, portrays children clearly disobeying their parents with little fear. The children are really young adults. The labor they are being asked to do, chopping wood and doing dishes, is not factory labor, yet the cartoon implies that the amendment is applicable. By their clothing, hair, posture, and indolent nature, the urban-appearing youth distinguish themselves from their rural parents. At the center of the cartoon, the fringes on the young woman's hammock, the glimpse of her thigh, and the chocolates on her lap suggest that she needs the character development honest labor could bring. The message is that the Child Labor Amendment subverts everything. Children will disobey and ignore their parents while being transformed into lazy, decadent, but

A cartoon showing the supposed results of the Child Labor Amendment. Cartoon clipping found in the Julia Lathrop Papers, folder—Papers, Child Labor, 1925.

perhaps modern, adults who smoke cigarettes and bob their hair. Government intrusion in the home is dangerous.[31]

Cardinal William O'Connell, archbishop of Boston, also used the home as a trope when he propelled the Catholic Church into opposing the Child Labor Amendment.[32] In early October Cardinal O'Connell issued a circular letter to all churches in the Boston area condemning the amendment. Understanding that women provided the energy on both sides of the amendment, the cardinal requested that each parish clergy "select two of your women parishioners" to attend an informational meeting against the amendment. Furthermore, he "recommended" that all parish clergy warn their parishioners of "the dangers hidden" in the amendment and of their duty to vote. The day following the Cardinal's announcement, Boston mayor James Curley, who had been a proponent of the amendment, denounced it as "a Bolshevik scheme." The next week the archdiocesan newspaper the *Pilot* proclaimed: "Parental control must not be subordinated to the will of Congress and to purposes, real or assumed, on the part of any supreme dictator, flashing his message from Washington to the farthest corners of this great country, with follow-up calls by a horde who would molest the peaceful tranquility of the American home." The *Pilot* went on to echo other arguments against the amendment—that it was socialistic, would sovietize the United States, was contrary to the ideals of the American founders, and would impose serious dangers on individual liberty.[33]

The Catholic hierarchy, and many parishioners, also feared that once Congress forbade child labor, government would be obliged to expand children's educational opportunities, and that federal control of education would result. Concurrent discussion of a possible federal department of education led many Catholics to interpret the amendment as a threat to parochial schools. These fears influenced Catholic voters.[34] For example, Mrs. Francis Slattery, a leader in the League of Catholic Women and member of the Sentinels of the Republic, claimed that the league had registered 162,000 Catholic women to vote.[35]

Clearly, the home was more than a simple physical space in these arguments. It was the metaphorical, and vulnerable, source of national well-being. It was the embodiment of the patriarchal family. The opponents of the Child Labor Amendment understood the physical and emotional space of the patriarchal home to be the inviolable ground on which democracy and the nation were built and on which the federal government could not step. In the words of a Baptist minister writing in the *Manufacturers*

Record, "The family has made the state, not the State the family." Or, as a
member of the Sentinels of the Republic wrote, "The Government at
Washington can never be any stronger than the Homes it comes out of.
Let us maintain all the government we can at home, where we can keep
our eyes on it."[36]

According to these opponents of the Child Labor Amendment, the home
was supposed to be a place in which each man exercised his own form of
government. Opponents of the amendment argued that it threatened male
exercise of power and constituted a radical program that "impose[d] a
condition in which no man is master of his home because of the constant supervision of Government agents."[37] A man's children were part of
his dominion. The Child Labor Amendment threatened his dominion
much as a foreign nation would threaten the United States. The legislated
bureaucracy of the Child Labor Amendment would create a "big national
father in Washington," subverting the authority of each individual father.[38]

Antiamendment arguments erroneously portrayed the idealized and
patriarchal home, rather than the factory or cotton field, as the site where
child labor took place. Over and over again, opponents of the amendment
used the blueberry-picking and table-setting analogies: If the amendment
passed, boys would not pick blueberries for their mothers, and girls would
not help set the family table. The work that made children's cheeks rosy
would be denied them, and their character development would be flawed.
Young men would be denied the opportunity to work their way through
college, and the children of widows would be unable to help their virtuous
mothers.[39]

It is ironic but not surprising that the middle- and upper-class activists
who populated the anti–Child Labor Amendment movement were not
members of working-class families who depended upon children's labor
for financial subsistence. Amendment opponents advocated a family
economy—a family system in which each family member contributes
wages or labor—while refusing to acknowledge the realities of one. Child
labor, as amendment opponents saw it, consisted of children helping out.
For many working-class Americans, however, the family economy meant
that children worked long hours, often outside the home, in wage-earning
jobs so that their families could survive.[40] Amendment opponents effectively controlled the terms of the argument in such a way that the conditions of child labor were rarely debated. They successfully used arguments
that focused attention on amendment proponents rather than on manufacturers or an economic system.

There is little suspense to this story. In the advisory referendum of November 1924, the voters of Massachusetts resoundingly defeated the Child Labor Amendment by almost a 3:1 ratio in what was nearly a record turnout. The referendum question received more votes than any other referendum on the ballot. With very little additional prodding, the state legislature voted against the amendment.[41] Amendment proponents were correct in their original analysis that the Massachusetts vote would be nationally decisive, but the statewide results were not what they wanted.

The arguments used against the Child Labor Amendment in Massachusetts echoed throughout the rest of the 1920s in the continued national debate. The Citizens Committee to Protect Our Homes and Children blurred into the National Committee for the Rejection of the Twentieth Amendment, with headquarters in the Washington, D.C., building of the National Association of Manufacturers. The newspapers and magazines of farmers' organizations, manufacturing organizations, and the national activists of the Woman Patriots, the Sentinels of the Republic, the MPIL, and like-minded organizations warned that radicals who sought to subvert the United States via the Child Labor Amendment threatened the American home and the American family. Opponents left behind the more reasoned rhetoric used against the Child Labor Amendment in the early phases of the legislative battle. Red Scare antiradicalism, which had served so effectively in Massachusetts, soon dominated the debate.

Proponents of the amendment, originally confident of their success, were sure that accusations of radicalism had caused the amendment's defeat. The effectiveness of this strategy surprised them, for they had never believed it viable. Alice Stone Blackwell labeled the arguments against the amendment "beneath contempt." Others, even an opponent of the amendment, called the rhetorical strategies "indefensible," "a 'hang-over' from the orgy of post-war propaganda," "ludicrous," "absolutely astounding," "a slough of reaction," and "a wanton disregard for truth." Harriet Taylor Upton, a prominent member of the Republican National Committee, wrote, "Never did I know of such remarkable propaganda nor see such results from such propaganda."[42]

Despite this public criticism, the charges were effective. Dorothy Kirchwey Brown, who chaired Massachusetts' proamendment campaign, once had felt that the accusations needed no comment, but by the end of October 1924 she wrote in frustration, "They are succeeding to an alarming extent."[43] Mrs. Alaysia Davis of the General Federation of Women's Clubs feared for women's future political activities nationwide and in her home of Vermont: "The women are meeting such bitter opposition . . . and they are so new at this work that I fancy they feel timid."[44] The impact was nationwide. From Florida, the state superintendent of the Children's Home Society wrote: "Unquestionably we are feeling the unfavorable reaction brought about by the Child Labor Amendment. Somehow, the Legislature seems to feel that all of us who are interested in child welfare are radicals and bolsheviks. It will take a long time to recover from this unfavorable reaction."[45]

Not everyone, however, felt that the defeat of the amendment was due to unfair propaganda. Margaret Robinson, writing in the *Manufacturers Record* in January 1925, claimed that the amendment was defeated due to "a real awakening throughout the country." Thomas Cadwalader, a lawyer and member of the Sentinels of the Republic, declared in 1927 that the amendment's death was part of a growing trend away from dangerous centralization.[46] The *Boston Herald* asserted that compliments were due to the Sentinels of the Republic, the MPIL, and the Citizens Committee to Protect Our Homes and Children.[47]

Proponents of the amendment blamed business interests for its defeat. Members of the Women's Trade Union League felt that the Citizens Committee to Protect Our Homes and Children was merely "a smoke screen" for industrialists who had interests in the South, where child labor was more prevalent.[48] Florence Kelley adamantly argued that opponents of the amendment were motivated by "the threatened loss of their privilege to continue to exploit."[49] Dorothy Kirchwey Brown said the same in her 1925 pamphlet *The Struggle for the Child Labor Amendment as Revealed by the Massachusetts Referendum*. The amendment lost, she argued, because of a "deliberately planned propaganda of fear" by those who profited from child labor, namely the interlocking membership of the National Association of Manufacturers (NAM), the Associated Industries of Massachusetts, and the Citizens Committee to Protect Our Homes and Children.[50] Massachusetts manufacturers who had textile mills in the South had sought to slow the Child Labor Amendment, Brown charged, in order to prevent stringent child labor laws from being implemented in the southern states.[51]

Brown noted that the vast majority of personal and organizational attacks made by Child Labor Amendment opponents had been directed at women and women's organizations but remained convinced that "the real animus of the attacks on women's organizations" was fear of losing the benefits of child labor. "The cry 'bolshevist' was raised against women leaders for the purpose of weakening their leadership and shattering the coherence of the women's groups, in order to defeat the legislative proposals that women were supporting. Its inspiration was economic."[52] She traced the attacks to the *Woman Patriot* (the five-woman board of directors—including Margaret C. Robinson—were named individually) and the reprinting of its articles by manufacturing newspapers and Henry Ford's *Dearborn Independent*.[53] In Brown's analysis, the attacks upon progressive women and their organizations were a strategy adopted by manufacturers acting out of economic self-interest.

Child labor was a profitable business. Children were significantly cheaper to employ than adults and were less likely to unionize or otherwise effectively resist their employer. The few available statistics on children's wages show that laborers under sixteen generally earned one-fourth to one-half of what adult laborers earned. For example, in the Tennessee cotton goods and hosiery industry, boys earned an average of $5.20 a week, girls $6.05, women $13.38, and men $18.27.[54] In the Georgia textile industry, the weekly wages of fourteen and fifteen year olds ranged from $5 to $8; adult males averaged $15.79, and women averaged $12.77.[55] The Department of Commerce figured that on a national basis, men who worked full time in industry earned $924 annually, women $495, and children $281.[56]

The profit motive, however, was more complex than amendment proponents envisioned. The issues were not purely economic. Most of the individuals and groups opposing the Child Labor Amendment used the same arguments to oppose a federal department of education, the extension of the Sheppard-Towner Act, and the existence of the Children's Bureau. Many amendment opponents understood government regulation of private business to be part of the same bureaucratic and centralizing trend that promoted a wide array of government social welfare programs. Members equated government influence in the home with the nationalization and regulation of businesses by the federal government. Men were to control their families just as business owners were to control mercantile fleets, railroads, and small businesses. According to amendment opponents, when government interfered with the exercise of male power, either in the home or in the factory, it threatened an intricate and interdependent network of male power in the home, family, state, and capital. The freedom of capital from government intrusion into the workplace depended upon the freedom of individual men from government intrusion into their homes. Opposition to the amendment included but went beyond the profit motive, for the organized opposition believed that the expansion of government threatened both unfettered capitalism and unfettered male power.[57]

Opponents of social welfare legislation conflated a variety of legislative measures into a single subversive menace. John Edgerton, president of the National Association of Manufacturers, called the Child Labor Amendment, the Sheppard-Towner Act, and the proposed education department a "triple program" that "aims to destroy our form of government."[58] The Sentinels of the Republic also conflated these measures and understood them as a historical crisis in which "Federal paternalism and other forms of communism threaten[ed] the bulwarks of the national structure."[59] The Woman Patriots called the three measures "a unified agency and program of revolution by legislation. They are as deliberate a conspiracy to destroy this Republic as any plot ever hatched to overthrow a government by force and violence."[60] This conflation enabled antiradicals to easily dismiss and discredit their opponents with code words needing little explanation or evidence.

A COMPLETE LEGISLATIVE PLOT

The Sheppard-Towner Act was an integral part of the feared subversive legislative plot. Sheppard-Towner, first passed in 1921 and implemented by the Children's Bureau, dedicated matching funds for states to provide visiting nurses, nutrition, and developmental and hygiene education for pregnant women and new mothers. The National League of Women Voters and the WJCC lobbied on its behalf. While it originally had few detractors except for the Woman Patriots, when the act came up for renewal in 1927 it faced fierce opposition and could only garner a two-year renewal.[61]

Those opposing the Child Labor Amendment used similar arguments to oppose the Sheppard-Towner Act. The MPIL, the Woman Patriots, the Sentinels of the Republic, and later the DAR claimed that the statute allowed government agents to infiltrate the American home. It nationalized American women and children as one step in the radical takeover of the United States. The issues again were dangerous federal centralization, the erosion of state and parental rights, burgeoning bureaucracies, and subversion. Mrs. George Madden Martin, a Kentucky author and General Federation of Women's Clubs dissident, warned that "it involve[d] the same principle of nationalized, standardized care of children and Federal interference between parent and child" as the Child Labor Amendment.[62] Opponents of Sheppard-Towner accused its advocates of un-Americanism and called the statute Bolshevistic, much as opponents of the Child Labor Amendment had done. Senator James Reed of Missouri claimed the two measures were part of the "cradle to the grave" legislative onslaught on American individualism.[63] The *Boston Herald* claimed, "There is plenty of evidence that the Sheppard-Towner bill . . . was inspired originally by Russian propaganda."[64] The American Medical Association, which also opposed the act, called it an "imported socialistic scheme."[65] Members of Congress—such as William King of Utah, Frank Greene of Vermont, and James Reed of Missouri—variably called the act socialist or Bolshevist.[66]

The Woman Patriots, who went on record against the Sheppard-Towner Act as early as 1921, emphasized this theme in a 1926 petition submitted to the *Congressional Record* by Delaware senator Thomas Bayard. In their thirty-five–page petition, they argued that the Sheppard-Towner Act, the Child Labor Amendment, and the education bill were "masked as 'welfare' and 'women's' measures, and entrusted to certain women's organizations to engineer . . . but are none the less straight imported communism." The act was part of the "Engels–[Florence] Kelley program" for the "central control and standardization of children." It was part of the "worst form of communism . . . the feminist phase," which included "arousing women against men, wives against husbands, and providing community care for children, legitimate and illegitimate, to 'remove the economic foundations of monogamous marriages.'"[67] Senator Bayard sent the petition "throughout the country." The national DAR endorsed it and successfully requested that Bayard use his frank to send a copy to each state regent.[68]

The foes of Sheppard-Towner understood the statute as another intrusion into the family home and an erosion of patriarchy. The editor of the *Woman Patriot* warned that the goal of the statute was to "substitute the State for the father." It enabled women to turn to an authority, an authority beyond the reach of the men in their lives, on matters that took place in the home. This angered activist Elizabeth Lowell Putnam, who argued that it was the duty of "the husbands and fathers of the country," not women or the federal government, to ensure that women received "proper care."[69] The possibility that women might be heads of households, for a multitude of reasons, never entered these discussions.

Because many of the same organizations and individuals that supported the Child Labor Amendment also supported the Sheppard-Towner Act, personal and organizational vilifications easily transferred from one campaign to another. The *Woman Patriot* called Florence Kelley "the Socialist-Feminist generalissimo of the campaign for the Child Labor Amendment, Maternity Act, etc." If the truth were known about Kelley, it went on, her influence "would be acknowledged by all informed persons as greater than that of Marx or Engels."[70] Both campaigns also accused the WJCC, Grace Abbott, and Julia Lathrop of being subversive and un-American.

Like the Child Labor Amendment, the Sheppard-Towner Act faced vigorous resistance in Massachusetts. Of the five states that initially refused the matching funds, only Massachusetts challenged the act's constitutionality in court. Massachusetts resident Harriet A. Frothingham, a member of the Sentinels and the Woman Patriots, also filed suit, claiming that her rights had been violated by the use of taxpayer monies to support Sheppard-Towner programs. Though neither case was successful, Frothingham's made it as far as the Supreme Court.[71]

Another campaign that effectively used many of the same political players and rhetoric was against a federal department of education. First introduced in 1919 and then reintroduced throughout the 1920s, this proposal was part of various educational reform efforts. Though this campaign did not receive the publicity that other legislative campaigns did, opponents of a department considered its possible creation to be part of a subversive plot as well as a likely outcome of the Child Labor Amendment. They argued that the proposed department was a dangerous federal incursion into the home, a violation of parental rights by female government agents, an expansion of undesirable bureaucracy and centralization, and a potentially subversive propaganda measure.[72]

For example, in 1921 the Woman Patriots warned that the bill proposing such a department would cause the "nationalization of all American schools under the Federal dictatorship." In 1923, they called the proposed department part of a "radical congressional program." By 1928, as the Woman Patriots grew increasingly extreme, they claimed that a federal department of education would bring "Sovietism" or "occupational bloc rule." The *Woman Patriot* claimed that it had proof that a "radical, pacifist, minority professional block of teachers seeks federal department of education to create 'new world order.'"[73] The Sentinels of the Republic, in a more reasoned tone, routinely listed a federal department of education in the legislation it opposed. Such a department, it claimed, would subordinate parents to "a central power at Washington."[74] The *Manufacturers Record* feared that such a department would bring the "nationalization, or

Russianization, of American children." Communists, the journal warned, "are determined to lay their destroying hands on the childhood of the free United States."[75]

All of these legislative proposals were associated with the Children's Bureau. Though a federal department of education was never part of the Children's Bureau program, its opponents assumed it would be an inevitable result of the Child Labor Amendment, which was a goal of the Children's Bureau. Because of this, groups such as the Woman Patriots, the Sentinels of the Republic, and the *Manufacturers Record*—as well as organizations like the Federation of Democratic Women—variably and repeatedly called for dissolution of the Children's Bureau and criticized the bureau's first two directors, Julia Lathrop and Grace Abbott. They argued that the Children's Bureau was socialistic, dangerously bureaucratic, and largely staffed by subversive and childless women.

Moves to challenge the Children's Bureau or impugn its staff generally took place within arguments against the legislation it endorsed. For example, when speaking against the Sheppard-Towner Act, Mrs. George Madden Martin characterized the bureau as an "over-parent" and as "abhorrent." "But then," she went on, "the whole doctrine of Karl Marx is abhorrent to those Americans who prefer a democracy and believe in representative government."[76] While speaking against the Child Labor Amendment, Charles Crisp of Georgia told Congress that the Children's Bureau had "interlocking connections" to "the great network of interlocking radical, pacifist, and bureaucratic organizations and activities."[77] The Woman Patriots warned that "the pacifist internationalist Federal Children's Bureau" was really just "a socialist propaganda agency," created by the crafty lobbying skills of Florence Kelley as part of her Soviet-directed plan to subvert the nation. In their petitions against the Sheppard-Towner Act and the Child Labor Amendment, the Woman Patriots argued that subversives such as the Hull House's Jane Addams, New York settlement house leader Lillian Wald, socialist and child labor opponent Owen Lovejoy, and socialist journalist Anna Louise Strong were affiliated with the bureau.[78] The Woman Patriots accused the bureau of modeling itself on the work of "the soviet feminist chief" Aleksandra Kollontai, a prominent Russian feminist who participated in the Bolshevik revolution and whose book, in Russian, was listed in a Children's Bureau bibliography.[79]

Opponents tried to dissolve the Children's Bureau. Senator William King of Utah, who had opposed the Child Labor Amendment, the Sheppard-Towner Act, and the proposed department of education, proposed a bill in

1927 to repeal the 1912 Act establishing the Children's Bureau. James Reed of Missouri and A. Piatt Andrew of Massachusetts also voiced congressional opposition. Mrs. Mortimer West of the Federation of Democratic Women urged all Democratic members of Congress to abolish "this fifth wheel on the Federal System, called a 'Children's Bureau,' which . . . has waged political campaigns to secure national control of children."[80]

The Woman's Constitutional League of Virginia received the most attention from the Children's Bureau. The league, whose slogan was "For Home and Constitutional Government; Against Feminism and Communism," had ties to the Sentinels and Woman Patriots via its secretary, Dr. Anna Moon Randolph. The group claimed that the Children's Bureau violated the Fourth Amendment to the Constitution, sought to "take the control of children away from their parents," and spent federal monies printing and distributing communistic propaganda. In a resolution sent to the Children's Bureau, the Woman's Constitutional League warned that similar resolutions had been adopted by the New Jersey DAR, the California State Society of the Sons of the American Revolution, the MPIL, the Sentinels of the Republic, and the Woman Patriots.[81] Eventually the Daughters of 1812, the Women's Constitutional League of Maryland, the national DAR as well as several additional state affiliates, and the American War Mothers joined the effort to dissolve the Children's Bureau.[82]

Opponents knew that the people who staffed the Children's Bureau and who filled the membership rolls of the organizations endorsing these measures were women. Opponents used the endorsement of the Children's Bureau and these measures by the rank and file of most of America's largest women's organizations as proof of women's political inadequacies and of the folly of female suffrage. Legislative opponents routinely pointed out that most employees of the Children's Bureau were "abnormal" women—single and childless. They emphasized that many of the women had been trained in the settlement house movement, where women lived together. These accusations may have included veiled fears and allegations of lesbianism.

In a sense, the opponents of these measures may have been right, for these measures and their female proponents *were* a threat. The women who advocated protective labor legislation and government regulation of industry hoped to temper capitalism and its effects upon women and children. Some were socialists. Many of the women hoped to see familial power distributed differently. Some—Grace Abbott and Florence Kelley, for example—were happily single. Enactment of a Child Labor

Amendment, the programs of the Sheppard-Towner Act, and the dictates of a federal department of education would have created sources of authority on child rearing and family life outside the family, sources to which women and children could turn in times of vulnerability, perhaps even in defiance of the men in their lives. The Sheppard-Towner Act gave women an alternative institutional base from which to draw personal and economic assistance. The Child Labor Amendment recognized the educational needs of children and the concept of childhood as a time separate from considerable work responsibilities, as would a federal department of education. It would thus be more difficult for fathers to direct and profit from children's labor. Each piece of legislation questioned men's capacity and right to always protect, advise, and control the women and children in their lives.

These social welfare measures, however, were not death blows to male power. While they provided alternative power sources that women and children could attempt to use to their own advantage, women and children remained dependent upon authorities outside themselves. As Gwendolyn Mink points out, this string of legislation placed women in a dependent relationship to the state and demanded cultural conformity.[83] The social welfare professionals and programs were frequently condescending and discriminatory, had clear ideas about racial and ethnic norms, and sometimes blamed women for their own problems. Antiradicals and Red Scare antifeminists interpreted social welfare programs as dangerous interventions because their theory of governing was built on a gendered sexual division of labor, the role of the male citizen as head of household, and a man's proprietary relationship over his physical property as well as his spouse and children. They considered familial forms of social control advantageous but public state forms detrimental. This theory of governing, however, ignored the role that the social welfare state, like previous forms of the liberal democratic state, played in enforcing gender hierarchy. While social welfare legislation threatened to reshape the power of men within individual families, it posed little threat of a female overthrow of either families or the state.[84]

The word most often used to deride and emphasize the dangers of these legislative measures, ironically, was *paternalistic*. While government paternalism was thought detrimental to individual persons and the nation, individual and collective patriarchy was defined as healthy and thus was vehemently protected. Many historians, and I agree, refer to this series of legislative measures as a consequence of maternalism, or politicized motherhood, on the part of progressive women. Conversely, however, what seems to have been at play among the opponents of these legislative measures is a *politicization of patriarchal fatherhood* by both men and women. Legislative opponents of these measures believed them to be part of a slippery slope of government centralization that would begin the usurpation of individual patriarchy. The usurpation of collective patriarchy could be next.

In her analysis of social control and family violence, Linda Gordon has argued that the late nineteenth-century defense of family autonomy grew from opposition to the increasingly obvious permeability of the public and private realms that accompanied an industrial capitalist society. As urban society "created more individual opportunities for women, the defense of family autonomy came to stand against women's autonomy in a conservative opposition to women's demands for individual freedoms."[85] The Red Scare defense of family autonomy is related, for it grew from fears of a politically radical conflation of public and private, enmeshed with fears of widespread implementation of feminism (as they understood feminism to be).

For Red Scare antifeminists, the ludicrousness and danger of female autonomy, when combined with a social welfare state, were most evident in the ironic fact that "the big national father in Washington" would be staffed and directed by women. Legislative opponents feared that *female* bureaucratic agents would undermine patriarchy by worming their way into American homes and exercising paternalistic government decrees. Male power in the home was threatened by a subversive female arm of the federal government staffed by unnatural and childless women. In the analysis of antifeminists and antiradicals, the perversion of state paternalism was ultimately exemplified by the femaleness of that paternalism.[86]

The gendered antistatism developed in these Red Scare years included hostility to growing government bureaucracy and social welfare measures, but it was inconsistent. It did not include hostility toward a growing military, domestic spy networks, public highways, or mail delivery. As Robin Muncy has pointed out, the Massachusetts effort to challenge the constitutionality of the Sheppard-Towner Act's grants-in-aid programs was accompanied by statewide spending of federal monies to fight white pine rust.[87] Antistatists also failed to acknowledge the ways in which their elite economic and racial status was buttressed by the state. The selective nature of antistatism during the 1920s reinforced its antifeminist and antiradical nature.

Opposition to feminism, radicalism, and the expansion of government worked together to permeate conservatism in the 1920s. Antiradicals urged defeat of the Child Labor Amendment, the Sheppard-Towner Act, and the proposed federal department of education as a necessary reassertion of individual and collective male power against an ever-growing and increasingly feminist government. Embedded in arguments against these measures were fears about the possibly subversive consequences of women's involvement in and restructuring of both politics and government. Red Scare antifeminism limited feminist influence in governmental policy in the postsuffrage decade and raised disturbing questions about the soundness of the female citizenry.

CHAPTER 6

The Woman Citizen

Dupe or Subversive?

After the tumultuous 1925 convention of the National Council of Women (NCW), minister, reformer, and NCW leader Anna Garlin Spencer commented on the mounting attacks upon individual women and women's organizations.

> At first only the women members . . . [who] said "Peace" when we were at war were attacked by . . . slander. Now, no group of women is so conservative and socially respectable as to escape public attack in prominent newspaper front page articles, attack[ed] as "traitors" and "bad citizens," if they espouse the cause of our own participation in international matters. It looks as if the powers of evil fear a United Womanhood, organized for definite social progress, and wish to destroy the unity now existing among many groups of women.[1]

The attacks were escalating, she argued, because of women's growing political and international involvement and because of the potential in women's united political action.

Maud Wood Park, who chaired the Women's Joint Congressional Committee (WJCC) and presided over the League of Women Voters, had a similar analysis. Women's organizations and women voters, she complained, had been unfairly and maliciously maligned. While men had always found women "more or less mysterious," many men were responding to female voters with "fear" rather than "curiosity or indulgence." The result was, she said, "a sorry picture": "Men of wealth, economic and political power, men of military rank and prowess, screaming aloud in fear of women voters. Hissing 'Bolshevist!' through chattering teeth at every woman prominent in public life. And then attempting to spread their own panic through the poison of slander and innuendo . . . seeking to terrorize the women of their own families as they themselves are terrorized or have some axe to grind." All of this, she argued, was because women voters wanted "the kind of legislation that considers human beings and human happiness above and before dollars and cents, or politicians' fate."[2]

The consequences of women's votes were as yet unclear, and the contentious attacks upon many individual women and women's organizations were part of the post–Suffrage Amendment struggle to shape the newly enfranchised woman citizen. A cross-class alliance of women led by middle-class women who advocated disarmament and the expansion of the social welfare state was the manifestation of all that many Red Scare antifeminists, antiradicals, conservatives, militarists, and manufacturers had feared. Though this alliance had existed before the war, it was now armed with the power of the vote. For these opponents of progressive women, the political involvement of the newly enfranchised woman was acceptable only when contained within narrow boundaries. When outside those boundaries, women's political activism meant subversion and social upheaval.

Behind the widespread attacks upon individual women and progressive women's organizations were a sometimes contradictory but complex set of antifeminist fears. Some military and patriot groups believed that feminism, and perhaps simply femaleness, was a subversive state that had to be carefully monitored. Many assumed women's lack of political understanding and feared that women's "natural" inclination toward benevolent-sounding but radical goals (like the Child Labor Amendment) made them easily duped and dangerous political actors. At the same time, progressive women's political skills were feared. Their opponents charged that their subversive political vision, combined with their growing strength and expertise in pressure politics, made them an ominous force. The newly enfranchised political woman, antiradicals charged, required careful monitoring. Red Scare antifeminists took the lead.

Misled American Women

The fervor and effectiveness of the attacks upon women's peace organizations and the social welfare legislation that many women endorsed were amplified by simultaneous attacks upon a wide array of women's organizations.

Red Scare antifeminists attacked many women's organizations for the legislation they endorsed and for the ways they chose to organize women and use the newly gained franchise. The wholesale failure of U.S. women to use their franchise correctly was supposed proof that the vast majority of U.S. women were political simpletons, duped by a small but interlocking directorate of subversive women who took their cues from Russia.

Opponents of progressive women's organizations contended that subversives had infiltrated and now led the vast majority of American women's organizations. Though antiradicals conceded that most U.S. women were not insidious, socialist, pacifist, and un-American, they insisted that the leaders of women's organizations were. The involvement of rank-and-file women in women's organizations therefore endangered the nation, for they were unknowing supporters of radicalism (presumably, the descendants of the parlor Bolsheviks of 1919). The real purpose of "this class of feeder societies," according to *What's What*, a publication of Boston's Industrial Defense Association, was "to provide recruiting stations for extreme Radicalism among the educated classes. They are points of contact with the established order of things, and they serve as the opening wedges in Communism's attack upon society."[3] One author claimed to quote a "peculiarly frank socialist" who said, "The ladies are helping to braid the rope which, if it is ever finished, will surely hang them."[4]

Antiradicals charged that the duping of the rank-and-file members of U.S. women's organizations had dire consequences for women and the nation. U.S. women were unknowingly championing dangerous legislation. Dr. Anna Moon Randolph of the Virginia Women's Constitutional League wrote,

> Some women are easily influenced by those they think have superior knowledge, instead of doing their own thinking. . . . Consequently a whole room full of apparently intelligent women blithely endorse such paternalistic measures as the Sheppard-Towner Maternity Act, Federal Education Bill, Child Labor Amendment, Equal Rights Amendment, together with welfare bills and disarmament, which upon investigation are found to be of foreign origin and when carried out will pave the way to the destruction of our Government. . . . It is an old, old story that women are used as dupes and tools for destructive work from the days of Sampson's Delilah to the Feminist Lobby of today.[5]

Margaret Robinson, writing in the *Woman Patriot* and *Dearborn Independent*, warned that women, by failing to inform themselves, were "working to transform themselves and the rest of us from *citizens* into *subjects*."[6] The women of the majority of U.S. women's organizations were allowing themselves to be manipulated. And, as the president of the National Association of Manufacturers claimed, this was being done "by minorities manipulated from abroad through interlocking directorates of susceptible organizations."[7]

Opponents of progressive women's organizations, echoing the accusations of the spider web chart, charged that an "interlocking directorate," a "dictatorship," or a "female bloc" led most women's organizations. Furthermore, the "female bloc" was dangerous because it was led by subversive women. As Haviland Lund wrote in the *Dearborn Independent*, "Leadership of women's organizations has fallen into the hands of radicals to an alarming extent."[8] As Nancy Cott points out in *The Grounding of Modern Feminism*, the existence of a female bloc was a highly contested issue, condemned by both mainstream politicians and right-wing "patriots" as divisive and antithetical to Americanism: "The right wing's purposeful contamination of the notion of sexual politics with the radioactive quality of class warfare" infected the notion of woman as a political group with un-American connotations.[9]

The most recognizable head of the feared female dictatorship was the WJCC. Opponents of the WJCC recognized its strength but warned of its insidious nature. Margaret Robinson called it "powerful and with a reputation for unscrupulous methods."[10] According to the *Woman Patriot*, the WJCC was "an almost perfect device for misrepresenting the organized women of the country before Congress."[11] Many opponents used the WJCC as an example of female lobbying gone bad and thus of representative government destroyed. Mrs. George Madden Martin, who criticized the state of women's organizations as a whole, warned that women involved in such lobbying efforts were "directly responsible for the deterioration in character in the individual Congressman" and were "denying to his constituents their political rights." Women's lobbying threatened to upset the nation's "constitutional equilibrium."[12]

Opponents also accused the National League of Women Voters (LWV) and its president Maud Wood Park of undemocratic behavior. The LWV's endorsement of the Child Labor Amendment, the Sheppard-Towner Act, a proposed federal department of education, protective labor legislation, and disarmament was proof to some of its radical nature and the dangers of female suffrage. Members of the War Department's Military

Intelligence Division (MID) sought information on the LWV but were never able to prove its disloyalty.[13] Despite that failure, War Department officials Lieutenant Colonel Barnes and Major General Helmick criticized the LWV's patriotism.[14] R. M. Whitney charged that the LWV was part of the Communist Party's system of interlocking directorates designed to overthrow the United States. The National Reserve Officers Association and the Daughters of the American Revolution (DAR) also attacked the LWV.[15]

The LWV responded to attacks much more directly than any other women's organization, perhaps because Maud Wood Park, its first president, chaired the WJCC's Special Committee on Attacks and was shrewdly aware of the possible impact and widespread nature of the attacks. Belle Sherwin, the LWV's second president, reported to regional director Marguerite Wells that "attacks of one form or another keep us busy most of the time." In 1927 the LWV issued an "attack kit" to all state presidents, outlining the best means by which to address accusations of subversiveness.[16]

The leadership of the American Association of University Women, which included individual women listed on various versions of the spider web chart, also felt it necessary to address accusations of radicalism. Speakers at the 1927 national convention told of the wide-ranging accusations against progressive women's organizations but encouraged members to maintain their relationships with other women's organizations such as the LWV and the WJCC.[17]

For some, particularly former antisuffragists, the manipulation of U.S. women by the radical leaders of progressive women's organizations was one of the dire consequences of female suffrage. In a pamphlet entitled *Political Dictatorship in Women's Clubs*, one author wrote, "Suffrage changed all previous values. As club leaders tasted of the fruits of political power, idealism waned. Democracy in women's clubs vanished and political dictatorship took its place."[18] Both Anna Moon Randolph of the Virginia Women's Constitutional League and Mrs. George Madden Martin of Kentucky, a prominent author and General Federation of Women's Clubs (GFWC) dissident, felt that women did not have what it took to be political actors. Women behaved according to a particularly female herd instinct, blindly following their leaders. Now that woman was an enfranchised citizen, this trait led her to "assume greater possibilities for mischief."[19]

The widespread infiltration of American women's organizations and the increased risks wrought by suffrage brought new responsibilities to all women. "It was high time," proclaimed a pamphlet of the Massachusetts Public Interests League (MPIL), "for a new DECLARATION OF INDEPENDENCE by the organized women of the United States." Margaret Robinson scolded a large meeting of the DAR and the American Legion Auxiliary, "It is not greatly to our credit as organized women that we have so long meekly submitted to radical dictatorship." Anna Moon Randolph felt the same and encouraged each woman to ask herself whether she was part of any organizations "furthering legislation destructive to [her] Country."[20]

PURGING WOMEN'S ORGANIZATIONS

Attempts to cleanse U.S. women's organizations of subversive elements and influences accompanied the challenges of Margaret Robinson and Anna Moon Randolph. Inside U.S. women's organizations—most notably the GFWC, the NCW, and the DAR—women debated disarmament and legislative policy and questioned the propriety of women's expanding political interests. Organizations expelled purportedly radical women, those favoring disarmament and transformative social legislation. When reforms or purges failed to accomplish what was sought, alternative women's organizations were founded.

The largest women's organization of the 1920s, the GFWC, was not exempt from dissension. Founded in 1890 to promote women's benevolence and civic programs, the white, predominantly middle-class organization waited to endorse suffrage till 1914. By 1920, it represented a million members. The organization was interested in social welfare programs. Its endorsement of the creation of the Children's Bureau can be understood in that light. The federation joined the National Council for the Prevention of War (NCPW) and became a founding member of the WJCC.[21] The GFWC felt the pressures of antiradical sentiment and cautiously withdrew from the NCPW in 1922 after Brigadier General Fries's allegations that the NCPW was out to establish communism. Later the organization joined Carrie Chapman Catt's Conference on the Cause and Cure of War but was one of the most reticent participants.[22] The GFWC was only a relatively reformist organization.

The most visible signs of dissension within the GFWC came between 1926 and 1928 when the Woman's Club of Louisville, Kentucky, led a revolt from within. The Louisville group questioned the appropriateness of the

GFWC's legislative program—a program that in 1922 had included endorsement of the Child Labor Amendment, a federal department of education, independent citizenship for women, and the Sheppard-Towner Act—and sought to restrict all lobbying. They accused the national GFWC of undemocratic behavior and radical tendencies.

The Woman's Club of Louisville was active and prominent and had a history of antiradicalism. In 1922, the 700-member club warned the Associated Industries of Kentucky of the GFWC's involvement with the NCPW. The Associated Industries later reprinted the *Dearborn Independent* articles about the subversiveness of U.S. women's organizations, which the Woman's Club helped to circulate.[23] Georgia Martin, a prominent author who went by the pen name of Mrs. George Madden Martin, was a member of the club and a leader of what was to be called the "Louisville rebellion." Martin also sat on national and state Democratic Party committees. Her national presence in opposition to the Sheppard-Towner Act, the Children's Bureau, and the Child Labor Amendment certainly must have spurred the actions of the local group.[24]

After declaring themselves not bound by the policy decisions of the national and state GFWC, the Louisville women accused the GFWC of steamrolling policies through national conventions, forcing the endorsement of subversive legislation upon unknowing women through its membership in the WJCC, and general un-American behavior. According to Martin, the Louisville protest was "the first protest from within against those un-American and unpatriotic forces which through control at the top are responsible for the mass of paternalistic, socialistic, and unconstitutional legislation which has been and is being demanded in the name of organized women." Martin named the Child Labor Amendment, the Sheppard-Towner Act, uniform marriage and divorce laws, and a federal department of education as examples of the insidious legislation her group sought to oppose. The dissident group received endorsements from the national American Legion Auxiliary, the MPIL, and the Woman Builders of America and tried to gain the support of Assistant Secretary of War and American Legion leader Hanford MacNider.[25]

Eventually the Louisville club left the GFWC and its Kentucky state affiliate—or was expelled, depending on whose claims one accepts—and made a "declaration of independence." The dissident women claimed to act against "tyranny" and "taxation without representation" and in favor of "local self-government," using their language to make further claims to patriotism. The GFWC did not entirely back down from its legislative program but did withdraw from the WJCC in 1928. The accusations of the Louisville "insurgents" and their supporters resonated within the context of other accusations of dictatorship and radicalism in women's organizations.[26]

The NCW also faced internal attempts by insurgent women's groups to reshape the organization and purge it of subversive elements. A coalition of suffrage and temperance workers had founded the NCW and the International Council of Women (ICW), of which the NCW was a part, in 1888. By the 1920s, the NCW included thirty-eight diverse women's organizations, including the WILPF. Organizers hoped that the May 1925 convention of the ICW, held in Washington, D.C., would spotlight the wonderful activities of U.S. club women. Instead, it provided an opportunity for many U.S. women to renounce pacifism as un-American, prompted the creation of a Red Scare antifeminist women's organization, and illuminated racial and political divisions among U.S. women.[27]

The NCW's ties to women's peace organizations shook the organization. In 1924 the DAR, the American Legion Auxiliary, and the Daughters of 1812 issued resolutions of censure against the organization and threatened to withhold dues and donations unless the WILPF withdrew from the NCW. The DAR also applied pressure by refusing the use of their Constitution Hall for the 1925 ICW convention—the site of which had already been advertised. For the NCW, money was a further factor because Congress was considering their appropriation request and demanding information on possible "disloyal" members. In January 1925, after intense debate internally and after substantial pressure from the NCW, the WILPF resigned from the organization.[28]

The forced withdrawal of the WILPF failed, however, to quell dissension within the NCW. At the much-anticipated international convention of May 1925, the U.S. delegates were caught up in debates over pacifism, patriotism, and additional publicity surrounding the refusal of a black women's chorus to sing before a segregated audience. Delegates unsuccessfully offered resolutions endorsing the League of Nations and international disarmament. The American Legion Auxiliary, the National Women's Relief Corps, the Ladies of the Macabees, and the National American War Mothers threatened to withdraw from the NCW because of the presence of peace activists. Cornelia Ross Potts, president of the National Patriotic Council, stood across the street from the convention and claimed that the "red flag of Russia ought to be flying over the auditorium." A group led by Potts met across the street from the ICW convention and were addressed by Brigadier General Amos Fries (of spider web chart fame). Potts issued what the *New York Times* called a "virtual accusation that the international organization was an unpatriotic body." Another group of women, known as the Club Women's Protective Committee and led by Sara I. Coe, expressed its fear of "the pacifist-Socialist influence within the National Council of Women" but encouraged all women to stay in the NCW "to the end that this pacifist-Socialist control be destroyed or enlightened from within" and "to restore democratic methods." Like-minded women were successful in prohibiting the inclusion of disarmament literature from the NCW's exhibition hall.[29]

The DAR played an important role in the internal debates of the NCW and others. Its threat to withdraw, its disapproval of the WILPF, and its refusal to allow the NCW to meet at Constitution Hall carried great weight, for it had become heavily involved in antiradicalism. In 1923, the DAR endorsed the military preparedness plan of Secretary of War John Weeks. In 1924, DAR president-general Mrs. Anthony Wayne Cook sent copies of Richard Whitney's *Reds in America* and *Peace at Any Old Price*, supplied by the American Defense Society, to all state regents and national officers. Between 1924 and 1925, the DAR demanded the removal of the WILPF from the NCW. At the 1925 Continental Congress, a resolution was passed recommending that a "definite, intensive campaign be organized in every state to combat 'Red' internationalists." In 1926, the DAR led the lengthy effort to keep peace activist Lucia Ames Mead, whom one state regent called "a serious menace," out of the southeastern United States. State regents and officials were sent copies, at Grace Brosseau's request, of the lengthy Woman Patriot petition against the Sheppard-Towner Act. By the mid-1920s, the DAR had joined the wave of anti-radicalism that denounced pacifism and social reform legislation as un-American and sought to rein in the consequences of female suffrage. While some progressive women within the organization led campaigns in hope of reform, antiradical women verbally attacked and expelled them.[30]

Sometime in early 1927, the national DAR and Margaret Robinson began distributing *The Common Enemy*, a pamphlet compiled by New York resident Fred Marvin.[31] While the pamphlet mentioned no names, it claimed that communists, Bolshevists, socialists, liberals, and pacifists "differ[ed] only on the question of tactics." Socialists, liberals, and pacifists chose legislative action, but while the legislation they endorsed might appear to "cure some alleged political, moral, social or economic ill," it was actually intended to "merely centralize government, or in some manner destroy the proper functioning of the constitution." Once such legislation was in place, "dupes" would be placed in government bureaus and "directed" in their actions by destructive influences." Already, the pamphlet warned, "the Socialist-Radical-Ultra-Pacifist groups" had been highly successful in "boring from within." U.S. organizations were being used by the "world revolutionary movement which proposes to destroy civilization and Christianity." Many of the manipulated groups were prominent women's organizations.[32]

Because it did not name names, *The Common Enemy* was relatively tame. Yet for Carrie Chapman Catt, its distribution was the final straw. Catt's rejoinder, published in the *Woman Citizen* and reported across the country, was the most public response to the Red Scare antifeminist harangues. Catt defended the political goals of social change held by many American women and turned the tables by forcing the DAR to defend its vision of women's political and patriotic duties.[33]

Catt concentrated on defending Florence Kelley and Jane Addams, whom she described as "the two persons most cruelly persecuted in the literature of the anti-Reds" and "the hardest to defend." Both were originally reluctant—Addams thought it might be best to "let me be 'thrown to the lions' as it were"—but quickly changed their minds. Kelley was glad to have something to "counterbalance the portrait of an abhorrent villain in which I have learned to recognize my character in caricature."[34]

In June and July 1927—not long before the August executions of anarchists Nicola Sacco and Bartolomeo Vanzetti—the *Woman Citizen* published two articles by Catt: "Lies-at-Large" and "An Open Letter to the DAR." In the first article Catt ridiculed those who leveled charges of Bolshevism: "In the women's organizations listed as dangerous and deceitful," she charged, "even Diogenes with his lamp could not find a Bolshevik." Yet the group of men and women who made such charges were "well-financed" and "venomous to an astonishing degree," and they "take themselves seriously and perform as though they actually believe what they say." The best example of Catt's sarcastic tone is found in her conclusion: "The only certain conclusion that can be drawn from the situation is that *probably* we did descend from apes, and *maybe* not long ago."[35]

In "An Open Letter to the DAR," Catt took a more serious tone. The noble qualities of the fathers of the Revolution, she claimed, had become "atrophied in their Daughters." She accused the DAR of assisting in a campaign that "made slanderous, mendacious and brutal attacks upon thousands of Americans who never saw a Bolshevik in their lives . . . until a veritable wave of hysteria is sweeping the country." Catt dissected *The Common Enemy* and the Woman Patriots' lengthy and widely distributed petition against the Child Labor Amendment. She systematically refuted charges against Addams, Kelley, and Rose Schneiderman, denying that they were Bolsheviks or communists, testifying to the good character of all three women, and listing the many prominent individuals who praised the women. Catt accused the DAR of being duped and called on their patriotic sensibilities: "It is your privilege as free citizens to campaign in support of your opposition to these views, but there is no excuse whatsoever for calling those who differ with you Bolsheviks, Reds and conspirators,

Woman Citizen, June 1927. The caption of this cartoon, which accompanied an article by Carrie Chapman Catt, reads, "Even Diogenes with his lamp could not find a Bolshevik in the women's organizations listed as dangerous."

aiming to tear down the nation." A search for "the real Bolsheviks instead of bogies," Catt claimed, would better serve the nation.[36]

Catt clearly took the influence of the DAR more seriously than that of other Red Scare antifeminist organizations. Her assault against the DAR took many by surprise and was widely reported. Catt was in San Francisco when the first article appeared, and reporters stampeded her hotel.[37] Grace Brosseau, president-general of the DAR, originally said little except that "the D.A.R. needs no defense from me or anyone else." Within weeks, however, Brosseau publicly renewed the DAR's commitment to "fight communist propaganda and subversive influences, no matter from what sources they emanate." Neither Catt nor her "tirade," Brosseau insisted, would deter the DAR in its efforts. Brosseau claimed the support of President Calvin Coolidge and Secretary of State Frank Kellogg.[38]

Responses to Catt's "Open Letter to the DAR" varied. Fred Marvin, author of *The Common Enemy,* predicted that Catt's attack on the DAR "will be as effective as the blows of a puny child against the hardened muscles of [boxer] Gene Tunney." Catt wrote, he accused, because of a bruised ego: "Once she was the bright star of all women's organizations. . . . The rabble was not permitted even to touch the hem of her skirt. . . . But times have changed. . . . She has, to use a rather crude expression in connection with Mrs. Catt, 'hit the skids.'" George L. Darte, the adjutant-general of the veterans' organization the Military Order of the World War and a frequent speaker at DAR meetings, agreed. Darte called the articles "diatribes" and claimed that Catt was simply "peeved to the point of anger uncontrolled."[39] Hermine Schwed, of the National Association for Constitutional Government and a frequent contributor to the *Dearborn Independent,* went further. In a lengthy pamphlet, *The Strange Case of Mrs. Carrie Chapman Catt,* she argued that Catt, though not a communist, was "a broadcaster for the communists."[40]

Others were more enthusiastic. The *New York Times* endorsed the article and cautioned against the "zeal" of the well-meaning DAR women.[41] Catt received many letters thanking her and praising the article. The *Woman Citizen,* the monthly magazine of the LWV, collected and reproduced positive comments from around the country.[42] Eleanor Roosevelt recommended that the Women's Committee of the Democratic Party read and circulate the article. She also wrote to the *Woman Citizen,* expressing her conviction that a lack of "calm judgement," as exhibited by the DAR, "is far more dangerous than any activities of Russian agents and Communist propagandists."[43]

The furor over the DAR, however, had only begun. Another contro-
versy—which received far greater attention—would soon divide the DAR
and open it up to further public ridicule. In April and March 1928, Helen
Tufts Bailie used speaking opportunities around Boston to charge that
Massachusetts and national DAR leaders had a blacklist of "undesirable"
speakers and organizations that local DAR chapters were supposed to
avoid.[44]

Helen Tufts Bailie of Cambridge, Massachusetts, was an active Unitarian and a member of the WILPF and the DAR. Bailie apparently burst
into the news media unexpectedly in 1928, but her charges and accompanying publicity were no accident. She does not appear to have been active
previously in Massachusetts legislative campaigns, but she was a longtime
personal opponent of fellow Cambridge resident Margaret Robinson.
Bailie's assault against the DAR was well organized, long researched, and
highly coordinated. Her Unitarian circles, which included peace activist
Lucia Ames Mead, served her well.[45]

When the DAR blacklist was published nationally, it was simply too
broad and too long to be taken seriously. As Bailie publicized it, the blacklist had six categories—"doubtful speakers (men)," "doubtful speakers
(women)," "labor organizations," "organizations interlocking with radical
groups either thro their directorates or legislative programs," "socialist-
communist organizations," and "workers schools and colleges"—listing 131
men, 87 women, and 306 organizations to be avoided. Individual names
were followed by one or more categorizations—for example, communist,
socialist, pacifist, feminist, radical. At least one person on the list, Mt.
Holyoke College president Mary Woolley, was a DAR member. (See
Appendix B for the complete blacklist.)

Bailie first registered dissatisfaction about the DAR in her diary entry
of March 22, 1927, complaining about and listing quotations from a DAR
publication. Bailie did not specify the source of these quotes, but they came
from Fred Marvin's *A Common Enemy*. She asked herself, "What ass is
responsible for all this? . . . Are American women such boobies?" In April
she wrote, "Shall soon embark upon a counter-thrust to 'The Common
Enemy.'" In May she presided over her local DAR "covered-dish lun-
cheon" and purposely invited someone who she knew was "counter to
orders from Washington" to be the main speaker, Reverend Talmadge
Root of the Massachusetts Federation of Churches. Later she hoped to
invite Lucia Ames Mead, another blacklisted speaker, to lecture on international relations.[46]

In December 1927, Bailie requested information from Carrie Chapman Catt on those she believed to be the source of DAR propaganda—Margaret Robinson, Fred Marvin, Edward Hunter of Boston's Industrial Defense Association, and Californian H. M. Haldeman of the Better America Federation.[47] Bailie went on to build alliances with other dissatisfied DAR members in New England. She organized meetings, visited likely signatories of her protest petition, and later sought the assistance of Jane Addams.[48]

On February 2, 1928, Bailie mailed her protest to DAR president-general Brosseau and wrote in her diary: "I have mailed to Mrs. Brosseau the letter of protest that I drafted about a month ago, feeling that it is the honorable course to take, though I guess it will have no effect."[49] Brosseau's response, which denied blacklists and the constraint of debate within the DAR, failed to satisfy Bailie. Soon she and her colleagues mailed protest letters to DAR and WILPF units and individuals across the nation, seeking financial and organizational support.[50] Bailie worried about the costs but "jumped up, howling with delight" when she received positive responses.[51] Eventually Bailie led a nationwide attempt to reform and challenge the DAR. Bailie and others distributed a series of publications listing complaints against the DAR. DAR units from Connecticut, Oregon, Massachusetts, and Indiana expressed support, and some women resigned. Some of the most public resignations were by individuals who themselves were listed or had spouses listed on the blacklist.[52]

In a widely publicized "trial" at the 1928 DAR Continental Congress, the DAR "totally expelled" Bailie for the publication of her pamphlet *Our Threatened Heritage*.[53] The pamphlet, the DAR's National Board of Management claimed, contained statements "derogatory to the good name of the society, belittled its work, falsely accused its officers of unauthorized acts, stated that its officers were duped and hypnotized and contained propaganda contrary to the expressed policy of the society in regard to its patriotic work."[54] Another woman, Eleanor St. Omer Roy, an office secretary for the WILPF and a DAR member, was charged with "aid[ing] and abet[ting] Mrs. Helen Tufts Bailie in her efforts to disturb the harmony of the Society." She received notice from the DAR National Board that her actions were "reprehensible and that she is hereby advised to avoid such action in the future."[55] Mary P. MacFarland, a DAR and LWV member, president of the New Jersey American Association of University Women, and wife of the General Secretary of the Federal Council of Churches of Christ (an organization on the blacklist), also publicized the blacklist and issued pamphlets stating her case. MacFarland received a summons to appear before the DAR's executive committee but declined to do so.[56]

The creators of the DAR blacklist were variably identified as Edward Hunter of the Industrial Defense Association (based in Boston), Fred Marvin, and Margaret Robinson. The blacklist was most widely attributed to Marvin, whom Bailie called "the tutelary divinity of the DAR." In a deposition for the DAR, however, Marvin denied that he had prepared the list.[57] Boston minister Talmadge Root, whose Massachusetts Federation of Churches appeared on the blacklist, accused the MPIL of having a blacklist in March 1928, approximately one month before Bailie's accusations. Margaret Robinson denied the existence of an MPIL blacklist, but in a letter to the Boston *Herald* replied, "Our league would consider itself at perfect liberty to make lists of pinks, reds or yellows—if it saw fit."[58] Edward Hunter did not hesitate to claim the blacklists: "Every man or woman named on the list of doubtful speakers is known by me to be working, either directly or indirectly, in the interests of organizations which exist to undermine the Government of the United States and Christianity." According to Hunter, it was the responsibility of his organization to distribute such information.[59] While who actually compiled the list is unclear, it is clear that Red Scare antifeminists turned to each of these organizations for resources and information on the activities of progressive U.S. women.[60]

The consequences and appropriateness of U.S. women's advocacy of peace were the most public point of contention surrounding the blacklist, even though many men and many other types of organizations were listed on the blacklist. By 1928, the DAR generally limited its political actions to antiradicalism and the endorsement of a strong military defense, and that is how the organization was understood. Two sympathetic cartoons in the *Washington Post*, which appeared during the Continental Congress that expelled Bailie, convey the issues at work and the DAR understanding of patriotic womanhood. In both, female peace advocates are portrayed as unattractive, grouchy women. In the first, the DAR is represented as patriotic and majestic, the strong and classical bearers of a huge flag, easily capable of overwhelming the weak, shrill, outside soapbox sentiments of pacifist women. The second contrasts DAR and pacifist mothers, sons, and even their dogs. The DAR mother appears kind, gentle, and loving, while her upright and responsible son, compared by the cartoon to Charles Lindbergh, marches off to military training. The pacifist mother, cut off by her fence, appears unattractive, unpleasant and harsh, while her shiftless and poorly dressed son smokes cigarettes. Her dog growls, is shaggy and unkempt—a dog of the lower class. The DAR dog is well-groomed, trained, and happy.[61]

Despite these cartoons favoring the DAR, the blacklists made the DAR a target of ridicule and derision.[62] William Allen White, a prominent author and editor known for his opposition to the Ku Klux Klan, claimed that the blacklist went "out of its way" to include opponents of the Klan. In a comment picked up by the Associated Press, he asserted, "The DAR

The Black Sheep Protests the "Blacklist."

Washington Post, April 21, 1928.

has yanked the Klan out of the cow pasture and set it down in the break-
fast room of respectability, removing its hood and putting on a transformation. . . . Mrs. Brosseau is a lovely lady with many beautiful qualities
of heart and mind, but in her enthusiasm she has allowed several lengths
of Ku Klux Klan nightie to show under her red, white, and blue."[63] His
comments were echoed by a cartoon in the *Baltimore Sun,* in which a Klan
member points the way for the DAR, his "goil friend." The derision,
laughter, and ridicule increased when the *Nation* organized a blacklist

Washington Post, April 22, 1928. This cartoon compares the pacifist and the DAR
"Mothers of Main Street."

party. Those listed in the blacklist, representatives of blacklisted organizations, and the now-famous DAR dissidents—over 900 people—were invited to the Level Club in New York City. Nearly 1,000 people attended and were entertained by African American poet James Weldon Johnson, the master of ceremonies. Those attending passed resolutions against repealing the Law of Gravity and declared that the only "respectable and tolerated revolution" was that of the earth on its axis.[64]

Baltimore Sun, April 7, 1928.

While the DAR was ridiculed and criticized, most progressive women's organizations limited their public rejoinders to accusations that the DAR and its members must have received the blacklist from someone else. Carrie Chapman Catt, in her "Open Letter to the DAR," recognized that the DAR distributed what others had printed and wrote: "The Daughters! Why, those Daughters are dupes themselves!!" DAR dissidents Helen Tufts Bailie and Mary P. MacFarland used "dupe" language also. The language appears a direct reference to the DAR's accusation that pacifists and other progressive women were dupes. Perhaps each believed such language would be successful because it was the same language and accusation that had been used against progressive women's organizations.[65]

WOMEN'S POLITICS AND SOCIAL TRANSFORMATION

The conviction that women were not yet fit for electoral politics lay behind many of the attacks upon progressive U.S. women and women's organizations. Red Scare antifeminists argued that U.S. women were well intentioned but duped. Given the opportunities of the ballot, women's natural womanly kindness and blindness led them to support radical legislation that would bring about Bolshevism. Femaleness handicapped women in such a way that it was best for them to avoid electoral politics.

This belief, however, was inseparable from the self-serving motives of manufacturing and military interests, who stood to lose money and influence owing to women's political effectiveness. Concerns about what women would do with the suffrage they had so recently gained lay at the core of the long series of attacks, from within and outside women's organizations, upon politically active and progressive-minded women in the 1920s.

This chorus of innuendoes and accusations was directed against women and women's organizations seeking to use suffrage to reconfigure social and political life. Women's political activities and women themselves were labeled subversive once women gained the governmental access to begin challenging institutions that they believed permitted and benefited from war, poverty, and inequality. As the Special Committee on Attacks of the Women's Joint Congressional Committee concluded, "As long as women's organizations contented themselves with work that contemplated merely palliative measures of a philanthropic sort, no criticism was encountered, but when they sought to discover the causes and remedies for poverty, sickness, unequal opportunity, and war, the opponents shouted: 'radicalism,' 'socialism,' 'communism,' 'bolshevism,' 'pacifism'; and tried by innuendo to discredit social, industrial, and war-preventive measures."[66]

In the battle for suffrage, U.S. women had created a powerful and effective lobbying network. The creation of the Children's Bureau and the 1921 passage of the Sheppard-Towner Act showed that this lobby still had strength and would support other measures. Historians have generally assumed that by the 1924 election the strength of this lobbying coalition had dissipated. It may be true that politicians and activists expressed skepticism about women's willingness to vote as a bloc as early as 1924, but the long series of attacks upon progressive U.S. women and their organizations illustrates that the legislative impact of a voting female citizenry was still being contested throughout the 1920s.[67] Even after the 1924 election, militarists, manufacturers, antiradicals, and the MID continued to devote organizational efforts and monies to influencing the woman citizen.

The 1920 passage of the Nineteenth Amendment clearly failed to settle the question of what the woman citizen was supposed to do and be. Despite the efforts of progressive women to define the woman citizen, the Red Scare stories of radicalism, Bolshevik women, and the nationalization of women and children continued to reverberate throughout the 1920s, shaping the political contexts in which U.S. women entered the electorate. Red Scare antifeminists, though few, remained an effective political force.

Conclusion

In 1925, an article entitled "Rebels in Retirement" appeared in *Collier's* and was reprinted in the *Literary Digest*. "Where are the spitfires of yesteryear?" the author asked. What had become of the radicals once endangering the nation? The taming influence of family and domesticity, the author claimed, had transformed them. Political activists who had once espoused radicalism in all aspects of their lives had been made proper Americans by the adoption of motherhood, fatherhood, and traditional gender roles. Gender orthodoxy led to political orthodoxy. Marie Ganz, once a popular soapbox orator who threatened death to mining executives, was now "a picture of complete domestication." Becky Edelson, who once was "vituperative, direct, defiant," was now a "sedate wife . . . domesticated." Frank Tannenbaum, onetime organizer of the unemployed, also had a wife and child and was turning to academia. Those who didn't fit the picture—Alexander Berkman, Emma Goldman, and Bill Haywood—were in Europe and had been barred from the country. Apparently, the only path to political redemption was the renunciation of radicalism and the adoption of domesticity.[1]

"Rebels in Retirement" traces the path of the post–World War I Red Scare. The scare began when wartime urgency carried into postwar domestic politics, when Americans feared Russian radicalism was infiltrating the United States, and the apparent national crisis demanded that the manly heroes who had displayed their patriotism in war combat radicalism at home. In this crisis, women were potential liabilities. Russian Bolshevism—rapidly infiltrating its way into the nation—manifested itself not only in political chaos but also in gender and sexual chaos. Women's natural weaknesses, accompanied by their supposed lack of political know-how in the postsuffrage decade, endangered the security of the nation. Nontraditional gender roles were used as proof of un-American radicalism. The preservation of individual and social patriarchy, on the part of both men and women, became an act of patriotism. The domesticity apparently embraced by the radicals discussed in the above article could then unquestionably serve as proof of their patriotic and proper citizenship.

The connections made between un-American gender roles and un-American politics during 1919, as well as the sense of wartime urgency, appeared again in 1923 when antiradicals began to attack progressive women and progressive women's organizations as radical and subversive. The radicalism of labor seemingly was defeated. In 1924, women were to vote in national elections for the second time. The Progressive movement had been reborn in the presidential candidacy of Robert La Follette. Congress was debating a possible increase of military appropriations at the same time that the U.S. peace movement was expanding. Individuals promoting business and a nonregulatory, antibureaucratic government were rising to leadership in the Republican Party. Organized and progressive women, those women assumed to be voters, promoted disarmament, government restrictions on business, and the formation of government bureaucracies to solve social welfare problems—issues with formidable opponents.

These opponents were made formidable partly by effective political communication. Antiradical organizations were not large, but they had great influence. Their extensive use of radio in the Child Labor Amendment campaign, one of the first political debates in which radio was used, reached many people. They also spread and legitimated their ideas by the selective use of government contacts. Senator Thomas Bayard of Connecticut, for example, could be trusted to insert antiradical petitions or statements into the *Congressional Record.* Most Americans were (and are) unaware that nearly anything can be inserted into the *Congressional Record.* Use of the *Congressional Record,* however, gave antiradicals legitimacy and prestige and allowed them to imply that they had the support of government. MID referrals to antiradical organizations and publications also had amplified impact. The involvement of the War Department in antiradical networks further strengthened their claims to legitimacy and government endorsement.

Aided by this strength, antiradicals used Red Scare antifeminism to limit and shape the newly enfranchised female citizenry to their own advantage. The endorsement of the Child Labor Amendment and other social welfare legislation by many of the same women and women's organizations that questioned military policies led many antiradicals to conclude that the majority of U.S. women's organizations were subversive. When questions of peace arose, military and veterans groups entered the debate, joining other figures who had been there all along. Many antiradicals sincerely believed that U.S. women and women's organizations posed a threat to the nation. Culpability lay even in the hands of well-meaning U.S. women, for unbeknownst to them their political involvement was directed by leaders connected to Moscow.

Red Scare antifeminism illustrated the intensity and persistence of the conviction that wives and children were the property of individual men and that this relationship was essential to social order. The Bolshevik challenge to private property was assumed, with very little basis in reality, to erase the proprietary relationship of men to wives and children. Conversely, the feminist challenge to male proprietary relationships was assumed to lead to other erosions of private property relationships. The assumption that women would then become the property of the state revealed the inability of antiradicals and Red Scare antifeminists to imagine women belonging, not to men or to the state, but to themselves. Antiradicals' assertion that feminists actually wanted women to become state property revealed their distortion of feminism. It also revealed the extent to which patriarchy and patriarchal thinking pervaded politics and the notion of a sound state.

Despite and because of this endorsement of patriarchy, politically conservative women played a vital role in the development, funding, and staffing of antiradicalism. These women, often with roots in the antisuffrage movement, generally were highly educated women of intellect and sincere political ideology. They cultivated connections with other conservative organizations and active participation in political debate. Despite their forays into public politics, however, these women remained convinced that male headship in both family and state was vital. Female headship, particularly in government bureaus, destroyed both family and nation. The belief that they were the final guardians, whose task it was to protect the nation when men failed to do so, particularly when it was other women who posed such a subversive threat, energized their activism. These women, exemplified by Margaret Robinson, shaped the gendering of antiradicalism and antistatism in the 1920s. By so doing, they helped to defeat the Child Labor Amendment and other progressive legislation.

Their very existence and success belie the notion of a united womanhood and force us to explore the ideological, economic, social, racial, and political benefits that they derived from patriarchy.

The gendering of conservatism—the ideological conflation of a noninterventionist government with the preservation of private and social patriarchy—profoundly shaped the politics of the 1920s. Progressivism and its faith in the government's ability to improve society were left behind. Pieces of legislation attempting to ameliorate social conditions via government intervention in the home or neighborhood, such as the Child Labor Amendment, the Sheppard-Towner Act, the Children's Bureau, or a proposed federal department of education, were labeled socialistic efforts to pervert male power by nationalizing women and children and were for the most part defeated. The probusiness presidency of Calvin Coolidge mirrored this aversion to a bureaucratic and regulatory government.

Inherent in the gendering of conservatism in the 1920s was the gendering of antiradicalism—the belief that either government or feminist challenges to male power were subversively radical and that inherent to political radicalism was gender upheaval. Feminist women became susceptible to accusations of radicalism, and such accusations were often used to discredit feminists and radical movements. The historical importance of the gendering of antiradicalism is that it was a vital element in the transformation and continuation of the post–World War I Red Scare throughout the 1920s. During the years of 1919 and 1920, the country effectively rid itself of many dissident radicals. Most were either deported, jailed, or scared into submission. No longer were socialists and anarchists the most visible enemy, and progressive women became the targets of antiradicalism in the 1920s because militarists, business interests, and conservatives feared that the newly enfranchised and as yet electorally unpredictable women would do them legislative damage. Red Scare antifeminists targeted progressive women and enabled the fears and energies of the Red Scare to continue throughout the 1920s, until it was clear that the hopes of progressive women that their ballot could transform the nation were no longer viable.

In this gendered antiradicalism, class was not primary—but neither was gender, ethnicity, or race. Red Scare antifeminists understood the sexual, racial, social, economic, political, and gender structures of society to be so integrally entwined that a transformation of one would lead necessarily to a transformation of them all. They consequently assumed that anyone who sought to revolutionize any social relationship of power sought to revolutionize them all. As guardians of the nation, they sought to protect a precarious but vital web from any form of radicalism.

Consequently those accused had little effective recourse in the face of these accusations. The women involved consulted lawyers, discussed libel suits and their own discouragement, and tried to illuminate the flaws in their opponents' arguments.[2] Factual denials seemed to get them nowhere. As proponents of the ERA would discover in the 1970s and 1980s, "facts" had little strength or relevance when weighed against understandings of "natural" gender roles and their relationship to civic soundness.[3] The numerous publications and articles designed to be exposés failed to convince those who truly believed that democracy and the nation were at risk that their concerns were groundless.[4] With "facts" seemingly so irrelevant, certainly more was at stake than the supposed subversive connections of reform-minded U.S. women.

The ineffectiveness of "facts" when weighed against ideas about the "nature" of gender also is revealed in the distorted vision of feminism that emerges from these arguments. Antifeminist attacks were directed not at the basic feminist principles of equality or autonomy but at a caricature of feminism in which women—ugly, man-hating, power-loving, and sexually deviant women—simply reversed gender hierarchies of power and then gloated over their ascendancy. However, antifeminists had to carefully avoid extreme misogynistic attacks upon women because of the high level of women's involvement and leadership in antifeminism. As Sara Diamond has pointed out, the high level of female leadership in the contemporary Christian Right has fostered a similar tendency.[5]

Most of the women targeted by Red Scare antifeminism did not consider themselves feminists. Ignoring this, Red Scare antifeminists accused all progressive and radical women of feminism, and disavowal of the term *feminism* was no protection against their attacks. It is thus ironic that those women actively claiming the label of feminism in the 1920s were exempt from most charges of radicalism. The lesson that Doris Stevens, an activist in the National Woman's Party, drew from the DAR's blacklisting of Carrie Chapman Catt was for all feminists "to keep their skirts clear of all other movements"—which the National Woman's Party (NWP) proceeded to do. The NWP, which focused its efforts exclusively on the Equal Rights Amendment, was included in the spider web chart but was generally not included in the wide array of attacks on progressive women and progressive women's organizations. The NWP and progressive women became further distinct by disavowing protective labor legislation. In the words of historian Nancy Cott, though most NWP members "did not hold consistently laissez-faire views, the single-mindedness of their espousal of equal rights made them appear to."[6] The NWP appeared to align itself, politically and ideologically, with the political opponents of progressive women. It failed to come to the support of the viciously attacked progressive women and instead, in 1928, formally aligned itself with the political party of many of those who had done the attacking. The general omission of the NPW in lists of radicals reinforces the argument that many of the attacks upon U.S. women's organizations were motivated by concerns about the widespread results of female suffrage.

Feminism flounders today, just as it did in the 1920s, to organize, to clarify its purpose, and to recognize and celebrate differences among women. One of the lessons of this period of pervasive antifeminism may be that patriarchy is a complex web of more than gender. As feminism flounders, however, we need to remember that those who wrestle with hierarchy and social divisions, despite their frequent failings, pose an encouraging threat. The level of antifeminism is an indicator of the success and strength of feminism. An ever-broadening social vision, though it may solicit attacks, is key to feminism's success.

Red Scare antifeminism had dissipated by the end of the 1920s. Many of the conservative women who provided much of the energy for the movement grew elderly or died. Groups of younger women did not replace them. Many of the organizations simply disappeared. And while women had a concrete impact on electoral politics after suffrage, as Kristi Anderson has argued, by the end of the decade militarists, manufacturers, and conservatives no longer saw organized women as a legislative threat.[7] The state-expanding social welfare measures of the Sheppard-Towner Act, the Child Labor Amendment, and much of the Children's Bureau's energy had been beaten down. Large numbers of women no longer expressed active interest in peace and disarmament issues. By the end of the decade, the intensity of Red Scare antifeminism was dying down. That is not to say, however, that the link between antifeminism and antiradicalism disappeared. As others have shown, scattered women like Ida M. Darden and Elizabeth Dilling played pivotal roles in linking the two Red Scares of the twentieth century.[8] And during the Cold War, gender continued as an effective weapon in questioning political orthodoxy of both men and women.

During the post–World War I Red Scare, issues of family life, gender roles, and sexuality intruded into what was, on the face of it, a matter of pure politics. This is a lesson, however, that there is no such thing as "pure politics." Family life, gender roles, and sexuality are issues of political import. Indeed, they are at the very core of our political understandings and discussions. During perceived crises of civic loyalty gender's centrality becomes more overt. The broadening and complicating of our analytical skills and frameworks to include (or perhaps simply notice) the conflation of family, gender, sexuality, and politics can only improve our understandings of the historical and contemporary United States.

Many of our current political debates, like those of the 1920s, are not only about economics or governmental policy or the relationship of the federal government to states. They are about our national identity and what family and gender roles we believe necessary for the security of the nation. Gender remains at the core of how we as a nation live and discuss patriotism, proper citizenship, and the needs of our nation.

Appendix A

Margaret C. Robinson Select Bibliography

"The Suffrage Prophets." *Unpopular Review* 4 (July 1915): 127–39.

"Against Woman Suffrage." *Zion's Herald,* October 20, 1915, pp. 1331–32.

"The Feminist Program." *Unpopular Review* 5 (April 1916): 318–31.

"Woman Suffrage in Relation to Patriotic Service." April 1917, Public
    Interests League of Massachusetts.

"Feminism and Defeat." *New York Times,* March 8, 1918, p. 10.

"Suffrage and Defeat." *New York Times,* March 16, 1918, p. 12.

"The Suffrage Amendment." *New York Times,* August 25, 1918, sec. 4, p. 2.

"Suffrage Amendment." *New York Times,* January 25, 1920, sec. 3, p. 2.

"Suffrage and Socialism." *New York Times,* March 21, 1920, sec. 5, p. 9.

"Winners at Chicago." *New York Times,* June 21, 1920, p. 14.

"Two Dangerous Bills." *America,* March 5, 1921, p. 477.

Christian Socialism: A Contradiction in Terms. February 23, 1923.
    Massachusetts Public Interests League.

"Is in Keeping with American Ideals." In "What Women Think of Open
    Shop." *American Industries,* May 1923, p. 21.

"The Youth Movement: What Is It?" *Iron Trade Review* (n.d.; possibly
    1923 or 1924).

"The Youth Movement in Colleges with Its Trend to Socialism and
    Other Evils." *Manufacturers Record* 86 (July 10, 1924): 61–62.

"A Woman's Warning to Men and Women on the Child Labor
    Amendment." *Manufacturers Record* 86 (September 4, 1924): 87.

"A Woman's Warning to Men and Women on the Child Labor
    Amendment." *Daily Bulletin: Issued by the Manufacturers Record* 52
    (September 10, 1924).

Letter to the Editor. November 18, 1924. *New York Times,* p. 24.

"Don't Ratify the Child Labor Amendment! Arguments Used against It Broadcasted to Sentinels of the Republic." Text of broadcasts, December 30, 1924, from WJY Radio.

"An Appeal to American Women." *Manufacturer's Record* 87 (January 8, 1925): 66.

"An Open Letter to 18 Women's Organizations Said to Have Endorsed the Labor Amendment." *Woman Patriot,* January 15, 1925, p. 32.

"Why Massachusetts Beat Child Control: New England Parents Believe They Can Manage Their Own Children." *Dearborn Independent,* March 7, 1925.

"The Responsibility of Being Led: A Friendly Message to Organized Women, by One of Them." *Dearborn Independent,* May 23, 1925. Reprinted as pamphlet by the Massachusetts Public Interests League. Also in *Woman Patriot,* July 1, 1925, pp. 98–101.

"American Pulpit Captured by Radicals." *Dearborn Independent,* January 9, 1926, pp. 6, 21–22.

Statement of Mrs. B. L. Robinson. In *Extension of Public Protection of Maternity and Infancy Act: Hearing before the Committee on Interstate and Foreign Commerce, House of Representatives,* pp. 26–30. 69th Congress, 1st session, January 14, 1926. Washington, D.C.: Government Printing Office, 1926.

"Club Women Linked with Communists." *New York American,* February 8, 1927, p. 3.

"The Responsibility of Being Led." Address before the Women's Patriotic Conference on National Defense. February 10, 1927. Catt-LOC Papers, container 27, folder 5.

"An Open Letter to Mrs. Florence Kelley." *Woman Patriot* 11 (June 1, 1927): 88.

"Defends 'Blacklist.'" *Boston Herald,* March 18, 1928.

"Keep Facts in View." *Christian Leader,* March 24, 1928, pp. 363–65.

Appendix B

Speaker Blacklist

The following are the DAR blacklists as found in various manuscript collections. The list "Doubtful Speakers (Men)" is found in the Catt Papers, reel 2, frame 399. The list "Doubtful Speakers (Women)" is found in the WILPF Records, series C, box 5 (reel 42, frame 828). The lists of "labor organizations," "organizations interlocking with radical groups either thro their directorates or legislative programs," "socialist-communist organizations," and "workers schools and colleges" are found in the Bailie Papers, box 2, blacklist folder.

Unless noted, I have retained the spelling and categorization as listed on each blacklist. Additions indicated on the women's list come from "D.A.R. Roll of Doubtful Women," *Boston Daily Advertiser,* April 5, 1926, pp. 3–4, which was supplied to the paper by Helen Tufts Bailie.

DOUBTFUL SPEAKERS (MEN)

Brent Dow Allison, pacifist, poet of Youth Movement
Judge George W. Anderson, National Council, Peoples Legislative
    Service
Bishop William Anderson, pacifist
Norman Angell, English socialist
William E. Austil (F.Y.P.), pacifist
Roger Baldwin, communist
Harry Elmer Barnes, socialist, pro-German
Jacob O. Bonatall, communist
Victor Berger, socialist

Leslie Blanchard, pacifist
Paul Blanchard, socialist
Rev. Benjamin Brewster, D.D., Christian socialist
Edward Brewster (F.Y.P.), pacifist
John Brophy, communist
Robert Bruere, socialist
J. M. Budish, socialist
Ralph Chaplin, communist
Stuart Chase, socialist
August Claessons, communist
Professor George A. Coe, pacifist
Harry W. L. Dena, communist, socialist, pacifist, defeatist
Max D. Danish, socialist
Clarence Darrow, socialist
Rev. Charles F. Dole, pacifist
Paul Douglas, socialist
W. E. B. DuBois, Negro socialist
Robert W. Dunn, communist
Jason A. Duncan, socialist
William F. Dunne, communist
J. Louis Engdall, communist
Sherwood Eddy, pacifist, pro-German
Edmund C. Evans, socialist
Edward W. Evans, socialist, pacifist
Morris L. Ernst, socialist
Robert Fechner, pacifist
Irving Fisher, socialist
Lovett Fort-Whitman, Communist
William Z. Foster, communist
Felix Frankfurter, socialist, denounced by Roosevelt as Communist
     sympathizer
O. Ben Gerig, pacifist
Ben Gitlow, socialist
Manuel Gomez, Filipino communist
Norman Hapgood, socialist
Thomas Que Harrison, leader of Youth Movement, pacifist
Arthur Garfield Hayes, socialist
Paxton Hibben, pro-Soviet
Stanley High, leader of Youth Movement, internationalist

Sidney Hillman, socialist
Morris Hillquist, leading socialist
Rev. Richard W. Hogue, Church socialist
John Haynes Holmes, pacifist socialist
Frederick C. Howe, socialist
Samuel Guy Inman, pacifist
Eldon E. Janes, pacifist
William H. Johnston, socialist
Bishop Paul Jones, pacifist, Christian
John [blank], socialist
Dr. David Starr Jordan, socialist, pacifist
Horace M. Kallen, socialist
Stanley Kelley, leader of Youth Movement
Fritz Kunz (Order of Star of the East)
George S. Lackland, socialist
Algernon Lee, socialist
Alfred Baker Lewis, socialist
Rabbi Harry Levi, pacifist
Frederick J. Libby, pacifist, communist sympathizer
Kenneth Lindsey, leading English socialist
Henry R. Linville, socialist
Louis P. Lochner, German socialist
Robert Morse Lovett, socialist
Albert Morse Lovett, socialist
Bishop Francis J. McConnell, pacifist
James C. McDonald, pacifist
Rabbi Judah L. Magnes, socialist
Dudley Field Malone, socialist
Benjamin C. Marsh, pacifist socialist
Harold Marshall, leader of Youth Movement
James A. Maurer, socialist
John Howard Mellish, Christian socialist
Alexander Meiklejohn, socialist
John Mez, of Germany
Bert Miller, communist
Spencer Miller Jr., socialist
Robert Minor, communist
Henry R. Mussey, socialist
A. J. Muste, socialist

Scott Nearing, leading socialist, communist
W. A. Neilson, pacifist
Reinhold Neibuhr, pacifist
Freemont Older, socialist
Moissaye J. Olgin, of Russia, communist
Harry A. Overstreet, socialist
Kirby Page, pacifist
Jacob Panken, socialist
George Lyman Paine, pacifist
William Pickens, socialist Negro
Amos Pinchot, radical Progressive
Henry W. Pinkham, pacifist
Roscoe Pound, socialist
Raymond Robins, pro-Soviet
Dr. E. Tallmadge Root, Christian socialist
Professor E. A. Ross, socialist
C. E. Ruthenberg, leading communist
J. B. Salutsky, socialist
John Nevin Sayre, pacifist, socialist
Upton Sinclair, communist
Clarence R. Skinner, socialist
Ronnie Smith, of England, socialist
John Spargo, socialistic
Rev. Harold E. B. Speight, pacifist
Edward A. Steiner, Christian socialist
Norman Studer, communist
Norman Thomas, leading socialist
Wilbur K. Thomas, pacifist
Alexander Tractonberg, communist
John Vanvaerenewyck, socialist
Oswald Garrison Villard, socialist
B. Chauncey Vladich, socialist
Frank P. Walsh, communist
Harry F. Ward, socialist
James P. Warbasse, socialist
Harry Waton, socialist
Charles Frederick Weller, pacifist
George P. West, socialist
William Allen White, socialist

Abraham Wirin, pacifist
Rabbi Stephen S. Wise, radical pacifist
Bertram D. Wolf, communist
Leo Wolman, socialist

Doubtful Speakers (Women)

Grace Abbott, internationalist, socialist, feminist
Jane Addams
Florence Allen, judge, socialist
Mary Anderson, socialist
Gertrude Baer, WILPF, speaker for German Youth Movement
Mrs. Frederick P. Bagley, Education Bill, Chairman of Campaign
Dr. S. Josephine Baker, director of Children's Bureau
Emily Greene Balch, WILPF
Rose Baron, communist
Jennie Loitman Barron, socialist
Mrs. O. H. P. Belmont, NWP, Pres., revolutionary-feminist
Alice Stone Blackwell, socialist
Harriet Stanton Blatch, communist
Susan Brandeis, radical
Sophonisba Breckenridge, pacifist, socialist
Mina Bruere, radical
Jennie Buell, member national committee La Follette-Wheeler
    Campaign
Lucy P. Carner, radical
Marie Carroll, Speaker for Fellowship of Youth for Peace
Carrie Chapman Catt, internationalist, feminist, editor of Women's Bible
Fannie M. Cohn, communist
Mrs. Mabel Costigan, socialist
Mrs. J. Sargeant Cram, pacifist, socialist
Margaret B. Crock of England, pacifist
Mary Ware Dennett, founder of Voluntary Parenthood League
Dorothy Detzer, National executive secretary, WILPF
Madeline Z. Doty, communist
[Crystal Eastman, communist]
Elizabeth Glendower Evans, pacifist, feminist, internationalist, socialist
Mrs. L. K. Elmhurst, radical pacifist
Sara Bard Field, revolutionary feminist

Louise Adams Floyd, socialist
Elizabeth Gurley Flynn, communist
Zona Gale, socialist
Mrs. Kate Crane Gartz, communist
Mabel Gillespie, socialist
Elizabeth Gilman, treasurer Wheeler Committee, Supporter of ACLU
Josephine Goldmark, socialist
Ann Guthrie, radical pacifist
Beatrice F. R. Hale, of England, feminist
Dr. Alice Hamilton, internationalist, socialist
Marguerite Harrison, radical
Rebecca Hourwich, communist
Mrs. Hannah Clothier Hull, international pacifist
Inez Hayes Irwin, feminist radical
Isabel Kendig, socialist
Susan Kingsbury, socialist
Freda Kirchwey, communist-feminist
Julia Lathrop, feminist, internationalist, socialist, pacifist
Agnes Brown Leach, feminist, pacifist
Lulu Levin, communist
Lucy Briddle Lewis, pacifist, feminist
Lola Maverick Lloyd, pacifist, socialist
Lucia Ames Mead, pacifist, socialist
Nelle Sees Nearing, socialist
Agnes Nestor, socialist
Mrs. Gordon Norris, radical
Alice Paul, revolutionary feminist
Dorothy P. Pemroy, radical
Jeannette Rankin, pacifist, radical
Mrs. William Z. Ripley, radical
Mrs. Raymond Robbins [Robins], socialist
Anna Rochester, radical
Maude Royden, of England, pacifist, Christian socialist
Margaret Sanger, leader of birth control movement
Tony Sender, of Germany, socialist
Rose Schneiderman, communist
Maude Schwartz, communist
Rosika Schwimmer, German propagandist

Viva Scudder, socialist
Belle Sherwin, radical
Mrs. V. G. Simkovitch, radical
Mrs. Anna Garlin Spencer, pacifist
Rose Pastor Stokes, communist
Anna Louise Strong, communist
Ida M. Tarbell, radical
Genevieve Townsend, radical
Mary Van Kleech [Kleeck], radical
Mrs. Henry Villard, pacifist
Mary Heaton Vorse, communist
Lillian D. Wald, communist
Bertha Poole Weyl, socialist
Charlotte Anita Whitney, communist
Elle Wilkinson, of England, socialist
Justius Wise, radical, strike leader
Amy Woods, radical, pacifist
Mary E. Woolsey, pacifist, radical

LABOR ORGANIZATIONS

Aerial Navigation Workers Industrial Union
Agricultural Workers Industrial Union
Amalgamated Bank of New York
Amalgamated Food Industrial
Amalgamated Society of Carpenters, Cabinet Makers & Joiners
Amalgamated Society of Engineers
Amalgamated Trust and Savings Bank
American Labor Press Directory
American Labor Monthly Pub. Co.
Amusement Workers Industrial Union
Boston Central Labor Union
Brotherhood of Metal Workers Industrial Union
Chemical Workers Industrial Union
Cloth Hat, Cap and Millinery Workers International Union
Construction Workers Industrial Union
Educational Workers Industrial Union
Finnish Federation of the Communist Party of America

Fishermens Industrial Union
Floricultural and Horticultural Industrial Union
Food Stuffs Workers Industrial Union
General Distribution Workers Industrial Union
Glass and Potter Workers Industrial Union
Health and Sanitation Workers Industrial Union
House and Building Construction Workers Industrial Union
Industrial Council of Trades Union
International Federation of Workers in Hotels, Restaurants, Clubs and
    Catering
International Marine Transport Union
International Metal Workers Federation
International Miners Association
Journeyman Bakers and Confectioners International Union of America
Labor Publication Society
Labor and Socialist International
Leather Workers Industrial Union
Lumber Workers Industrial Union
Metal and Machinery Workers Industrial Union
Municipal Transportation Workers Industrial Union
National Brotherhood Workers of America
National Labor Alliance
New York Knit Goods Workers
Oil, Gas and Petroleum Workers Industrial Union
Park and Highway Maintenance Workers Industrial Union
Pennsylvania State Federation of Labor
Public Utility Workers Industrial Union
Railroad Workers Industrial Union
Red International of Labor Unions
Shipbuilders Industrial Union
Syndicalist International Workingmen's Association
Textile and Clothing Workers Industrial Union
The League Workers (Industrial) of Union Struggle for the Liberation
    of the Working Class
Proletarian University of America
United Garment Workers of America
United Labor Council
Workers (International) Industrial Union
Workmens Council for the Maintenance of Labor's Rights

ORGANIZATIONS INTERLOCKING WITH RADICAL GROUPS
EITHER THRO THEIR DIRECTORATES OR LEGISLATIVE PROGRAMS

African Blood Brotherhood
All-American Cooperative Commission
American Association of University Women
American Association for Labor Legislation
American Birth Control League
American Christian Fund for Jewish Relief
American Committee for the Outlawry of War
American Committee for Relief of Russian Refugees
American Friends Service Committee
American League to Limit Armaments
American Neutral Conference Committee
American Peace Society
American Union Against Militarism
American Youth League
Amos Council Appeal Committee
Association for International Conciliation
Association to Abolish War
Children's Bureau—Federal
Chine-American Committee (Branch of Fellowship of Youth for Peace)
Christian Socialist Fellowship
Collegiate Anti-Militarism League
Conference for Democracy
Conference for Progressive Political Action
Conference of Youth Organizations
Cooperative League of U.S.A.
Council of Jewish Women
Council of Women for Home Missions
Emergency Foreign Policy Association
Emergency Peace Federation
Emergency Peace Foundation
Farmers Labor Party
Federal Council of Churches of Christ in America
Federal Department of Education—Committee for Federated Press
Federal Farmers Labor Party
Federation of Womens Board of Foreign Mission
Fellowship for a Christian Social Order

Fellowship of Faiths
Fellowship of Youth for Peace
Ford Hall Forum, Boston
Foreign Policy Association
Friends Disarmament Council
League for the Abolition of Capital Punishment
League for Jewish Women
League of Nations Non-Partisan Association, Inc.
League of Neighbors
Legal First Aid Bureau
Methodist Federation of Social Service
National Association for the Advancement of Colored People
National Association for Child Development
National Catholic Welfare Council
National Child Labor Committee
National Council for the Limitation of Armaments
National Council of Mothers and Parent-Teacher Associations
National Council of Women
National Federation of Progressive Women
National League of Women Voters
National Student Forum
National Womens Peace Party
Northern States Cooperative League
Peoples Council of America
Peoples Legislative Service
Peoples Reconstruction League
Philadelphia Yearly Meeting of Friends
Plumb Plan League
Proportional Representation League
Public Ownership League
Reconciliation Trips
Society for the Abolition of War
Student Friendship Fund
National Popular Government League
Teachers Union
Twentieth Century Club—Boston
Voluntary Parenthood League
Ukraine Farming and Machinery Corporation
Children in Germany

Union of the East and West
Wheeler Defense Committee
Womens Christian Temperance Union
Womens Committee for Political Action
Womens International Union Label League
World Alliance for International Friendship thro the Churches
World League of Youth
World Peace Association
Young Friends Society
Young Men's Christian Association
Young Women's Christian Association

SOCIALIST-COMMUNIST ORGANIZATIONS

American Association for the Advancement of Atheism
American Civil Liberties Union
    Branches:
    Cincinnati Civil Liberties Committee
    Connecticut League for Civil Liberties and Progressive Legislation
    Detroit Civil Liberties Committee
    Labor Defense and Free Speech Council of Western Pennsylvania
    Maryland Civil Liberties Committee
    New England Civil Liberties Committee
    Philadelphia Civil Liberties Committee
    Providence Civil Liberties Committee
    Seattle Civil Liberties Committee
    Southern California Branch A.C.L.U.
    Virgin Islands Civil Liberties Committee
Amalgamated Clothing Workers of America
American Friends of Russian Freedom
American Fund for Public Service, better known as the Garland Fund
American Labor Press Directory
California Non-Partisan Alliance for Progressive Political Action
Church Socialist League
Church League for Industrial Democracy
Committee of 48
Communist International
Conference for Filipino Independence
Conference to Perfect Plans for the Committee of 48

Fellowship of Reconciliation
First American Conference for Democracy and Terms of Peace
Foreign Language Communist Press
Friends of Freedom for India
Friends of Soviet Russia
General Defense Committee
Industrial Workers of the World
Inter-Collegiate Socialist Society
International Committee for Political Prisoners
International Association on Labor Legislation
International Association on Unemployment
International Federation of Trade Unions
International Committee of Women for Permanent Peace
International Federation of Students
International Labor Defense
International Labor News Service
International Ladies Garment Workers Union (Prosanis label)
International Press Correspondence
International Woman Suffrage Alliance
Inter-Parliamentary Union
International Workers Aid
Joint Amnesty Committee
Kuzbas
League for Amnesty of Political Prisoners
Labor Education Bureau, Inc., N.Y.
Jewish Socialist Labor Federation
Labor Defense Council
League for Democracy and Terms for Peace
League for Democratic Control
League for Industrial Democracy
    branches in 28 colleges
    Church League for Industrial Democracy
    Emergency Committee for Strikers Relief
League for Mutual Aid
League for World Peace
League of Youth Against Militarism
Mothers League of Jewish Women
Mooney Defense Committee
National Bureau of Information and Education

National Civil Liberties Union
National Consumers League
National Council for the Prevention of War
National League for Release of Political Prisoners
National Trade Union League
One Big Union of America
National Popular Government League
National Womans Party
Non-Partisan League
Pioneer Youth of America
Public Ownership Association
Rand School of Social Science
Road to Freedom Conference
Russian-American Industrial Corporation
Russian Famine Relief Conference
Russian Federation of the U.S.A.
Russian Friends of American Freedom
Russian Information Bureau
Russian Reconstruction Farms
Sacco-Vanzetti Defense Committee
Socialist Publication Society
Society for Cultural Relations in Foreign Countries of the Soviet Union
Socialist Youth International
Soviet Russian Red Cross Society
Speakers Service Bureau
Trade Union Educational League
Union Health Center, N.Y.
War Resisters International
War Resisters League
Womens Committee on World Disarmament
Womens International League for Peace and Freedom
Womens Peace Society
Womens Peace Union
Womens Trade Union League Unions
Womens International Federation of Trade
Workers (Communist) Party of America
Workers Defense Union
Workers Education Bureau of America
Young Peoples Socialist League—called Ypsels

Young Pioneers of America
Young Workers (Communist) League of America
Youngstown (Ohio) Workers Defense League

WORKERS SCHOOLS AND COLLEGES

Amalgamated Labor Classes—Chicago, Ill.
Amherst-Holyoke Classes for Workers
Amherst-Springfield Classes for Workers
Barnard Social Science Club, Barnard College
Berkeley Divinity School
Boston School of Social Science
Boston Trade Union League
Brookwood Labor College
Brookwood Workers College
Bryn Mawr Liberal Club
Bryn Mawr Summer School
Camp Tamiment Vacation School
Chicago Trade Union College
Commonwealth College, Arkansas
Dartmouth Round Table, Dartmouth College
Denver Labor College, Denver, Colo.
George Washington University Free Lance Club
Harvard Student Liberal Club
Hollins (Va.) Student Forum
Labor Bureau, N.Y.
Labor Educational Bureau, Inc., New York City
Labor College, Des Moines, Iowa
   Philadelphia, Pa. New York City
   Rochester, N.Y.
Labor School, Chicago, Ill.
Labor Temple School, New York City
   Seattle, Wash. Omaha, Neb.
Manhattan School
Meadville Theological School
Manument School
Miami University Round Table
Minneapolis Workers College
Milwaukee Workers College

Modern School, The
N.Y. University Law School Liberal Club
Northwestern University Liberal League
Oberlin College Liberal Club
Park College Social Science Club
Peoples College, Kansas City
Portland Labor College, Portland, Ore.
Pueblo Labor College, Pueblo, Colo.
Radcliffe Liberal Club
Rand School of Social Science
Rochester Labor College, Rochester, N.Y.
Sanford University Forum
School of the Open Gate
School for the Study of Marxism
Seattle Labor College, Seattle, Wash.
Social Problems Club of Columbia Univ.
Swarthmore Polity Club
Smith College Liberal Club
Trade Union College, New Haven, Conn.
Union Theological Seminar Contemporary Club
University of Chicago Liberal Club
University of Colorado Forum
Vassar College Political Association
Wellesley College Forum
Western College Forum
Workers Education Association, Detroit, Mich.
Workers Colleges, Minneapolis, Minn.
Workers School, N.Y.
Womens Trade Union College
Womens Trade Union League Training School
Workers University
Work People's College, Duluth, Minn.
   Smithville, Minn.
   New York City
Yale Liberal Club
New School for Social Research

Notes

Introduction

1. Walter O. Boswell to Mrs. Schatz, October 26, 1926, RG 165, 10110-1935/61, National Archives (hereafter NA); Kerr T. Riggs to John F. Madden, May 14, 1924, RG 165, 10110-1935/40, NA.

2. Weigand, "The Red Menace"; Swerdlow, *Women Strike for Peace;* Elaine Tyler May, *Homeward Bound.*

3. Cott, *The Grounding of Modern Feminism.*

4. A notable exception is Joan M. Jensen's "All Pink Sisters."

5. Robert K. Murray remains the eminent historian of the first Red Scare. Murray argues that the Red Scare was a moment of unnecessary national hysteria during which reason and democracy were forsaken. Murray, *Red Scare.* See also Murray B. Levin, *Political Hysteria in America.*

Other historians, while agreeing with Robert Murray that the scare was unnecessary, argue that it was part of larger and continuing nativistic and/or antiradical trends in U.S. history and culture. See Kovel, *Red Hunting;* Heale, *American Anticommunism;* David H. Bennett, *The Party of Fear;* Preston, *Aliens and Dissenters;* Higham, *Strangers in the Land;* Coben, "A Study in Nativism."

For historians Donald Johnson and Paul L. Murphy, the Red Scare is part of the larger story of the emerging civil liberties movement in the United States. Johnson, *The Challenge to American Freedoms;* Murphy, *World War I.* Richard Gid Powers presents the Red Scare as the beginning of anticommunism in the United States. Powers, *Not without Honor.*

A helpful guide to the social science literature on antiradicalism is William B. Hixson, *Search.*

For an interesting commentary on the impact of anticommunism, see Blanche Wiesen Cook, "The Impact of Anti-Communism."

6. My use of the term *patriarchy* relies heavily upon definitions developed by Judith M. Bennett and Linda Gordon. Bennett, "Feminism and History"; Gordon, *Heroes of Their Own Lives,* pp. vi–vii.

7. And despite the cautions of Cott to be careful in our use of the word *feminism,* many historians also have called these activist women feminists. Cott, "What's in a Name?"

8. Muncy, *Creating a Female Dominion.*

9. For example, see Dumenil, *The Modern Temper.*

10. A notable exception to the separation of black and white women's politics is the example of Jessie Daniel Ames and the Association of Southern Women for the Prevention of Lynching. Hall, *Revolt against Chivalry.* For information on black women's efforts against lynching, see Thompson, *Ida B. Wells-Barnett.*

11. For an indication of the breadth of black women's activism and the structural as well as cultural obstructions black women encountered, see Giddings, *When and Where I Enter;* Hine and Thompson, *A Shining Thread of Hope;* Gordon, "Black and White Visions"; Rouse, *Lugenia Burns Hope;* McMurry, *To Keep the Waters Troubled;* Gilmore, *Women and the Politics of White Supremacy.*

12. Examples include Kerber, *No Constitutional Right;* Bederman, *Manliness and Civilization;* Gilmore, *Women and the Politics of White Supremacy;* MacLean, *Behind the Mask of Chivalry;* Norton, *Founding Mothers and Fathers.*

CHAPTER 1

1. Strong, *I Change Worlds,* pp. 72, 80; Friedheim, *The Seattle General Strike,* pp. 124–25, 128. For more information on the Seattle labor scene, see Frank, *Purchasing Power.*

2. Friedheim, *The Seattle General Strike,* p. 113.

3. Murray, *Red Scare,* p. 65.

4. "Seattle to Face Army Rule," *New York Times,* February 8, 1919, pp. 1, 4.

5. Murray, *Red Scare,* p. 64; "Anarchists Tried Revolution," *New York Times,* February 9, 1919, p. 1.

6. "Ole Hanson," *Washington Post,* February 11, 1919, p. 5; Murray, *Red Scare,* p. 65; "The Fighting Mayor Who Would Banish Fear," *Current Opinion* 66 (April 1919): 225–26 (includes examples of photos); Blanche Brace, "Too Much Red in the Spectrum," *World Outlook* 6 (January 1920): 5–6, 56; *Town Crier,* February 15, 1919; "Barnes Booms Hanson," *New York Times,* February 13, 1919, p. 8; Leiren, "Ole and the Reds," p. 87; "Wanted—Men for Government Jobs," *Woman Patriot,* October 11, 1919, p. 2. See also *Literary Digest* 60 (March 8, 1919): 47–50; *Outlook* 121 (March 5, 1919): 376–77; *American Industries,* June 1919, pp. 37–38; *Unpartizan Review* 12 (July 1919): 35–45; "If Ole Hanson Were Mayor of New York," *New York Times Magazine,* September 28, 1919, sec. 7, pp. 8–9; *World's Work,* December 1919 through March 1920.

7. Woman Patriots' petition, *Congressional Record* (July 3, 1926), 69th Cong., 1st sess., 67:12950.

8. Friedheim, *The Seattle General Strike,* p. 147.

9. Filene, *Americans and the Soviet Experiment,* p. 61. N. Gordon Levin, Jr., *Woodrow Wilson and World Politics;* Foglesong, *America's Secret War against Bolshevism.*

10. David H. Bennett, *The Party of Fear,* p. 197. For a history of the debates surrounding World War I civil liberties, see Murphy, *World War I and the Origin of Civil Liberties.*

11. Murray, *Red Scare*, p. 67.

12. Ibid., p. 68.

13. The Overman committee included Lee Overman of North Carolina (chair), William King of Utah, Josiah Wolcott of Delaware, Knute Nelson of Minnesota, and Thomas Sterling of South Dakota. "Senate Orders Reds Here Investigated," *New York Times*, February 5, 1919, p. 1; Murray, *Red Scare*, pp. 94–98.

14. Murray, *Red Scare*, p. 98. New York lawyer Archibald Stevenson was named assistant counsel. Stevenson was known for his warnings of rampant radicalism among New York workers and for his release to the Overman committee of "Who's Who in Pacifism and Radicalism," a list containing the names of sixty-two prominent men and women. "Lists Americans as Pacifists," *New York Times*, January 25, 1919, pp. 1, 4.

15. New York State Legislature, *Report of the Joint Legislative Committee. Revolutionary Radicalism: Its History, Purpose and Tactics* (Albany, N.Y.: J. B. Lyon, 1920).

16. Ibid., p. 79; see also pp. 70–78. The bombing of Palmer's house is usually credited with transforming him into an enthusiastic red-baiter. Coben, *A. Mitchell Palmer*.

17. Murray, *Red Scare*, pp. 178, 165. See also Ellis, "J. Edgar Hoover"; Tuttle, *Race Riot*; Brody, *Labor in Crisis*; Russell, *A City in Terror*.

18. Murray, *Red Scare*, pp. 210–18; Schlesinger, *The Age of Roosevelt*, p. 43.

19. Attorney General Palmer, "The Case against the Reds," *Forum* 63 (February 1920): 174; Murray, *Red Scare*, p. 219.

20. Murray, *Red Scare*, p. 66; Leiren, "Ole and the Reds," p. 92.

21. Murray, "Ole Hanson," pp. 279–80; Brace, "Too Much Red," pp. 5–6, 56.

22. Leiren, "Ole and the Reds," pp. 77–78; "The Fighting Mayor," pp. 225–26; "Fighting the Reds in Their Home Town," *World's Work* 39 (December 1919): 123–26.

23. Murray, "Ole Hanson," pp. 279–80. For material on Roosevelt and masculinity, see Testi, "The Gender of Reform Politics"; Haraway, *Primate Visions*, chap. 3; Bederman, *Manliness and Civilization*, chap. 5.

24. Hanson, *Americanism versus Bolshevism*, pp. viii, 91, 247.

25. Ibid., pp. 283–84. The use of the family as the source, justification, and target of political obligation was not unique to Hanson. As Linda Gordon and Nancy Fraser argue, in the mid-nineteenth century the process of owning slaves and/or subsuming wives in coverture defined the civil citizenship of white male property owners. Robert Westbrook argues that war propagandists appealed to Americans to join the war effort in the cause of their private family; citizens were entreated to join in the public political obligations of war by exercising private moral obligations and protecting private (family) interests. Fraser and Gordon, "Contract versus Charity"; Westbrook, "Fighting for the American Family."

26. In 1924, Hanson moved to southern California, where he continued his real estate business. He died there in 1940. Murray, "Ole Hanson," pp. 279–80.

27. Leed, *No Man's Land*, p. 196.

28. "The Voice of the New Day," *American Legion Weekly*, November 28, 1919, p. 8; Pencak, *For God and Country*.

29. Pencak, *For God and Country*, pp. 149–53.

30. For information on the Wobblies and the Centralia Massacre, see McClelland, *Wobbly War*; Copeland, *The Centralia Tragedy of 1919*. McClelland and Copeland agree that the castration story was part of the Centralia myth rather than fact. Whether fact

or fiction, however, the common acceptance of the story of Everest's castration is what matters here.

31. Pencak, *For God and Country*, pp. 151–53; Rumer, *The American Legion*, pp. 93–95.

32. "Centralia," *American Legion Weekly*, December 12, 1919, p. 7.

33. "The Legion's War on Disloyalty," *Literary Digest* 63 (November 29, 1919): 19–20.

34. "The Awakening of Gulliver," *American Legion Weekly*, December 26, 1919, p. 34.

35. Dawley, *Struggles for Justice*, pp. 234–35, 238; Barrett, "Americanization from the Bottom Up." For a discussion of governmental efforts to ensure the wartime cooperation of unions, see Montgomery, *Fall of the House of Labor*, pp. 373–80.

36. Dawley, *Struggles for Justice*, p. 247.

37. Fine, "'Our Big Factory Family,'" pp. 281, 285. As Andrea Tone argues, gender was integral to all of the employee benevolence programs of industry. Tone, *The Business of Benevolence*.

38. The *Open Shop Review* was published in Chicago. In 1912, the National Founders' Association and the National Metal Trades Association (two of the nation's leading manufacturers' organizations) began recommending that all of its members send the journal to their employees. Bonnett, *Employer's Associations*, pp. 64, 127.

39. "How the Union Slugger Broke Up the Family," *Open Shop Review* 17 (July 1920): 285–86.

40. "Ma Becomes a Socialist," *Open Shop Review* 18 (February 1921): 45–50.

41. I. DeCalesta, "I Wanted to Know," *Open Shop Review* 17 (August 1920): 257–312; 17 (September 1920): 362–77; 17 (October 1920): 404–14; quotations on pp. 309 and 408.

42. Faragher, *Daniel Boone;* Bederman, *Manliness and Civilization*, pp. 1–10; Lackie, *Elizabeth Bacon Custer*.

43. As Gwendolyn Mink argues, this promise failed to take into consideration the "culturally plural, polyglot army" of white, black, and immigrant men that served the nation. Mink, *The Wages of Motherhood*, p. 17; See also ibid., pp. 13–23; Filene, "In Time of War"; David M. Kennedy, *Over Here*, pp. 188–89.

44. Kathleen Kennedy, *Disloyal Mothers and Scurrilous Citizens*.

45. See, for example, Kent, *Making Peace;* Roberts, *Civilization without Sexes*.

46. Susan Ware has found that female heroines abounded in the 1920s and 1930s, but without the politicized and patriotic edge available to men. Heroicized women were "independent and individualistic heroines from popular culture," excelling in aviation, athletics, Hollywood, or journalism. Ware, *Still Missing*, pp. 12–13. See also Cayleff, *Babe*.

CHAPTER 2

1. Diary of Alice Stone Blackwell, April 17, 1920. Library of Congress.

2. Foglesong, *America's Secret War against Bolshevism*, p. 25.

3. Overman Report, quoted in "Is Bolshevism in America Becoming a Real Peril?" *Current Opinion* 67 (July 1919): 4; Dr. Frank Crane, "Bolshevism and the Future," *World Outlook* 5 (November 1919): 40–41; Hornaday, *The Lying Lure of Bolshevism*, p. 5.

4. "New York Reds Potent in Russia," *New York Times*, February 13, 1919, pp. 1, 4. Earlier reports had told of "well-bred" women who attempted suicide for "fear

of outrage": "Bolsheviki Slow Up at Polish Frontier," *New York Times,* January 21, 1919, p. 4.

5. "Bolshevism Bared by R. E. Simmons," *New York Times,* February 18, 1919, p. 4; "Francis Confirms Bolshevist Horror," *New York Times,* March 9, 1919, pp. 1, 16; "Russia under Reds a Gigantic Bedlam," *New York Times,* March 11, 1919, p. 1; "Russian Noblewoman's Appeal to American Women," *New York Times Magazine,* February 1, 1920, p. 9. For other examples of these stories, see "Soviets Make Girls Property of State," *New York Times,* October 26, 1919, p. 5; "Reds to Allot Husbands," *New York Times,* January 5, 1919, p. 3. See also Foglesong, *America's Secret War against Bolshevism,* pp. 42–43; Lasch, *American Liberals,* pp. 121–27; Filene, *Americans and the Soviet Experiment,* p. 46.

6. Hubbard, *Socialism, Feminism, and Suffragism,* p. 230.

7. Ole Hanson, "Bolshevism and Readjustment," *American Industries,* June 1919, p. 37; "Bolshevist Marriage," *New York Times,* April 28, 1919, p. 14; "Some More Disproof Is Required," *New York Times,* April 24, 1919, p. 16.

8. U.S. Senate, Subcommittee on the Judiciary, *Brewing and Liquor Interests and German and Bolshevik Propaganda: Report and Hearings of the Subcommittee on the Judiciary, United States Senate,* 3 vols. (Washington, D.C.: Government Printing Office, 1919, no. 7597–7598), testimony of Louise Bryant, February 21, 1919, p. 541. Another denial was written by Alice Stone Blackwell. Letter to the Editor, *New York Times,* March 7, 1919, p. 12.

9. "Women in 1917 and After," *Blackwell Encyclopedia of the Russian Revolution* (New York: Blackwell Reference, 1988), pp. 34–36.

10. Maude Radford Warren, "Bolshevik Women," *Ladies' Home Journal* 37 (December 1920): 16–17, 176.

11. "Women Cruelest of Red Terrorists," *New York Times,* October 26, 1918, p. 5. Americans, for example, were fascinated by the Russian Women's Battalion of Death and its commander Maria Botchkareva. When Botchkareva's autobiography was published in the United States in 1919, that interest only increased. Jensen, "Minerva on the Fields of Mars," pp. 128–58.

12. Similar accounts of the gender inversions inherent to Communism occurred during the Cold War. Soviet women frequently were derided in the U.S. press as ugly and masculine. Cahn, *Coming on Strong,* p. 210; Elaine Tyler May, *Homeward Bound,* pp. 18–19.

13. Murray, *Red Scare,* pp. 166–67.

14. Hornaday, *The Lying Lure of Bolshevism,* p. 10.

15. Samuel Crowther, "Radical Propaganda: How It Works," *World's Work* 39 (April 1920): 620; "The Bolshevist Movement in America," *American Industries,* November 1919, p. 22; Crowther, "Radical Propaganda," p. 624; John Bruce Mitchell, "'Reds' in New York's Slums," *Forum* 61 (April 1919): 442–55.

16. Roosevelt, "Bolshevism and Applied Bolshevism," *The Works of Theodore Roosevelt,* vol. 19 (New York: Scribner's Sons, 1926), p. 356.

17. Lewis Allen Browne, "Bolshevism in America," *Forum* 59 (June 1918): 717.

18. Solomon, *Educated Women,* p. 142; "Information Wanted," *Woman Patriot,* March 29, 1919, p. 2; Woodworth Chum, "Radicalism in Our Universities," *Iowa Magazine,* February 5, 1920. The *Iowa Magazine* was a publication of the Greater Iowa

Association of Davenport, which later became the Davenport Chamber of Commerce. The organization, which was also aligned with the American Protective League, was founded to combat the growth of socialism in Dubuque and was hostile to the socialist city administration elected in 1920. Chum, author of this article, also led the attack against the National Nonpartisan League in Iowa. See Cumberland, "The Davenport Socialists of 1920."

19. Calvin Coolidge, "Enemies of the Republic: Are the 'Reds' Stalking Our College Women?" *Delineator* 98 (June 1921): 4–5, 66–67; Calvin Coolidge, "Enemies of the Republic: Trotzky [*sic*] versus Washington," *Delineator* 99 (July 1921): 10–11, 38–39; Calvin Coolidge, "Enemies of the Republic: They Must Be Resisted," *Delineator* 99 (August 1921): 10–11, 42; *Daughters of the American Revolution Magazine*, April 1921, May 1921; "Campaign against Radicalism in Women's Colleges," *Woman Patriot*, July 1, 1923, p. 7. Coolidge's warnings followed wartime and Red Scare attacks upon and dismissals of socialist academics. Gruber, *Mars and Minerva*. Coolidge's claim that "to make a home is to be a capitalist" was echoed in the late 1940s and 1950s. And as Elaine Tyler May argues, home ownership represented a validation of capitalism in Cold War contests. Suburban developer William J. Levitt, developer of suburban areas, argued that "no man who owns his house and lot can be a Communist. He has too much to do." May, *Homeward Bound*, chap. 7.

20. Peter Collins, "Bolshevism in America," *Current Opinion* 68 (March 1920): 324; "Radicalism Repudiated," *Bellman*, May 31, 1919, p. 594.

21. Collins, "Bolshevism in America," p. 324; "Declares Parlor Reds Most Dangerous Type," *New York Times*, January 13, 1920, p. 2.

22. Theodore Roosevelt, "Parlor Bolshevism," *The Works of Theodore Roosevelt*, vol. 19, pp. 351–52.

23. Edith Sellers, "Amateur Bolsheviki," *Living Age* 307 (November 20, 1920): 480.

24. "No Compromise with Bolshevism," *Saturday Evening Post* 194 (June 24, 1922): 23.

25. A. Mitchell Palmer, "The Case against the 'Reds,'" *Forum* 63 (February 1920): 183.

26. "Tragedy of the Parlor Bolsheviki," *New York Times* January 25, 1920, sec. 4, p. 6.

27. John Spargo, "The Psychology of the Parlor Bolsheviki," *World's Work* 39 (December 1919): 127–31.

28. Morlan, *Political Prairie Fire*. Historical interpretations of the NPL have leaned heavily on Morlan's populist interpretation. Official membership as of December 1919:

Minnesota	50,000	Idaho	12,000
North Dakota	40,000	Washington	10,000
South Dakota	25,000	Iowa, Kansas, Texas, and	
Montana	20,000	Oklahoma	11,300
Wisconsin	15,000	Nebraska	13,500
Colorado	12,000	TOTAL	208,800

For more information on women's involvement in the NPL, see Nielsen, "'We Are All Leaguers by Our House.'"

29. Morlan, *Political Prairie Fire*, pp. 109, 148, 256–61. See also Chrislock, *Watchdog of Loyalty*; LeSueur, *Crusaders*.

30. Minnie J. Nielson, *A Message to Minnesota Womanhood* (St. Paul: Minnesota Sound Government Association, 1920).

31. Jerry D. Bacon, *Sovietians: Wreckers of Americanism* (Grand Forks, N.D.: Jerry D. Bacon, 1920).

32. "The Non-Partisan League and Its Leaders," speech by Honorable Clarence B. Miller of Minnesota in the U.S. House of Representatives, June 8, 1918. Reprinted by the Government Printing Office, Washington, D.C.

33. "Farmers' Non-Partisan League," *American Industries*, February 1918, pp. 14–15.

34. "Are You Ready to Hand Over Your Farm to a Bunch of Socialist Adventurers?: That Is What Townleyism Means, Mr. Farmer," 1918(?), State Historical Society of Wisconsin, Library Pamphlet Collection, no. 91–1113.

35. Fred Marvin, *Are These Your Friends?* (Denver, CO: Americanization Press, 1922), cover.

36. *Red Flame*, April 1920, p. 217.

37. Ibid.

38. Morlan, *Political Prairie Fire*, p. 244; *North Dakota Leader*, July 10, 1920; July 5, 1919. For more information on the IVA, see Tweton, "The Anti-League Movement: The IVA."

39. Bacon, *Sovietians*, pp. 18–19; Remele, "North Dakota State Library Scandal."

40. *Red Flame*, March 1920.

41. Lemons, *The Woman Citizen*, pp. 121–22; Region Reports, Fifth Region, November 12–14, 1922, Board of Directors Meeting, Papers of the League of Women Voters, 1918–1974 (Frederick, MD: University Publications of America, Inc.), Part I: Minutes of the Board of Directors and the Executive Committees, 1918–1974 (hereafter LWV Papers).

42. "Another 'Nationalization of Women' Myth," *Woman Citizen* July 26, 1919, p. 189.

43. *North Dakota Leader*, March 6, 1920.

44. Lena Borchardt, "The Militant Mothers of Rutabaga County," in *The People Together*, ed. Meridel LeSueur (Minneapolis: People's Centennial Book Committee of Minnesota, 1958), pp. 17–19; Lena Borchardt, "Memoirs," Lena Borchardt Manuscript Collection, Minnesota Historical Society.

45. Marshall, *Splintered Sisterhood*, pp. 203–6. Thomas Jablonsky argues that anti-suffrage red-baiting began among antisuffragists when Dorothy Dodge resigned from the presidency in 1917 and Alice Hayes Wadsworth became president. As the "rhetoric of anti-suffragism shifted from a conservative but non-vindictive articulation of the female role in society to one filled with innuendo and character assassination," the Woman Patriots lost credibility and ignored their most potent argument: that women did not want to vote. Jablonsky, *Home, Heaven, and Mother Party*, pp. 98, 106–13. For more information on antisuffragists, see Marshall, *Splintered Sisterhood*; Green, *Southern Strategies*; Sims, "Beyond the Ballot"; Thurner, "'Better Citizens without the Ballot'"; Kraditor, *Woman Suffrage Movement*, chap. 2; Camhi, *Women against Women*; Stevenson, "Women Anti-Suffragists"; Kenneally, "Opposition to Woman Suffrage."

46. *Woman Patriot*, May 4, 1918, p. 6.

47. *Woman Patriot*, May 18, 1918, p. 1.

48. *Woman Patriot*, February 1, 1919, p. 2.

49. *Woman Patriot*, April 19, 1919, p. 8; April 27, 1918, p. 4; June 15, 1918, p. 8.

50. *Woman Patriot*, October 19, 1918, p. 5.

51. *Woman Patriot,* June 1, 1918, p. 6.

52. *Woman Patriot,* December 21, 1918, p. 4.

53. *Woman Patriot,* May 18, 1918, p. 4.

54. *Woman Patriot,* October 12, 1918, p. 4; October 19, 1918, p. 7; September 14, 1918, p. 4. For an examination of the use of white supremacy in antisuffrage arguments, see Lebsock, "Woman Suffrage and White Supremacy"; Kraditor, *Woman Suffrage Movement,* chap. 7. The assumption of both suffragists and antisuffragists that black women would be allowed to vote in the South, when black men were not, seems self-serving. Neither group recognized that black men had been and would continue to be excluded, or that black women would be excluded, from the electorate through legal and extralegal means.

55. *Woman Patriot,* August 23, 1919, p. 8. See also *Woman Patriot,* August 2, 1919, p. 6; October 11, 1919, p. 7. J. Edgar Hoover and the Bureau of Investigation also blamed radicals for inciting racial discontents. Ellis, "J. Edgar Hoover."

56. *Woman Patriot,* July 12, 1919, p. 4.

57. *Woman Patriot,* April 12, 1919, p. 1.

58. This discussion of Native American women by antisuffragists may have been a response to suffragists' own use of Native American women as political symbols. Suffrage advocates used Indian women both as evidence of women's past power and rights in the natural state (the justice argument, in which an image of noble squaws was used) and as examples of women's essential civilizing qualities (the expediency argument, in which Sacajawea and Pocahontas were used). False historical pictures were used to counter an equally false set of historical constructions and appropriations. Both appropriations used a similar concept of "civilization" as a key component in their arguments. Landsman, "The 'Other' as Political Symbol."

59. Kraditor, *Woman Suffrage Movement.*

60. Elaine Tyler May has shown that the containment of sex in a "safe" sphere also was important during the Cold War. May, *Homeward Bound.*

61. McMann, *Birth Control Politics,* pp. 2, 30, 42–43.

62. See, e.g., Chauncey, *Gay New York;* Ullmann, *Sex Seen;* D'Emilio and Freedman, *Intimate Matters;* Langum, *Crossing Over the Line;* Odem, *Delinquent Daughters;* Peiss, *Cheap Amusements.*

63. Montgomery, *Fall of the House of Labor,* p. 464; Montgomery, "Thinking about American Workers."

64. Schlesinger, *The Age of Roosevelt,* p. 60; MacKay, *The Progressive Movement of 1924,* pp. 162–74; Burgchardt, *Robert M. La Follette, Sr.,* pp. 111–16. In her article on attacks on women's organizations in the 1920s, Joan M. Jensen argues that the 1924 campaign of La Follette and the (re)birth of a reform movement frightened conservative politicians into attacks on feminists. Jensen, "All Pink Sisters," p. 213.

65. Hicks, *Republican Ascendancy;* Schlesinger, *The Age of Roosevelt,* pp. 57–60; Parrish, *Anxious Decades,* p. 66. William Morgan Butler, Coolidge's long-time Massachusetts assistant and Republican national chairman, owned several cotton mills in which children undoubtedly worked. Goldman, *National Party Chairmen and Committees,* pp. 365–67. Sklar, "Historical Foundations of Women's Power," p. 75.

66. Ward, "Against the Tide," pp. 59–61; DeBenedetti, *Modern American Peace Movement,* pp. 71–73, 95–96.

CHAPTER 3

1. *Springfield Union,* April 9, 1923, reprinted by the Massachusetts Public Interests League (hereafter MPIL), n.d., Children's Bureau Records, National Archives, box 24, folder 1.

2. Marshall, *Splintered Sisterhood.* See also Chafetz and Dworkin, "In the Face of Threat."

3. For varying definitions, analyses, and uses of the term *maternalism,* see Koven and Michel, "Womanly Duties," p. 1079; Skocpol, *Protecting Soldiers and Mothers;* Sklar, "Historical Foundations of Women's Power"; Boris, "What about the Working?" pp. 104–9; Ladd-Taylor, *Mother-Work,* p. 3; Gordon, *Pitied but Not Entitled;* Mink, *The Wages of Motherhood;* Gordon, "Putting Children First"; Kornbluh, "New Literature on Gender," p. 173; Brush, "Love, Toil, and Trouble."

4. Michel and Rosen, "The Paradox of Maternalism," p. 364.

5. Dunn and Woodard, *American Conservatism,* p. 109. See also Hodgson, *The World Turned Upside Down;* Himmelstein, *To The Right;* Nash, *The Conservative Intellectual Movement,* chap. 7; Kirk, *The Conservative Mind;* Rossiter, *Conservatism in America.*

Leonard J. Moore also points to the 1920s as pivotal, calling the era "a key turning point, or perhaps more precisely, a starting point, in the history of the modern Right." Moore, "Good Old-Fashioned New Social History," p. 560. For an excellent discussion on historians and the history of American conservatism, see the *American Historical Review* forum of April 1994: Brinkley, "The Problem of American Conservatism"; Yohn, "Will the Real Conservative"; Ribuffo, "So Much Conservatism." Michael Kazin also has issued a call to historians to treat conservatives, and conservative women specifically, in an analytically critical manner; Kazin, "The Grass-Roots Right."

6. Nancy MacLean discusses the politics and implications of studying right-wing women in "White Women and Klan Violence." Historians of women are beginning to pay attention to conservative women. For some examples, see Jeansonne, *Women of the Far Right;* Blee, "Ku Klux Klan Movement"; Blee, *Women of the Klan;* DeHart, "Gender on the Right"; Matthews and DeHart, *Sex, Gender;* MacLean, *Behind the Mask of Chivalry;* McEnaney, "He-Men and Christian Mothers"; Felsenthal, *Sweetheart of the Silent Majority;* Green, "From Antisuffragism to Anti-Communism."

7. Baker, "The Domestication of Politics," p. 641.

8. See MacLean, "White Women and Klan Violence"; Blee, "Ku Klux Klan Movement"; Blee, *Women of the Klan.*

9. The notable exception is the DAR, which has its own sizable but access-restricted archive.

10. *Woman Patriot,* May 1, 1923, p. 6.

11. *Woman Patriot,* October 1 and 15, 1922, pp. 10–11; February 15, 1923, p. 5; September 1, 1924, p. 7.

12. December 10, 1923 meeting, Sentinels of the Republic, Williams College; Mary G. Kilbreth to Rossiter Johnson, September 24, 1922, Rossiter Johnson Papers, Manuscripts and Archives Division, The New York Public Library, Astor, Lenox and Tilden Foundations.

13. *Woman Patriot,* September 1 and 15, 1922, p. 2.

14. "To Arms! To Arms! The New Crisis," n.d., Alexander Lincoln Papers, folder 5, Schlesinger Library, Radcliffe Institute (hereafter Lincoln Papers). Louis A. Coolidge was not, as far as I have been able to discover, a relative of Calvin Coolidge.

15. "Mustering Sentinels of the Republic," *National Magazine* 51 (October 1922): 229–30; "Sentinels of the Republic," n.d., Lincoln Papers, folder 7; Katharine T. Balch, "Plan of Organization for the Sentinels of the Republic," June 1923, Lincoln Papers, folder 2; Letter from Grace Abbott to Alma E. Shimer, September 12, 1929, Children's Bureau Records, box 8, folder 3.

Women whose membership in the Sentinels overlaps with other organizations include Margaret C. Robinson, Alice Robertson, Mary Kilbreth, Katharine T. Balch, Mrs. Rufus Dawes, Mary (Mrs. Louis) Frothingham, Harriet A. (Mrs. Randolph) Frothingham, Cornelia A. (Mrs. Rufus) Gibbs, Elizabeth Lowell Putnam, and Mrs. Francis E. Slattery.

16. Minutes, Annual Meeting, January 12–13, 1926, Lincoln Papers, folder 1.

17. Organizations such as the American Child Health Association and the National Education Association, which were not specifically female but supported measures of which the Sentinels disapproved, were described as being led by "he-women and she-men." Letter from Frank L. Peckham to Alexander Lincoln, June 5, 1928, Lincoln Papers, folder 2.

18. *Woman Patriot,* December 15, 1923, p. 1. January 12–13, 1926, "Meetings, 1924–1926," Sentinels of the Republic, Williams College.

19. *Do You Realize That in Every Country Woman Suffrage and Socialism Go Hand in Hand?* (Boston: Massachusetts Public Interests League of Anti-Suffragists, n.d.), National American Woman Suffrage Association Papers, reel 27, frames 294–95; *Is Woman Suffrage Pro-German?* (Boston: Massachusetts Public Interests League, September 16, 1918), Papers of Carrie Chapman Catt, Library of Congress, reel 17, frames 546–47 (hereafter Catt-LOC Papers).

20. "Aims to Preserve Ideals of Republic," *Springfield Union,* June 7, 1925, pp. 3–4, Lincoln Papers, folder 16, box 3.

21. *The Massachusetts Public Interests League* (Boston: Massachusetts Public Interests League, March 1, 1922), Children's Bureau Records, box 24, folder 1.

22. "Public Interests League Has Decided to Dissolve," *Chronicle,* May 30, 1932, Helen Tufts Bailie Papers, box 1, clippings folder—DAR, Sophia Smith Collection, Smith College (hereafter Bailie Papers).

23. For information on the DAR, see Peggy Anderson, *The Daughters;* Gibbs, *The DAR;* Strayer, *The D.A.R.* For the DAR's move to antiradicalism, see Morgan, "'Regions Remote from Revolutionary Scenes'"; Morgan, "'Home and Country,'" chap. 2.

24. Lora Haines Cook (Mrs. Anthony Wayne), a resident of Cookstown, Pennsylvania, had been both a local and a state regent and continued her activism in the DAR until her death in 1946. During her term as president-general, her husband donated $10,000 to the building of the DAR Constitution Hall. Before her presidency-general, Grace Lincoln Hall Brosseau (Mrs. Alfred J.) had been treasurer-general and had chaired several national committees. She and her husband, Alfred J. Brosseau, the president of Mack Trucks, Inc., lived in Greenwich, Connecticut, where she died in April 1959. Flora A. (Mrs. William Sherman) Walker also had been a state regent. Walker was from Seattle but moved to Washington, D.C., when Brosseau became

president-general and remained there while holding various posts in the DAR until 1957. Strayer, *The D.A.R.*, pp. 185, 245.

25. "A Message from the President General," *DAR Magazine*, September 1924, pp. 546–47; Gibbs, *The DAR*, pp. 103, 106, 113; Craig, "Redbaiting, Pacifism, and Free Speech"; "National Defense Committee: Annual Report," *DAR Magazine*, June 1928, p. 385; Strayer, *The D.A.R.*, pp. 121, 173; Gibbs, *The DAR*.

26. Strayer, *The D.A.R.*, p. 124.

27. Address before the Continental Congress, *DAR Magazine*, May 1927, pp. 333, 334.

28. *DAR Magazine*, March 1928, p. 147.

29. Strayer, *The D.A.R.*, p. 245.

30. "DAR Congressional Report of the National Defense Committee," *DAR Magazine*, August 1927, pp. 590–92. For example, see "National Defense Committee," *DAR Magazine*, November 1927, p. 695; "Americanism versus Internationalism," *DAR Magazine*, July 1928, pp. 433–37; "The Common Enemy," *DAR Magazine*, 1927, p. 766; Address of Mrs. William Sherman Walker, Ohio State Conference, March 16, 1927, reprint from Ohio Conference Report, Bailey Papers, box 1.

31. *DAR Magazine*, July 1928, p. 434.

32. For example, see "National Defense Committee," *DAR Magazine*, April 1928, pp. 250–52; "National Defense Committee," *DAR Magazine*, Dec 1927, pp. 901–4.

33. For an analysis of the gendered elements of the hostility toward women's peace efforts in World War I, see Kathleen Kennedy, *Disloyal Mothers and Scurrilous Citizens;* Zeiger, "She Didn't Raise Her Boy."

34. The original sixteen organizations were the DAR; Women's Overseas Relief Corps, G.A.R.; Women's Overseas Service League; Ladies of the G.A.R.; National Society, United Daughters of 1812; National Society of Colonial Dames of America; American Nurses Association; Service Star Legion; American War Mothers; United Daughters of the Confederacy; Women's Club of the Service Flag; American Women's Legion; Women's Auxiliary of Spanish-American War Veterans; Government Club of New York; Society of Sponsors of the United States Navy; and the American Legion Auxiliary. Breckinridge, *Women in the Twentieth Century*, pp. 86–87.

35. The National Committee on the Cause and Cure of War was, in the spectrum of women's peace organizations, very moderate. Schott, "'Middle-of-the-Road' Activists."

36. Proceedings of the Seventh Annual Conference of Post Commanders and Post Adjutants, Iowa Department, American Legion, February 22, 1927, pp. 48–50. See also Gibbs, *The D.A.R.*, pp. 115–17; Duffield, *King Legion*, pp. 240–45; Katherine Lewis, "America's Womanhood Declares for Adequate Defense," *American Legion Weekly*, March 20, 1925, p. 13; "Lack of National Defense Criminal, Women Told," *Washington Post*, February 23, 1925, p. 2.

37. *First Women's Patriotic Conference on National Defense*, souvenir ed. (Washington, D.C.: Women's Patriotic Conference, 1935), copy with Minnesota Historical Society; "National Should Set Arms Cut Example, Coolidge Declares," *New York Times*, February 24, 1925, pp. 1, 2; "These Women Must Save the Nation," *Manufacturer's Record*, March 5, 1925, p. 83; "Mrs. Macrae Urges Auxiliary Launch War on Pacifists," *Iowa Legionaire*, February 19, 1926, p. 11; "Women's Patriotic Groups to Discuss

National Defense," *Washington Post,* February 22, 1925, p. 12; "Coolidge, Generals and Weeks Demand National Defense," *Washington Post,* February 24, 1925, p. 1; "Strong Navy Urged by Admiral Phelps at Defense Session," *Washington Post,* February 25, 1925, p. 1.

38. Margaret C. Robinson, "The Responsibility of Being Led," an address before the Women's Patriotic Conference on National Defense, February 10, 1927, Catt-LOC Papers, container 27, folder 5; Records of the National Board of Management, April 16, 1927, DAR, *DAR Magazine,* May 1927, p. 384; "Patriotic Women Urge Quick Work on Cruisers," *Washington Post,* February 12, 1927, p. 1. For other information on the 1927 conference, see "Women's Patriotic Conference on National Defense," Weekly Bulletin of the American Legion National Legislative Committee, February 12, 1927, Hanford MacNider Papers, Herbert Hoover Presidential Library, box 2 (hereafter MacNider Papers); *New York Times,* p. 22; Proceedings of the Annual Conference of the Iowa DAR, March 9–11, 1927, pp. 16–17, State Historical Society of Iowa; R. L. Bullard to Carrie Chapman Catt, February 28, 1927, Catt-LOC Papers, reel 5, frame 156; weekly newsletter of the Better America Federation, April 8, 1927, Catt-LOC Papers, container 27, reel 17, frame 443; "Legion-Auxiliary Have Proved Right to Talk for Vets," *Iowa Legionaire,* August 5, 1927, p. 36; "Longworth Backs Cruiser Program," *New York Times,* February 10, 1927, p. 22; "Longworth Urges Bigger U.S. Navy; Holds Ratio Is Cut," *Washington Post,* February 10, 1927, p. 1; "The Woman's Patriotic Conference on National Defense," *DAR Magazine* 61 (1927): 270–73.

39. "500 Women to Confer on National Defense," *New York Times,* January 22, 1928, sec. 2, p. 2; "To Educate Women on Naval Bill," *New York Times,* January 29, 1928, p. 33; "Women Support Coolidge on Navy," *New York Times,* February 4, 1928, p. 25; "Women Hear Plea for Big Navy," *New York Times,* February 3, 1928, p. 12; Program of the Women's Patriotic Conference on National Defense, February 1–3, 1928, Bailie Papers, box 1, folder DAR; "Army and Navy Big Enough to Protect U.S. Urged by Reed," *Washington Post,* February 2, 1925, p. 1; "Patriotic Women Take Stand for Adequate National Defense," *DAR Magazine* 62 (1928): 145–50.

40. The DAR had 156,000 members in 1929; the American Legion Auxiliary had 200,000 members in 1925. Pencak, *For God and Country,* p. 276.

41. Robinson left no manuscript collection, but left a relatively large collection of published writings. See Appendix A for a bibliography of Robinson's written articles and articles about her.

42. Cott, *The Grounding of Modern Feminism,* pp. 4–5; Cott, "What's in a Name?"

43. Others have mentioned similarities among antifeminist and feminist women. For example, Faye D. Ginsburg, in *Contested Lives,* emphasizes the shared commitment to "woman's values" among contemporary anti- and proabortion activists. For analyses of female reformers, see Baker, "The Domestication of Politics"; Muncy, *Creating a Female Dominion;* Lemons, *The Woman Citizen;* Gordon, *Pitied but Not Entitled.*

44. *Boston Herald,* May 11, 1932, p. 15. Fernald, *Biographical Memoir,* pp. 305–6. "Benjamin Lincoln Robinson," *The National Cyclopaedia of American Biography,* vol. 12, 1904 ed. (Ann Arbor, MI: University Microfilms, 1967). Robinson was a student at the University High School (of Illinois State Normal School) in 1881 and in 1883. Letter from Jo Ann Rayfield, University Archivist, to author, December 19, 1994. Robinson's parents were William Henry Casson and Mary (MacMahon) Casson; 1870 and 1880 Federal Census Reports.

45. Charles A. Harper, *Development of the Teachers College in the United States* (Bloomington, IL: McKnight and McKnight, 1935), p. 125.

46. Allen F. Davis, *American Heroine;* "Julia Lathrop," *Notable American Women, 1607–1950: A Biographical Dictionary* (Boston: Radcliffe College, 1971), pp. 370–72. For information on the debates surrounding women's education, see Solomon, *Educated Women;* Rosenberg, *Beyond Separate Spheres.*

47. Hendricks, *James Harvey Robinson,* pp. 1–3.

48. *Boston Herald,* July 29, 1935; *Boston Herald,* May 11, 1932, p. 15; "William Hall Sherwood," *Baker's Biographical Dictionary of Musicians,* ed. Nicolas Slonimsky, 8th ed. (New York: Schirmer Books, 1991), p. 1699.

49. *Boston Herald,* July 29, 1935.

50. Robinson, "The Responsibility of Being Led," p. 14. For further information on McDougall, see Degler, *In Search of Human Nature,* pp. 34–35, 44, 161; "William McDougall," *Dictionary of American Biography,* vol. 11, suppl. 2, ed. Robert Livingston Schuyler (New York: Charles Scribner's Sons, 1958), pp. 405–7; McDougall, *Is America Safe for Democracy?*

51. Linda K. Kerber, "Annie Nathan Meyer," *Notable American Women,* pp. 473–74; Margaret C. Robinson, "Against Woman Suffrage," *Zion's Herald,* October 20, 1915, pp. 1331–32. *Zion's Herald* was a Boston Methodist weekly. See also Margaret C. Robinson, "The Suffrage Prophets," *Unpopular Review* 4 (July 1915): 127–39.

52. Robinson, "Against Woman Suffrage"; Margaret C. Robinson, "The Feminist Program," *Unpopular Review* 5 (August 1916): 318–31.

53. "Information Wanted," *Woman Patriot,* March 29, 1919, p. 2; "Campaign against Radicalism in Women's Colleges," *Woman Patriot,* July 7, 1923, p. 7.

54. Margaret C. Robinson, *The Responsibility of Being Led,* Massachusetts Public Interests League, 1925 (reprinted from *Dearborn Independent,* May 23, 1925), Bailie Papers, box 1, folder—Publications, MPIL (this is the same work as that cited in n. 38, above).

55. Robinson, "The Feminist Program." An understanding of the family as the check on male instability is not unique to Robinson. Mark Kann argues that this is a long-standing connection in American history. In the colonial period, family men were viewed as "bulwarks against disorder as well as patriots." In the early twentieth century, Theodore Roosevelt claimed, "No man can be a good citizen who is not a good father." Kann, *On the Man Question,* pp. 198–203.

56. Robinson, *The Responsibility of Being Led.* Robinson credited Harvard history professor Wilbur C. Abbott with the idea that feminists advocated government bureaucracy because they wanted jobs. Robyn Muncy argues that the attainment of jobs was an integral part of the development and maintenance of women's reform culture. "Both the old female guard and the new, then, continued to push for reform legislation because their professional and institutional interests encouraged them to do so." Muncy, *Creating a Female Dominion,* p. 159.

57. Margaret C. Robinson to Editor, "Two Dangerous Bills," *America,* March 5, 1921, p. 477.

58. Margaret C. Robinson, "Don't Ratify the Child Labor Amendment! Arguments Used against It Broadcasted by the Sentinels of the Republic," December 30, 1924, from WJY radio, Sentinels of the Republic Collection, Miscellaneous, Williams

College. See also Margaret C. Robinson to Editor, *Boston Herald*, May 1, 1924, Children's Bureau Records, box 16, folder 3.

59. Robinson, "Don't Ratify the Child Labor Amendment!"

60. Margaret C. Robinson, "A Woman's Warning to Men and Women on the Child Labor Amendment," *Manufacturer's Record*, September 4, 1924, p. 87, Children's Bureau Records, box 11, folder 17.

61. Margaret C. Robinson, "Is in Keeping with American Ideals," *American Industries* 23 (May 1923): 21. Most of this essay was reprinted in Portland's newspaper the *Spectator*, December 15, 1923, Children's Bureau Records, box 16, folder 3. *The Truth about the Red Movement* (Cleveland: *Iron Trade Review*, n.d.), Bailie Papers, box 1, folder—Pamphlets, DAR.

62. Robinson, "The Responsibility of Being Led," p. 4. For an account of the founding of the WJCC, see Cott, *The Grounding of Modern Feminism*, pp. 97–99.

63. Robinson, *The Responsibility of Being Led*. See also Margaret C. Robinson, "An Open Letter to 18 Organizations Said to Have Endorsed the Labor Amendment," *Woman Patriot*, January 15, 1925, p. 32. Robinson may have gotten the language of "interlocking directorates" from the spider web chart, a widely dispersed chart that alleged links between many women and women's organizations and claimed that they were part of a larger movement working for international socialism. See chapter 6 for a lengthier discussion of the spider web chart.

64. Robinson, "The Responsibility of Being Led," p. 13.

65. October 2, 1917, press release, Papers of the National American Woman Suffrage Association (NAWSA), Library of Congress, reel 29, frames 47–50 (hereafter NAWSA Papers); December 29, 1927, letter to Mrs. Helen Tufts Bailie from Carrie Chapman Catt, Catt-LOC Papers, reel 2, frames 397–98. For Catt's efforts to commit NAWSA to support World War I, see Scott and Scott, *One Half the People*, pp. 40–41; Eleanor Flexner, "Carrie Chapman Catt," *Notable American Women*, pp. 309–13; Alonso, *Peace as a Women's Issue*, chap. 3.

66. December 8, 1927, diary entry, Bailie Papers, box 3, personal journal; April 8, 1927, diary entry, ibid. Bailie's dismissal from the DAR will be discussed in greater detail in chapter 5.

67. December 8, 1927, diary entry; April 8, 1927, entry.

68. December 8, 1927, diary entry.

69. April 8, 1927, diary entry; December 8, 1927, entry. See also April 12, 1927, entry; December 13, 1927, entry; March 21, 1928.

70. December 21, 1927, letter from Helen Tufts Bailie to Carrie Chapman Catt, Catt-LOC Papers, reel 2, frame 396.

71. April 7, 1927, diary entry, Bailie Papers, box 3, personal journal. Bailie wrote, "What a woman to have in that family."

72. "Aims to Preserve Ideals," pp. 3–4.

73. October 2, 1917, press release, NAWSA; Cott, *The Grounding of Modern Feminism*, p. 10.

Chapter 4

1. Murphy, *Meaning of the Freedom of Speech*, pp. 189–90.

2. For a history of women's peace movements beginning in the early nineteenth century, see Alonso, *Peace as a Women's Issue*. For discussion of women's peace organizations and activities in this period, see ibid., chaps. 3 and 4; Zeiger, "Finding a Cure for War"; Zeiger, "She Didn't Raise Her Boy"; Early, "Feminism, Peace, and Civil Liberties"; Schott, *Reconstructing Women's Thoughts*.

3. Florence Watkins to Elizabeth Tilton, April 5, 1923, enclosure, Tilton Papers, Schlesinger Library, Radcliffe Institute, box 9, folder 246 (hereafter Tilton Papers). The NCMPTA is the predecessor of the modern Parent-Teachers Association. When the National Council for the Prevention of War (NCPW) and the Women's International League for Peace and Freedom protested, Secretary of War Weeks was forced to back down briefly. But the American Defense Society praised the patriotism and loyalty of Weeks and Fries and warned that peace groups were acting "directly along the lines laid down by Moscow." "Anti-War Council Denies Red Taint," *New York Times*, April 14, 1923, p. 5; Lucia Ames Mead to John W. Weeks, April 12, 1923, Records of the Women's International League for Peace and Freedom—U.S. Section, 1919–1959, Swarthmore College Peace Collection, Scholarly Resources microfilm edition (hereafter WILPF Records), reel 39, frame 26; "Says Fries's Critics Are Led by Moscow," *New York Times*, April 5, 1923, p. 21.

4. Florence Watkins to Mrs. Tilton, May 4, 1923, Tilton Papers, box 9, folder 246.

5. For discussions of the spider web chart, see Jensen, "All Pink Sisters," pp. 212–14; Murphy, *Meaning of the Freedom of Speech*, pp. 191–94; Cott, *The Grounding of Modern Feminism*, pp. 242, 249–50; Lemons, *The Woman Citizen*, pp. 215–18. Maxwell's original version included the Daughters of the American Revolution (DAR), but later versions did not.

6. See entry on Mrs. Lucia Ramsey Maxwell, Librarian, Chemical Warfare Service, pp. 15–18, in an untitled report from a private investigator. Catt-LOC Papers, container 27, reel 17, frames 503–27.

7. *Woman Patriot*, June 1, 1927, p. 4.

8. J. Edgar Hoover to Lucia Ramsey Maxwell, May 19, 1923, RG 165, 10110-1935/25, NA; R. M. Whitney to Lucia Ramsey Maxwell, June 14, 1923, RG 165, 10110-1935/26, NA.

Another version of a spider web chart, compiled and printed by Charles Norman Fay of Cambridge, Massachusetts, appeared in 1927. This version included both men and women but received the most attention because of its attacks on Jane Addams. See Allen F. Davis, *American Heroine*, pp. 264–65; Louise Bowen (Mrs. Joseph T.) to Jane Addams, January 24, 1927, Jane Addams Papers, series 1, Swarthmore College Peace Collection, University Microfilms edition (hereafter Addams Papers). Spider web language was also used in *What's What*, a publication of the Industrial Defense Association (IDA) of Boston. Nicholas Kelley Papers, New York Public Library. The IDA was also an active member in the fight against the Child Labor Amendment.

9. "Are Women's Clubs 'Used' by Bolshevists?" *Dearborn Independent*, March 15, 1924, p. 2; "Why Don't Women Investigate Propaganda?" *Dearborn Independent*, March 22, 1924, p. 1.

10. See n. 9.

11. Mary Anderson and Mary N. Winslow, *Woman at Work*, p. 189. Anderson recognized the material as coming from the *Woman Patriot* and threatened the paper with

a lawsuit. Quickly, the paper's editor named Haviland Lund as the author and claimed that the *Woman Patriot* had no connection to the *Dearborn Independent* articles. Many women wrote to the *Dearborn Independent* demanding a retraction and seeking information. Mary Anderson to Margaret Dreier Robins, March 20, 1924, Mary Anderson Papers, Papers of the Women's Trade Union League and Its Principal Leaders, Schlesinger Library, Radcliffe Institute, microfilm edition, reel 4, frame 226 (hereafter Anderson Papers); J. S. Eichelberger to W. J. Cameron, Editor, *Dearborn Independent*, Anderson Papers, reel 4, frame 231; Mary Anderson to Mrs. Philip N. Moore, March 21, 1924, Anderson Papers, reel 4, frame 227; J. S. Eichelberger to Mary Anderson, March 1924, Anderson Papers, reel 4, frame 228; Mary Anderson to Mrs. Theodore B. Pierce, *Dearborn Independent*, March 31, 1924, Anderson Papers, reel 4, frame 239; Lucia Ames Mead to Jane Addams, May 14, 1924, WILPF Records, Correspondence; Eva Perry Moore to Mrs. W. J. Cameron, Editor, *Dearborn Independent*, May 21, 1924, Anderson Papers, reel 4, frame 290.

Haviland Lund was someone known to most of the attacked women. She directed the Institute of Government in Washington, D.C., where Brigadier General Fries had spoken out against the National Council for the Prevention of War. At one point she was on the staff at the Department of the Interior, and when speaking before the Women's Democratic Club of New York City, she claimed to have warned President Harding about the Teapot Dome Scandal. She also represented the American Lovers of Music in the National Council of Women (NCW) and featured her NCW convention activities prominently in the *Dearborn Independent* articles. Mary Anderson to Mrs. Philip Moore, May 5, 1924, Anderson Papers, reel 4, frame 267; Florence Watkins to Mrs. Tilton, February 26, 1923, Tilton Papers, box 9, folder 246; "Warned Harding on Oil," *New York Times*, March 15, 1924, p. 4. See also "Peace Conference Motives Impugned in Hectic Session," *Washington Post*, January 26, 1925, p. 1.

12. The membership of the Special Committee varied. Initially it consisted of Maud Wood Park, Frances Fenton Bernard, and Cora W. Baker. By November 1926 it was composed of Maud Wood Park, Ethel Smith, Mary Stewart, Cora (Mrs. Henry) Baker, Flora Sherman of the General Federation of Women's Clubs, Mrs. Glen Levin Swiggett, and Mabel (Mrs. E. P.) Costigan. The names of all except Mary Stewart appear on the committee's final report.

13. Maud Wood Park to Mr. Secretary (John Weeks), April 2, 1924, LWV Papers, part 1, Pre-Convention Board Meeting, April 21–23, 1924, reel 1, frames 817–20; John Weeks to Maud Wood Park, April 10, 1924, ibid.; May 12 Report of the Special Committee of the Women's Joint Congressional Committee, Records of the Women's Joint Congressional Committee, Library of Congress, reel 3, frames 683–85 (hereafter WJCC Records); Alice Stone Blackwell to the Club Women of Massachusetts, "A Slander Squashed," May 9, 1924, Maud Wood Park Papers, Papers in the Women's Rights Collection, 1870–1960, Schlesinger Library, Radcliffe Institute, folder 231 (hereafter Park Papers); "Would Add 6,000,000 to Nation's Voters," *New York Times*, April 26, 1924, p. 8.

In 1927, after Weeks's death, the *Woman Patriot* intimated that Weeks's letter might have been a forgery and that "the pacifists, feminists and Socialists" suppressed a second letter in order to protect themselves. "The War Department Letter That Pacifists Conceal," *Woman Patriot*, June 1, 1927. Attacks by military officials upon the WILPF and NCPW continued even after the majority of attacks had been taken over by private citizens. In April 1926, Major General Eli A. Helmick warned of "the insidious arm of the soviet government of Russia" that reached into the United States via the NCPW, the WILPF, and other organizations. See Gladys E. Ryons to Hannah Clothier Hull, April 30, 1926, Hannah Clothier Hull Papers, 1889–1958, attacks folder, Swarthmore College Peace Collection, Scholarly Resources microfilm ed. (hereafter Hull Papers); Hannah Clothier Hull to Secretary of War Dwight Davis, May 3, 1926, Hull Papers, attacks folder; Dwight Davis to Hannah Clothier Hull, May 17, 1926, Hull Papers, attacks folder.

14. "Others Carry on War Department's Attack on Women," *New York World,* June 8, 1924, p. 1.

15. Gladys Harrison to Julia Lathrop, July 17, 1924, Julia Lathrop Papers, Rockford College, folder—Correspondence July to September 1924 (hereafter Lathrop Papers).

16. Foster, *The Women and the Warriors;* Alonso, *Peace as a Woman's Issue,* pp. 81–83, 90–93. For other sources on the WILPF, see Schott, *Reconstructing Women's Thoughts;* Bussey and Tims, *Pioneers for Peace;* Foster, *Women for All Seasons.*

17. Whitney, *Peace at Any Old Price,* pp. 3, 4.

18. Ibid.

19. Ibid., p. 23. Wenger, "Radical Politics." Affiliation with Schwimmer is also in an indictment of the WILPF by Fred R. Marvin, "Bootlegging Mind Poison," n.d. [sometime before Feb. 1924], Los Angeles, Better America Federation, Catt-LOC Papers, container 27.

20. Marvin wrote *The Common Enemy: Bootlegging Mind Poison,* printed by the Better America Federation, n.d., Catt-LOC Papers, container 27, reel 17, frames 467–73; *Are These Your Friends* (Denver, Colo.: Americanization Press, 1922), copy in New York Public Library; *My Country 'Tis of Thee, Underground with the Reds, Ye Shall Know the Truth, The Marvin Lectures on Government* (all self-published pamphlets); and *Fool's Gold: An Exposé of Un-American Activites and Political Action in the United States since 1860* (New York: Madison and Marshall, 1936).

Oswald Garrison Villard, "What the Blue Menace Means," *Harper's Magazine* 157 (October 1928): 537–38; See entry on Fred R. Marvin, pp. 4–11, in an untitled report from a private investigator, Catt-LOC Papers; "The DAR Upholds the Blacklist," *Outlook* 149 (May 2, 1928): 14; "The 'Black List' Fight Goes On," *Outlook* 149 (July 24, 1928): 369–70; "The Blue Menace," *Nation* 126 (April 18, 1928): 422; Helen Tufts Bailie, "Our Threatened Heritage," April 1928, enclosure in Nellie Fender to Jane Addams, May 2, 1928, Addams Papers, series 1, Swarthmore College Collection.

21. "Marvin, Red-Baiter, Loses Backing for His Daily Alarum," *Washington (D.C.) News,* July 1, 1929, clipping in Bailie Papers, box 1, clippings folder; "Fred Richard Marvin," *Who's Who in America, 1897–1942,* vol. 1 (Chicago: Marquis Publications, 1968), p. 785; Hapgood, *Professional Patriots;* Margaret Cobb, "The Soviet of Lady Patriots," *American Mercury* 15 (September 1928): 100. The DAR was not only involved with Marvin when it came to the blacklists. In 1928, for example, the Iowa DAR endorsed a resolution forwarded to them by the Key Men of America that condemned pacifism as socialist, communist, and un-American and supported an enlarged navy. Proceedings of the 29th Annual Conference, Iowa Daughters of the American Revolution, March 9–11, 1928, State Historical Society of Iowa.

22. F. H. Anspacher, Key Men of America, to Hanford MacNider, August 24, 1926, MacNider Papers, box 60, folder—Key Men of America. The Women's Joint Congressional Committee's Special Committee to Investigate Attacks subscribed, in secrecy, to the "Daily Data Sheet" of the Key Men of America in order to be better aware of what Marvin was saying; Minutes of the Special Committee, March 5, 1927, LWV Papers, part 3, series A, reel 1, frames 243–44.

23. "D.A.R. Blacklist Was Born in Hub," *Boston Daily Advertiser*, April 5, 1928, pp. 4–5; Hapgood, *Professional Patriots*, 177–180; Bailie, "Our Threatened Heritage"; see entry on Edward H. Hunter, pp. 19–21, in an untitled report from a private investigator, Catt-LOC Papers; *What's What*, October 1926, Nicholas Kelley Papers; May 15, 1927, diary entry, Bailie Papers. Hunter is also referred to with the middle initials A. and E. Also see Emily Greene Balch to Edward Hunter, March 16, 1927, WILPF Records, series C, box 5, reel 42, frame 801; Edward Hunter to Emily Greene Balch, March 21, 1927, ibid., frame 807.

24. "Would Investigate Women's Peace Plan," *New York Times*, May 12, 1924, p. 31; "Measure in House Aims at Peace Plan," *New York Times*, May 15, 1924, p. 6.

25. Hannah Clothier Hull to Louise Wells, January 5, 1924, WILPF Records, reel 39, frame 32; "Women Want Part in Bronx Memorial," *New York Times*, July 2, 1925, p. 19; Catherine E. Nagle to WILPF, June 1, 1924, WILPF Records, reel 39, frames 133–34.

26. Copy of a letter from A. C. Marshall, Dayton Employers' Association, to Mr. M. M. Taylor, February 11, 1924, WILPF Records, reel 39, frame 36; W. J. Burns to Rev. Miles H. Krumbine, May 9, 1924, WILPF Records, reel 39, frame 151; Amy Woods to Hon Harlan F. Stone, Attorney General, July 11, 1924, WILPF Records, reel 39, frames 149–50.

27. Marvin, *Bootlegging Mind Poison*.

28. William Scarlett to Jane Addams, May 10, 1924, Addams Papers, series 1, Swarthmore College Collection.

29. November 11, 1925, diary entry, Bailie Papers.

30. Edith Edwards to Marion Holmes, April 29, 1924, WILPF Records, reel 39, frames 58–60.

31. Copy of letter from Burt R. Shurley to Detroit clergymen enclosed with Detroit Branch W.I.L. to Jane Addams, May 25, 1924, Addams Papers, reel 16, frames 743–44.

32. Dorothy Detzer to Jane Addams, November 22, 1926, Addams Papers, series 1, Swarthmore College Collection.

33. Elizabeth (Mrs. Thomas B.) Hutton to Jane Addams, May 19, 1927, WILPF Records. For more information on this incident, see Nielsen, "Dangerous Iowa Women."

34. Hutton to Addams, May 19, 1927.

35. Allen F. Davis, *American Heroine*, pp. 265–66.

36. Ibid., pp. 264–65; Received by Jane Addams, Louise Bowen (Mrs. Joseph T.) to Charles Norman Fay, January 24, 1927, Addams Papers, series 1, Swarthmore College Collection; Charles Norman Fay to *Boston Herald*, May 17, 1927, Addams Papers, ibid.

37. "Assails Hull House," *New York Times*, November 11, 1926, p. 16; "Jane Addams," *Iowa Legionaire*, December 3, 1926, pp. 4–5.

38. "MacNider Hits Pacifist with War Warning," *Des Moines Register*, February 24, 1926, p. 1; "MacNider Condemns Pacifist Agitators," *New York Times*, March 19, 1926, p. 8.

39. Allen F. Davis, *American Heroine*, p. 266. Watkins's statements were further quoted and used by Mrs. Rufus Dawes, sister-in-law to the vice-president. Edith Abbott to Jane Addams, ca. November 10, 1926, Addams Papers, series 1, Swarthmore College Collection.

40. Allen F. Davis, *American Heroine*, p. 267; "Question Jane Addams on League for Peace," *New York Times*, August 23, 1928, p. 21; Emily Greene Balch to Mrs. I. E. Evans, February 18, 1927, and attachment, Addams Papers, series 1, Swarthmore College Collection.

41. William H. Wilson to Mrs. Paul B. Ryder, April 6, 1931, RG 165, 10110-1935/78, NA.

42. For examples of BI files, see RG 65, OG 82811, NA; RG 65, OG 25025, NA. BI investigators often confused the Women's Peace Party, the Women's Peace Union, and the WILPF. For examples of MID files, see December 12, 1923, report of Agent Davidson, RG 165, 10110-1935/27, NA; October 22, 1923, report of Agent Davidson and informant Mrs. Jennie Franklin, RG 165, 10110-1935/23, NA; J. Edgar Hoover to Director, MID, May 14, 1924, RG 165, 10110-1935/37, NA.

43. Lt. Col. Kerr T. Riggs to Col. John F. Madden, May 14, 1924, RG 165, 10110-1935/40, NA; Madden to War Department, RG 165, 10110-1935/38, NA.

44. The involvement of nongovernment organizations in domestic intelligence operations was not unprecedented. For examples, see Joan M. Jensen, *Army Surveillance in America*.

45. Anita Phipps to Assistant Chief of Staff, G-2, January 10, 1924, RG 165, PF 51440/2, NA.

46. Anita Phipps to Assistant Chief of Staff, G-1, June 25, 1924, RG 165, 10314-547/1, NA.

47. Colonel J. H. Reeves to Secretary, General Staff, July 17, 1924, RG 165, 10314-547/2, NA; Colonel G. C. Barnhardt to Secretary, General Staff, July 21, 1924, RG 165, 10314-547/3, NA.

48. Anita Phipps to Assistant Chief of Staff, G-1, July 28, 1924, RG 165, 10314-547/5, NA.

49. Anita Phipps to Assistant Chief of Staff, G-1, November 29, 1926, Rg 165, 10314-56/5, NA.

50. Anita Phipps to Secretary of War, January 8, 1927, RG 165, box 55, Women's Relations, NA. Phipps complained again in 1929 of the War Department's failure to use her expertise and pointed out the damage that this failure had caused. Anita Phipps to Assistant Chief of Staff, G-1, July 1, 1929, RG 165, box 55, Women's Relations, NA.

51. Secretary of War to Maude Wetmore, undated, RG 165, box 55, Women's Relations, NA.

52. For example, Colonel John M. Morgan to Chief of Staff, July 21, 1927, RG 165, box 55, Women's Relations, NA; Colonel Stanley H. Ford to Chief of Staff, G-1, July 13, 1927, RG 165, box 55, Women's Relations, NA.

53. Brigadier General Campbell King to the Chief of Staff, September 29, 1927, RG 165, box 55, Women's Relations, NA.

54. Dwight Davis, Secretary of War, to Lena Hitchcock, February 15, 1929, RG 165, box 55, Women's Relations, NA.

55. Informal Report of the February 25, 1929, meeting, RG 165, box 55, Women's

Relations, NA; February 25, 1929, War Department Press Release, RG 165, box 55, Women's Relations, NA.

56. James W. Good, Secretary of War, to Maude Wetmore, March 21, 1929, RG 165, box 55, Women's Relations, NA; Secretary of War to Mrs. John F. Sippel, October 19, 1929, RG 165, box 55, Women's Relations, NA. Cancellation notice sent in undated letters from the Secretary of War to Mrs. John F. Sippel and Mabel Boardman, RG 165, box 55, Women's Relations, NA.

57. O. A. Dickinson to Lt. Col. Walter Wilson, January 9, 1926, RG 165, 10261-257, NA; James Reeves to Adjutant General, February 13, 1926, RG 165, 10314-556/98, NA.

58. Walter O. Boswell to Mrs. Schatz, October 26, 1926, RG 165, 10110-1935/61, NA; Kerr T. Riggs to John F. Madden, May 14, 1924, RG 165, 10110-1935/40, NA.

59. Mary Kilbreth to Rossiter Johnson, September 24, 1922, Rossiter Johnson Papers, New York Public Library.

60. Lt. Col. Mark Brooks to Lt. Col. Joseph A. Marmon, January 14, 1926, RG 165, 10110-2515/7, NA; Dana Jones to Hanford MacNider, March 25, 1927, RG 165, 10110-1935/64, NA.

61. James Reeves to General Pershing, January 6, 1927, RG 165, 10314-562/7, NA; James Reeves to Adjutant General, April 5, 1927, RG 165, 10110-1935/65, NA; James Reeves to Adjutant General, April 14, 1927, RG 165, 10110-1935/67, NA; Col. Graham to Walter O. Boswell, May 8, 1926, RG 165, 10110-2520/9, NA; Mark Brooke to William R. Standiford, January 14, 1926, RG 165, 10314-556/72, NA; Mark Brooke to J. Alfred Moss, RG 165, 10314-556/71, NA; Mark Brooke to Rolland W. Case, RG 165, 10314-556/70, NA; Mark Brooke to John Pratt, RG 165, 10314-556/69, NA; Mark Brooke to Henry C. Rexach, RG 165, 10314-556/68, NA; Mark Brooke to Hugh A. Parker, RG 165, 10314-556/67, NA; Mark Brooke to George D. Holland, RG 165, 10314-556/66, NA; Mark Brooke to Joseph A. Marmon, RG 165, 10314-556/65, NA; Mark Brooke to Oliver A. Dickinson, RG 165, 10314-556/64, NA.

62. Kerr T. Riggs to Major Thompson, November 24, 1923, RG 165, 10110-2515/4, NA; Mark Brooks to Joseph Marmon, January 14, 1926, RG 165, 10110-2515/7, NA; Memo for Executive Officer, G-2, November 26, 1923, 10110-2515/5, NA; Hugh White, G-2, to KMA, June 12, 1928, RG 165, 10560-225/755, NA; Henry C. Rexach to Walter Boswell, April 16, 1926, RG 165, 10110-2520/15, NA.

Chapter 5

1. Muncy, *Creating a Female Dominion*. The creation of the Children's Bureau is told well by Lindenmeyer, *"A Right to Childhood."* Mother's pensions, an early success of women's politics, were not included in antiradical litanies against social welfare legislation. Mother's pensions were nearly all enacted before 1914, and battles over their implementation were settled before the Red Scare. Because of this early passage, generally 1911–14, they were not included in Red Scare antistatism.

2. *American Child*, April 1925, p. 6.

3. The claim of Don D. Lescohier and Elizabeth Brandeis that black children were four times as likely to work as white children is presumably national. In contrast, Joel Perlmann found that in 1915 Providence, Rhode Island, black children worked at the same rate as the children of native-born whites but were *less* likely to be employed

than immigrant children or the children of immigrant parents: 7.2 percent of native white children of native parentage, 13.3 percent of native white children of foreign parentage, 21.2 percent of foreign born children, and 8.1 percent of black children worked. Kriste Lindenmeyer attributes the differences to region. Black children in urban areas stayed in school longer than immigrant children because of job discrimination; black children in rural areas faced different forms of discrimination and worked in agriculture. Lescohier and Brandeis, *History of Labor*, 41; Perlmann, *Ethnic Differences*, pp. 171–75; Lindenmeyer, *"A Right to Childhood,"* pp. 110–12.

4. Lescohier and Brandeis, *History of Labor*, pp. 40–41.

Gainfully Employed Children, 10–15 Years Old, 1900–1930

	Total No.	Total %	% of Boys	% of Girls
1900	1,750,178	18.2	26.1	10.2
1910	1,990,225	18.4	24.8	11.9
1920	1,060,858	8.5	11.3	5.6
1930	667,118	4.7	6.4	2.9

These figures fail to include the number of working children under ten. *American Labor Year Book, 1925*, vol. 11 (New York: Rand School of Social Science, 1925), p. 41; *American Labor Year Book, 1926*, vol. 11 (1926), p. 68.

5. See also Ladd-Taylor, *Mother-Work*, chap. 3; Trattner, *Crusade for the Children*, pp. 163–86; Costin, *Two Sisters for Social Justice*, chaps. 5 and 6; Sherman, "Child Labor Amendment"; Chambers, *Seedtime of Reform*, chap. 2.

6. Costin, *Two Sisters for Social Justice*, p. 151; Chambers, *Seedtime of Reform*, p. 33. Lathrop expressed a similar sentiment to Owen Lovejoy in 1922. "I have been astonished to find the popular distaste for governmental activity in this part of the country and I suspect it is typical." Julia Lathrop to Owen Lovejoy, May 29, 1922, Lathrop Papers, folder—Papers 1922–1924 Child Labor.

7. See Representative Harry Hawes of Missouri, *Congressional Record* (April 25, 1924), 68th Cong., 1st sess. 65:7195; Committee on the Judiciary, Minority Report, House of Representatives, 68th Cong., 1st sess., Report 395, part 2, p. 4; Representative John McSwain of South Carolina, *Congressional Record* (April 25, 1924), 68th Cong., 1st sess., 65:7190.

8. Senator Joseph Ransdell of Louisiana, *Congressional Record* (June 2, 1924), 68th Cong., 1st sess., 65:10097; Senator Thomas Bayard of Delaware, *Congressional Record* (May 31, 1924), 68th Cong., 1st sess., 65:10005; Representative Fritz Lanham of Texas, *Congressional Record* (April 25, 1924), 68th Cong., 1st sess., 65:7198; for a similar rhetorical strategy, see Representative Charles Robert Crisp of Georgia, *Congressional Record* (April 25, 1924), 68th Cong., 1st sess., 65:7174.

9. Senator James Reed of Missouri, *Congressional Record*, (June 2, 1924), 68th Cong., 1st sess., 65:10088. See also Senator Joseph Ransdell of Louisiana, *Congressional Record* (June 2, 1924), 68th Cong., 1st sess., 65:10097; Representative John McSwain of South Carolina, *Congressional Record* (April 25, 1924), 68th Cong., 1st sess., 65:7190; Representative Harry Hawes of Missouri, *Congressional Record* (April 25, 1924), 68th Cong., 1st sess., 65:7195; Representative Charles Robert Crisp of Georgia, *Congressional Record* (April 25, 1924), 68th Cong., 1st sess., 65:7174; Proposed Child Labor Amendments

to the Constitution, Hearings before the Committee on the Judiciary, House of Representatives, 68th Cong., 1st sess. (Washington, D.C.: Government Printing Office, 1924).

10. Joseph Deal of Virginia, *Congressional Record* (June 3, 1924), 65:10371. See also Senator James Reed of Missouri, *Congressional Record* (June 2, 1924), 68th Cong., 1st sess., 65:10083–88; Senator William King of Utah, *Congressional Record* (May 31, 1924), 68th Cong., 1st sess., 65:10007; Thomas Bayard of Delaware, *Congressional Record* (May 31, 1924), 68th Cong., 1st sess., 65:9962–76; *Woman Patriot*, September 1, 1926, p. 136.

11. For information on Florence Kelley, see Trattner, *Crusade for Children,* pp. 33–48; Louise C. Wade, "Florence Kelley," *Notable American Women, 1607–1950: A Biographical Dictionary* (Boston: Radcliffe College, 1971), pp. 316–19; Goldmark, *Impatient Crusader;* Sklar, *Florence Kelley.*

12. See *Congressional Record* (May 31, 1924), 68th Cong., 1st sess., 65:10007; *Congressional Record* (June 3, 1924), 68th Cong., 1st sess., 65:10365–72; "American Men and Women: Attention!" n.d., Dorothy Kirchwey Brown Papers, Schlesinger Library, Radcliffe Institute, box 3, folder 65 (hereafter D. K. Brown Papers); Charles Gow to Mr. and Mrs. Day, October 8, 1924, D. K. Brown Papers, box 2, folder 55; "Socialist Dictated Draft of Child Labor Amendment," *Woman Patriot,* June 11, 1925, pp. 8–9; "An Examination of the Proposed Twentieth Amendment to the Constitution of the United States (The So-Called 'Child Labor' Amendment)," Children's Bureau Records. Senator Thomas Walsh later ridiculed this strategy: "Is not her name Wischnewetsky? That may be Polish. Anyway, it has a Russian sound. Ergo, she is a Russian, a communist, an intriguing tool of Moscow, diabolically successful in throwing the spell of her occult powers over 61 hard-boiled Senators and 297 Representatives." Walsh's defense of Florence Kelley is found in *Congressional Record* (January 8, 1925), 68th Cong., 2nd sess., 66:1441.

13. Trattner, *Crusade for the Children,* p. 167.

14. Sherman, "Child Labor Amendment"; Trattner, *Crusade for the Children,* pp. 168–70.

15. Trattner, *Crusade for the Children,* pp. 174–78; Owen Lovejoy to Raymond G. Fuller, September 29, 1924, D. K. Brown Papers, box 3, folder 57. Poster comparing Massachusetts and Georgia found in Curtis and Mallach, *Photography and Reform,* p. 18. Original in possession of the Milwaukee Art Museum.

16. Massachusetts Committee on Ratification of the Child Labor Amendment, D. K. Brown Papers, box 2, folder 55. Dorothy Kirchwey Brown also campaigned, in her position on the Child Welfare Department of the LWV, for the repeated renewal of the Sheppard-Towner Act. Her husband, LaRue Brown, an assistant U.S. Attorney General, was also involved in pro–Child Labor Amendment efforts, as was her father, George W. Kirchwey, professor of law and dean at Columbia Law School.

17. Lathrop characterized the amendment's opposition as extraordinary and, despite her early doubts that it would pass, assured Edith Abbott that "sooner or later we shall come out ahead." Julia Lathrop to Edith Abbott, October 29, 1924, Papers of Grace and Edith Abbott, box 3, folder 11 (hereafter Abbott Papers). Dentist comment: Julia Lathrop to Florence Kelley, July 2, 9124, Lathrop Papers, folder—Papers 1922–1924 National Consumer's League. Dorothy Kirchwey Brown, however, was worried about Lathrop and wrote to John Ryan that "Miss Lathrop is frightfully tired and

I hate to have her use herself up in such a cause as this." Dorothy Kirchwey Brown to John Ryan, October 16, 1924, D. K. Brown Papers, box 3, folder 60. Lathrop flier: Papers of the Boston Women's Trade Union League, Papers of the Women's Trade Union League and Its Principal Leaders, Schlesinger Library, Radcliffe Institute, microfilm edition (hereafter BWTUL Papers), frame 34.

18. Ethel Smith to Agnes Nester, October 23, 1924, Records of the New York Women's Trade Union League, Papers of the Women's Trade Union League and Its Principal Leaders, Schlesinger Library, Radcliffe Institute, microfilm edition (hereafter NYWTUL Papers), reel 12, frames 415–17; Ethel Smith to Lida Hafford of the General Federation of Women's Clubs, October 23, 1924, BWTUL Papers, frame 52; Ethel Smith to Agnes Nester, October 23, 1924, NYWTUL Papers, reel 12, frames 415–17; Ethel Smith to Mabel Leslie, October 28, 1924, NYWTUL Papers, reel 12, frames 439–40.

19. Ethel Smith to Agnes Nester, October 23, 1924, NYWTUL Papers, reel 12, frames 415–17.

20. "Don't Ratify the Child Labor Amendment! Arguments Used against It Broadcasted to Sentinels of the Republic," by Louis Coolidge and Margaret C. Robinson, Tuesday, December 30, 1924 from WJY, Sentinels of the Republic Papers, Williams College, miscellaneous files (hereafter Sentinels Papers); "The Child Labor Amendment: An Appeal to the Christian Men and Women of Massachusetts," radio address by Louis A. Coolidge, October 10, 1924, Lincoln Papers, box 2, folder 14; "Sentinels of the Republic," n.d., Lincoln Papers, folder 5—Sentinels of the Republic—History.

21. "Receipts of Citizens Committee to Protect Our Homes and Children," D. K. Brown Papers, box 3, folder 65; Dorothy Brown to Mrs. Caspar Whitney, December 5, 1924, New York League of Women Voters, D. K. Brown Papers, box 3, folder 61; Dorothy Brown to Carrie Chapman Catt, December 31, 1924, D. K. Brown Papers, box 3, folder 61. Though I can trace the money this far, I've been unable to figure out where the MPIL or the Sentinels of the Republic got their money.

22. Julia Lathrop to Mrs. Mumford, November 8, 1924, Lathrop Papers, folder— Correspondence 1924, October–December.

23. For discussions of the rejection of the amendment, see Sherman, "The Rejection of the Child Labor Amendment"; Costin, *Two Sisters for Social Justice,* pp. 155–58; Trattner, *Crusade for the Children,* pp. 171–86; Chambers, *Seedtime of Reform,* pp. 38–47.

24. *Examination of the Proposed Twentieth Amendment to the Constitution of the United States (The So-Called 'Child Labor' Amendment)* (Boston, Mass.: Citizens Committee to Protect Our Homes and Children, n.d.), cover, p. 2, Children's Bureau Records, part 5, reel 19, box 24, folder 1. Identical language is used in the following: Alexander Lincoln to Pastor James Gordon Gilkey of the South Congregational Church, September 12, 1924, enclosure, Springfield, Massachusetts, D. K. Brown Papers, box 3, folder 65; Associated Industries of Massachusetts to all members, August 27, 1924, D. K. Brown Papers, box 3, folder 65.

25. "Men and Women of Massachusetts." For an example of a use of King's words, see "American Men and Women." For other accusations of un-Americanism, Russian origin, or Bolshevism, see Mrs. Josephine Morton to the Editor, *New York Times,* June 22, 1924, sec. 8, p. 19; George Stewart Brown to the Editor, *New York Times,* July 20, 1924, sec. 8, p. 13.; Felix Rackeman, "A Menace to Our Nation Few Understand,"

Manufacturers Record 86 (August 28, 1924): 70; "Who Are the Active Workers for the Child Labor Amendment?" *Manufacturers Record* 86 (November 13, 1924): 62–63; "Communistic Fight for the Amendment," *Manufacturers Record* 87 (January 15, 1925): 55; "Denies Child Labor Is a Federal Affair," *New York Times*, August 18, 1924, p. 16; *New York Times*, July 19, 1924, p. 20; "The Child Labor Amendment," *Women Lawyers Journal* 14 (January 1925): 14; "The Child Labor Amendment," *Ohio Journal of Commerce*, December 1, 1924, p. 182; reprint from the *Miami Herald*, reprinted as "The So-Called Child Labor Amendment," *Manufacturers Record* 86 (December 11, 1924): 67; reprint from the *Corvallis (Ore.) Gazette-Times*, "An Amendment That Originated in Russia," *Manufacturers Record* 87 (January 8, 1925): 68.

26. "Says Amendment Would Invade Home," *New York Times* December 7, 1924, p. 19.

27. Margaret C. Robinson, "Why Massachusetts Beat Child Control: New England Parents Believe They Can Manage Their Own Children," *Dearborn Independent*, March 7, 1925, Lincoln Papers, box 2, folder 14.

28. "Citizens Committee to Protect Our Homes and Children," (Boston, Mass: n.d.), Lincoln Papers, box 2, folder 14.

29. Speech of Rep. Henry L. Shattuck of Boston on behalf of the Citizens Committee to Protect Our Homes and Children, Edison radio station, October 31, 1924, D. K. Brown Papers, box 3, folder 65.

30. "Says Amendment Would Invade Home," p. 19.

31. Cartoon clipping found in Lathrop Papers, folder—Papers, Child Labor 1925.

32. Amendment proponents initially assumed that the Catholic Church in Massachusetts would support the amendment. Father John Ryan, a nationally known figure and a faculty member at Catholic University, was a member of the National Child Labor Committee (NCLC) and supported the amendment. His public presence and close ties with the NCLC assured many amendment supporters of the blessing of the Catholic Church. McQuade, *American Catholic Attitude*, pp. 81–82; Trattner, *Crusade for the Children*, pp. 176–77.

33. McQuade, *American Catholic Attitude*, pp. 81–97; the *Pilot*, a joint reprint of the issues of October 4 and 11, 1924, cover and p. 2, Elizabeth Lowell Putnam Papers, 1887–1935, Schlesinger Library, Harvard University (hereafter E. L. Putnam Papers), box 16, folder 295; Beatty, *The Rascal King*, pp. 240–41; Huthmacher, *Massachusetts People and Politics*, p. 70.

34. James A. Emery, general counsel for the National Association of Manufacturers and author of anti–Child Labor Amendment pamphlets, also was Catholic. This increased the discussion between Catholic officials and others against the amendment. McQuade, *American Catholic Attitude*, p. 87; Huthmacher, *Massachusetts People and Politics*, pp. 70–71.

35. Notes of January 12 and 13, 1926, meeting, Sentinels of the Republic meeting, 1924–1926 file, Sentinels Papers. Despite Slattery's efforts, Catholic women were not united on every political issue. A group of Catholic women, tied to the National Woman's Party, supported the Equal Rights Amendment and attempted to push the Catholic church in that direction. Kenneally, "Women Divided."

36. Russell Johnson Pirkey, "Sovietism, the Self-Appointed Protector of the home,"

Manufacturers Record 87 (February 26, 1925): 77; Hon. Frank L. Greene to Louis Coolidge, September 26, 1922, Sentinels Papers.

37. Marian Bruce Clar, "The Radical Trail in Welfare Laws," *Dearborn Independent,* March 6, 1925, p. 8.

38. Senator Joseph Ransdell of Louisiana, *Congressional Record* (June 2, 1924), 68th Cong., 1st sess., 65:10097. Laws regulating child labor in France in the mid-nineteenth century also were understood to infringe upon paternal power. Auslander, *Taste and Power,* pp. 187–88.

39. For examples of the blueberry and table-setting arguments and similar representations, see Margaret C. Robinson, "Don't Ratify the Child Labor Amendment!"; Representative Joseph Deal of Virginia, *Congressional Record* (June 3, 1924), 68th Cong., 1st sess., 65:10366; Senator James Reed of Missouri, *Congressional Record* (June 2, 1924), 68th Cong., 1st sess., 65:10089; Representative Charles Robert Crisp of Georgia, *Congressional Record* (April 25, 1924), 68th Cong., 1st sess., 65:7174; Committee on the Judiciary, Minority Report, House of Representatives, 68th Cong., 1st sess., Report 395, part 2, p. 8; Associated Industries of Massachusetts to All Members, August 27, 1924, D. K. Brown Papers, box 3, folder 65 (the same language is used in Alexander Lincoln to Mr. James Gilkie, September 12, 1924, D. K. Brown Papers, box 3, folder 65); "The Child Labor Amendment the Devil's Best Scheme for Ruination of Manhood and Womanhood," *Manufacturer's Record,* September 11, 1924, p. 2.

40. Historian Vivan Zelizer argues that child labor reformers emphasized children's "sentimental value" while opponents of reform emphasized children's economic usefulness. Zelizer, *Pricing the Priceless Child,* p. 57.

41. Sherman, "Child Labor Amendment," pp. 11–12; "Massachusetts Ratifies Dry Act," *New York Times,* November 10, 1924, p. 2.

42. Dorothy Kirchwey Brown to Mrs. Blair Banister, September 29, 1924, D. K. Brown Papers; Alice Stone Blackwell, "What the American Woman Thinks," *Woman Citizen,* November 29, 1924, p. 15; "Indefensible Tactics," *Independent* 114 (February 21, 1925): 199; William L. Chenery, "Child Labor: The New Alignment," *Survey* 53 (January 1, 1925): 379; "Child Labor Truths," *Woman Citizen,* January 24, 1925, p. 20; William Allen White, "What Halts the Child Labor Amendment?" *Woman Citizen,* February 21, 1925, p. 10; Wiley H. Swift, "Misinformed Massachusetts," *Survey* 53 (November 15, 1924): 177–78; Julia Lathrop to Mrs. Walter Miller, December 13, 1924, General Federal of Women's Clubs, Lathrop Papers, folder—Correspondence 1924, October–December; Harriet Taylor Upton, "What Halts the Child Labor Amendment?" *Woman Citizen,* February 21, 1925, p. 9; "An Unworthy Campaign," *Christian Science Monitor,* October 16, 1924, clipping found in Lillian Wald Papers, folder—Florence Kelley, collateral, New York Public Library. See also "The Child Labor Amendment's Defeat," *New Republic* 42 (May 20, 1925): 330.

43. Dorothy Kirchwey Brown to Senator Henry Cabot Lodge, October 30, 1924, D. K. Brown Papers, box 3, folder 60.

44. Alaysia H. Davis to Mrs. (Florence) Arthur Watkins, November 3, 1924, WJCC Records, reel 1, frame 380.

45. Marcus Fagg to Katharine F. Lenroot, May 27, 1925, CB Papers, part 5, reel 7, box 7, folder 1.

46. Margaret C. Robinson, "An Appeal to American Women," *Manufacturers Record* 87 (January 8, 1925): 66; Thomas F. Cadwalader, "The Defeat of the Twentieth Amendment," *Annals of the American Academy of Political and Social Sciences* 129 (January 1927): 65–69.

47. "To Whom Credit Is Due," *Boston Herald,* January 30, 1925, clipping in Paul Kellogg Papers, folder 197, Social Welfare History Archives, University of Minnesota.

48. Ethel Smith to Mabel Leslie, October 21, 1924, WJCC Records, reel 1, frame 366; Ethel Smith to Mabel Leslie, October 28, 1924, NYWTUL Papers, reel 12, frames 439–40; Ethel Smith to Mabel Leslie, September 8, 1924, NYWTUL Papers, reel 12, frame 157.

49. Florence Kelley, "Objections, Secret and Public," *Woman Citizen,* December 27, 1924, p. 13. See also Harriet Taylor Upton, "What Halts the Child Labor Amendment?" *Woman Citizen,* February 21, 1925, p. 9; Alice Stone Blackwell, "Massachusetts—'No,'" *Woman Citizen,* November 29, 1924, pp. 14–15, 28; "What New Wind of Doctrine," *Woman Citizen,* December 27, 1924, p. 18; "The Profit Motive and the Child Labor Amendment," *Social Service Bulletin* 15 (January 1, 1925): 1; "Child Labor, the Home and Liberty," *New Republic* 41 (December 3, 1924): 32–33.

50. *The Struggle for the Child Labor Amendment as Revealed by the Massachusetts Referendum,* Massachusetts Organizations Associated for Ratification of the Child Labor Amendment, 1925. See copies of this pamphlet in D. K. Brown Papers, box 4, folder 76; BWTUL, frames 156–67. A typewritten and hand-edited partial copy can be found in "What Happened in Massachusetts?" 1925, Records of the National Consumers League, reel 48, frames 546–50, p. 1. The pamphlet is unsigned, but I'm fairly certain that Brown wrote it. By December 6, 1924, only one month after the referendum, Brown had already submitted a lengthy article, later rejected, to the *Woman Citizen* expressing her frustration and anger. "I know it was much too long," she wrote to Marguerite Owen of the National League of Women Voters, "but in fighting fervor of my rage I could not bear to leave out a single insult." Dorothy Kirchwey Brown to Marguerite Owen, December 6, 1924, D. K. Brown Papers, folder 3, box 58; Marguerite Owen to Dorothy Kirchwey Brown, December 23, 1924, D. K. Brown Papers, box 3, folder 58. Kathryn Kish Sklar helped me to determine that Florence Kelley did not write the pamphlet but instead helped with revisions; personal letter, June 25, 1995. For other compiled lists of amendment opponents, see Ethel Smith, "Who Is For? Who Against?" *Woman Citizen,* December 27, 1924, pp. 14, 25; "The Profit Motive," pp. 1–3, CB Papers, part 5, reel 10, box 11, folder 37; Senator Thomas Bayard of Delaware, *Congressional Record* (January 28, 1925), 68th Cong., 2nd sess., 66:2571–73.

51. Arden Lea argues that in the 1916 Federal Child Labor Act debate, New England textilists supported federal child labor restrictions in order to defend themselves against competition from southern manufacturers, who enjoyed an economic advantage because of looser child labor laws. It may be that by 1924, facing expanded federal regulation on many fronts and imbued by antiradicalism, these same industrialists opposed the amendment. It also may have been the case that by 1924, as Brown claims, enough southern mills were owned by northern textilists that it was to their economic advantage to oppose the amendment. Lea, "Cotton Textiles."

52. *Struggle for the Child Labor Amendment,* pp. 8–9.

53. Ibid., p. 5. The five members of the Woman Patriots' Board of Directors were Mary G. Kilbreth, Margaret C. Robinson, Harriet A. (Mrs. Randolph) Frothingham, Katharine T. (Mrs. John) Balch, and Cornelia A. (Mrs. Rufus) Gibbs.

Kilbreth, who chaired the Woman Patriots Board, lived in New York City but spent a great deal of time lobbying and testifying in Washington, D.C. She was also a member in the Sentinels of the Republic and was involved in the activities of the MPIL. At one point she was president of the New York Association Opposed to Woman Suffrage, and she became the association's national president in 1919.

Frothingham, whose lawsuit designed to halt the Sheppard-Towner Act will be discussed later, was a Massachusetts resident, a Sentinels of the Republic member, and a donor and head of Emmanuel Memorial House Settlement in Boston. Mary Anderson, head of the Women's Bureau, initially suspected Frothingham of compiling the 1928 DAR blacklist (to be discussed in chapter 6), but Frothingham denied it. Mary Anderson to Mrs. Randolph Frothingham, May 4, 1928, Anderson Papers, reel 4, frame 341; Mrs. Randolph Frothingham to Miss Mary Anderson, May 14, 1928, Anderson Papers, reel 4, frames 342–43.

Balch, was one of the incorporating member of the Sentinels of the Republic as well as its longtime board secretary. She lived in Milton, Massachusetts, where she was a member of the MPIL.

54. Children are here defined as those under sixteen; 12.3 percent of Tennessee children aged ten to fifteen were employed in 1920. Wage figures are from 1928. *Child Labor: White House Conference on Child Health and Protection* (New York: Century Company, 1932), p. 84; *American Labor Year Book, 1930,* vol. 11 (New York: Rand School of Social Science, 1930), p. 44; *American Labor Year Book, 1925,* vol. 11, p. 41.

55. In 1920, 20.8 percent of ten to fifteen year olds were employed. Wage figures are from 1928. *American Labor Year Book, 1925,* vol. 11, p. 41; *Child Labor: White House Conference on Child Health and Protection* (New York: Century Company, 1932), p. 84; *American Labor Year Book, 1930,* vol. 11, p. 42.

56. Paul F. Brissenden, *Earnings of Factory Workers, 1899–1927* (Washington, D.C.: Government Printing Office, 1929), p. 85. These wage figures are from 1923.

57. In this work, the term *patriarchy* refers to systems of male power—whether manifested in tradition, legislation, economics, language, or elsewhere—but firmly grounded, learned, and first exercised in the family household. *Patriarchy* originally referred to the power a father had over wife and children; in contemporary usage often it refers to any and all forms of male power. I have chosen to stay with the word *patriarchy* because of its origin in the family, but I want to avoid all-encompassing and ahistorical generalities about male power. Part of the historical specificity (and one of the ironies) of the use of the term *patriarchy* by these upper- and middle-class activists is that they made broad claims about an essentialized man and essentialized male power. At the same time, they often balked at and sometimes vigorously resisted extending such power to men of all races and classes. In practice, the patriarchal power they defended and relied upon for the development of political theory was limited to men of specific racial and economic backgrounds.

58. John E. Edgerton to Mrs. Frederick G. Bursch, April 29, 1926, Catt-LOC Papers, reel 17, frames 486–90.

59. "To Arms! To Arms! The New Crisis!" n.d., Lincoln Papers, folder 5. Margaret C. Robinson also linked these three bills in her legislation testimony against the Sheppard-Towner Act; see "Extension of Public Protection of Maternity and Infancy Act: Hearing before the Committee on Interstate and Foreign Commerce, House of Representatives," 69th Cong., 1st sess., January 14, 1926 (Washington, D.C.: Government Printing Office, 1926), statement of Mrs. B. L. Robinson, p. 29.

60. "A Petition for the Rejection of the Phipps-Parker Bill Proposing an Extension of the Maternity Act," *Congressional Record*, 69th Cong., 1st sess., 68:12919. The Jesuit journal *America* also linked these bills as part of a general bureaucratic and socialistic tendency. See "The Maternity Bill and the School Bill," *America* 26 (November 19, 1921): 112; "The Sheppard-Towner Program," *America* 26 (December 10, 1921): 182.

61. One of the first public detractors of the Sheppard-Towner Act was Alice Robertson, the first woman in Congress after the passage of the Nineteenth Amendment. Oklahoma representative and Sentinels of the Republic member Robertson called the act "German paternalism." Cott, *The Grounding of Modern Feminism*, p. 111. For more information on the Sheppard-Towner Act, see Ladd-Taylor, "Federal Help for Mothers," pp. 217–27; Ladd-Taylor, *Mother-Work*, chap. 6; Lemons, *The Woman Citizen*, pp. 153–80; Lemons, "Sheppard-Towner Act," pp. 776–86; Muncy, *Creating a Female Dominion*, pp. 93–123; Chepaitis, "First Federal Social Welfare Measure"; Rosen, "Federal Responsibility or Governmental Tyranny?"; Lindenmeyer, *"A Right to Childhood,"* chap. 4.

62. George Madden Martin, "Dangers in the Maternity Bill," *Woman Citizen*, December 1926, pp. 17, 42–43. Martin also wrote against the Child Labor Amendment in manufacturing journals. See George Madden Martin, "The American Woman and the Proposed Twentieth Amendment," *Manufacturers Record* 87 (January 8, 1925): 73–74.

63. Senator James Reed of Missouri, *Congressional Record* (June 2, 1924), 68th Cong., 1st sess., 65:10088.

64. *Boston Herald*, February 24, 1922, quoted in Chepaitis, p. 172.

65. Lemons, *Woman Citizen*, p. 164. For discussions of the medical establishment's opposition to the Sheppard-Towner Act, see Muncy, *Creating a Female Dominion*, pp. 135–44.

66. Chepaitis, "First Federal Social Welfare Measure," pp. 142–48.

67. Thomas M. Bayard of Delaware, *Congressional Record* (July 3, 1926), 69th Cong., 1st sess., 67:12919, 12940, 12946, 12948. A copy of the reprint of the petition, with an accompanying index, is found in the CB Papers, part 5, reel 10, box 11, folder 43. See also "Resolution against Towner Bills," *Woman Patriot*, January 22, 1921, p. 6; "To Readers," *Woman Patriot*, November 15, 1921, p. 4.

68. "Accuracy of Petition Defended in Senate," *Woman Patriot* 1 (February 1, 1927): 17–18. The Woman Patriots learned of this when their president, Mary Kilbreth, met with Grace Brosseau, DAR president-general. Katharine Balch, who along with Kilbreth was a member of both the Woman Patriots and the Sentinels of the Republic, told this to Alexander Lincoln, Sentinels president, in a December letter: "This brings in a new and influential group for the fight." Katharine Balch to Alexander Lincoln, December 20, 1926, Lincoln Papers, box 2, folder 9.

69. Ladd-Taylor, *Mother-Work*, p. 171.

70. "Baby Act 'Threatened with Destruction' Sobs Mrs. Kelley," *Woman Patriot* 10 (November 1, 1926), p. 1.

71. The most lengthy and detailed discussion of the legal battle is found in Chepaitis, "First Federal Social Welfare Measure," pp. 142–60, 180–208, 272. See also Lemons, *Woman Citizen*, pp. 171–72; Ladd-Taylor, *Mother-Work*, p. 184; Muncy, *Creating a Female Dominion*, pp. 134–35; Lindenmeyer, *"A Right to Childhood,"* pp. 93–94. The Sentinels of the Republic supported Frothingham in her lawsuit. Because of the lack of historical evidence, however, it is unclear how the suit was initiated. In an undated history, the Sentinels claimed credit for instigating the suit. "History of the Sentinels," n.d., Lincoln Papers, folder 5. See also Minutes of the Sentinels Annual Meeting, January 12–13, 1926, Lincoln Papers, folder 1.

72. Dumenil, "'The Insatiable Maw of Bureaucracy'"; Ross, *Forging New Freedoms*, pp. 66–70; Munger and Fenno, *National Politics*, pp. 2–5; Cubberly, *Public Education*, pp. 740–43.

73. "Resolution against Towner Bills," p. 6; "Radical Congressional Program in Next Session," *Woman Patriot* 7 (December 1, 1923): 1; "N.E.A. Bloc Dictatorship, Not Federal Control, Aim of Education Bill," *Woman Patriot* 12 (May 15, 1928): 1.

74. Iredell Meares, "The Power That Lurks in the Proposed Department of Education Bill," n.d., Lincoln Papers, box 8. See also Minutes of the Sentinels Annual Meeting, January 12–13, 1926, Lincoln Papers, folder 1.

75. "Do These Women Know They Are 'Dupes' of the Reds?" *Manufacturers Record* 87 (May 7, 1925): 84.

76. Martin, "Dangers in the Maternity Bill," p. 42. See also Gordon, *Pitied but Not Entitled*, pp. 93–96.

77. Charles Robert Crisp of Georgia, *Congressional Record* (June 3, 1924), 68th Cong., 1st sess., 65:10369. Crisp, speaking of "interlocking connections," was using the language of the spider web charts.

78. Thomas M. Bayard of Delaware, *Congressional Record* (July 3, 1926), 69th Cong., 1st sess., 67:12927, 12933–35; *Congressional Record* (May 31, 1924), 68th Cong., 1st sess., 65:9963, 9968–72.

79. Thomas Bayard of Delaware, *Congressional Record* (May 31, 1924), 68th Cong., 1st sess., 65:9967, 9972. See also John Edgerton, National Association of Manufacturers to Mrs. Frederick G. Bursch, April 29, 1926, Catt-LOC Papers, reel 17, frames 486–90; Lemons, *The Woman Citizen*, pp. 212–13. For biographical information on Kollontai, see Archie Brown, ed., *The Soviet Union: A Biographical Dictionary* (London: Weidenfeld, 1990), pp. 172–74. Very few women in the United States had heard of Kollontai. Julia Lathrop spent a great deal of time and energy writing to the Library of Congress to try and find out who she was. Henry J. Harris, Library of Congress, to Julia Lathrop, August 6, 1924, Lathrop Papers; Julia Lathrop to Librarian of Congress, September 27, 1924; Julia Lathrop to Herbert Putnam, Library of Congress, October 19, 1924. See also "Who Is Madame Kollontai," *Woman Voter's Bulletin* 6 (May 1926): 5–7.

80. W. F. Bigelow, editor, *Good Housekeeping*, to Julia Lathrop, February 4, 1928, Lathrop Papers, folder—Correspondence 1928, January–June; Costin, *Two Sisters for Social Justice*, pp. 129–31; Muncy, *Creating a Female Dominion*, pp. 128, 132–33. Another

opponent of the Children's Bureau was Elizabeth Lowell Putnam. Putnam, whose political career began in the pure milk movement in Massachusetts, was an opponent of the Sheppard-Towner Act, the Child Labor Amendment, and the Children's Bureau. While a member of the Woman Patriots and Sentinels of the Republic, she also tried to use her status as Calvin Coolidge's cousin to work for repeal of the Children's Bureau. See Michel and Rosen, "The Paradox of Maternalism"; Rosen, "Federal Responsibility or Governmental Tyranny?" pp. 82–137.

81. See Woman's Constitutional League of Virginia Resolution, March 31, 1927, in the Information Files of the Children's Bureau, classification 1-6-2. This action resulted in a long correspondence between Fletcher Harper Swift, professor of education at the University of California–Berkeley, and Grace Abbott of the Children's Bureau. Swift was asked by the California Sons of the American Revolution to investigate the charges of the Woman's Constitutional League of Virginia. Swift apparently did so and subsequently endorsed the Children's Bureau. He later wrote to Grace Abbott:

> The noble and courageous Sons tabled the matter, and thus ran thoroughly true to form. I was so disgusted with the lack of courage displayed on this occasion and so convinced that the Sons of the American Revolution are willing to openly champion no progressive social movement that I decided then and there to never attend another meeting and to resign from the Board of Managers. (Fletcher Harper Swift to Grace Abbott, October 10, 1929)

This series of correspondence is in the central file of the Children's Bureau, classification 1-6-2 for 1929. I am grateful to Aloha South at the National Archives for helping me find this material.

82. *Woman Patriot* 11 (May 1, 1927): 65–71.

83. Mink, *The Wages of Motherhood*, 7.

84. In the formulation of this section, I have drawn heavily upon the following works: Gordon, "Family Violence"; Fraser, *Unruly Practices*, chap. 6. See also Griswold, *Fatherhood in America*, p. 57; Boris and Bardaglio, "The Transformation of Patriarchy," p. 81; Taub and Schneider, "Perspectives on Women's Subordination," pp. 117–39.

85. Gordon, "Family Violence," p. 191.

86. Senator Joseph Ransdell of Louisiana, *Congressional Record* (June 2, 1924), 68th Cong., 1st sess., 65:10097.

87. Muncy, *Creation of a Female Dominion*, p. 135.

CHAPTER 6

1. Anna Garlin Spencer, "Reasons Why the National Council of Women of the United States Should Be Preserved," December 18, 1925, LWV Papers, part 3, series A, reel 12, frames 173–76.

2. Maud Wood Park, "Organized Women and Their Program," an unpublished submission to the *Dearborn Independent*, accompanying Maud Wood Park to W. J. Cameron, April 26, 1924, LWV Papers, part 3, series A, reel 4, frames 750–60.

3. *What's What*, October 1926, pp. 1, 2, Nicholas Kelley Papers. See also Whitney, *La Follette, Socialism, Communism*.

4. Hermine Schwed, "How They Put It Over in Clubs," *The Truth about the Red Movement,* a publication of the Cleveland *Iron Trade Review,* Bailie Papers, box 1, folder—Pamphlets, DAR.

5. Dr. Anna Moon Randolph, *Parallels for Thinking Men and Women* (Newport News, Va.: Women's Constitutional League, 1926), Catt-LOC Papers, container 27. For another example of "dupe" language, see Whitney, *La Follette, Socialism, Communism,* p. 20.

6. Margaret C. Robinson, "The Responsibility of Being Led," *Dearborn Independent,* May 23, 1925; Margaret C. Robinson, "The Responsibility of Being Led," *Woman Patriot,* July 1, 1925, pp. 98–101. This speech was also reprinted in pamphlet form by the MPIL: Bailie Papers, box 1, folder—Publications, MPIL. See also Mrs. George Madden Martin, "American Women and Paternalism," *Atlantic Monthly* 133 (June 1924): 744–53.

7. John Edgerton, "Defend American Womanhood by Protecting Their Homes," speech before the Women's Industrial Conference, January 19, 1926, Mary Van Kleek Papers, box 71, folder 118, Sophia Smith Collection, Smith College.

8. "Are Women's Clubs 'Used' by Bolshevists?" *Dearborn Independent,* March 15, 1924, p. 2. See also Mrs. Lilla Day Monroe, "Big Business: The Great Magician," *Industry,* October 24, 1925: 1–7.

9. Cott, *The Grounding of Modern Feminism,* pp. 260, 113–14. Denise Riley makes a similar argument in *"Am I That Name?"* contending that one of the reasons for feminism's lack of continued success after World War I was the reluctance to categorize "woman" as a class. Class language became the domain of Marxism and fascism and was avoided by progressives because of its unpatriotic connotations.

10. Mrs. H. H. Amsden, "Political Dictatorship in Women's Clubs," Boston, Massachusetts Public Interests League, 1927, Bailie Papers, box 1, folder—Publications, MPIL.

11. "A Petition for the Rejection of the Phipps-Parker Bill (S. 2696, H.R. 7555) Proposing an Extension of the Maternity Act," *Congressional Record* (July 3, 1926), 69th Cong., 1st sess., 68:12933.

12. Mrs. George Madden Martin, "The American Woman and Representative Government," *Atlantic Monthly* 135 (March 1925): 363–71. See also the response of Ethel Smith, "Are We a Menace?" *Woman Citizen,* June 13, 1925, pp. 15, 24–25.

13. C. H. Mason to Walter O. Boswell, MID, November 16, 1926, RG 165, 10110-2592/2, NA; James Reeves to General Pershing, December 17, 1926, RG 165, 10314-593, NA; Lt. Col. William Graham to Walter Boswell, January 28, 1927, RG 165, 10314-593/4, NA.

14. Minutes of Executive Committee Meeting, January 6–9, 1926, p. 11, LWV Papers, part 1, reel 2, frame 231; Dwight Davis, Secretary of War to Miss Sherwin, May 17, 1927, LWV Papers, part 3, series A, reel 14, frame 951; Minutes of Executive Committee Meeting, June 22–24, 1926, p. 19–20, LWV Papers, part 1, reel 3, frames 472–73; D. E. Nolan to Major General Henry Allen, January 12, 1926, and enclosures, RG 165, 10314-556/63, NA.

15. Whitney, *La Follette, Socialism, Communism,* pp. 16–17; Minutes of the Board of Directors Meeting, May 2–3, 192?, pp. 9–10, LWV Papers, part 1, reel 4, frames 101–2.

16. Belle Sherwin to Marguerite Wells, February 11, 1927, LWV Papers, part 3,

series A, reel 9, frames 840–41; Marguerite Wells to Gladys Harrison, July 9, 1927, LWV Papers, part 3, series A, reel 9, frames 865–69; Minutes of the Board of Directors Meeting, January 19, 1927, p. 25, LWV Papers, part 1, reel 4, frame 26.

By the end of the year, executive secretary Gladys Harrison wrote, "According to our reports anything approaching direct charges against the League have just about dropped out of the speeches of the patrioteers. I think they have found it does not do to challenge us direct." Gladys Harrison to Marguerite Wells, November 10, 1927, LWV Papers, part 3, series A, reel 9, frames 882–83.

17. American Association of University Women, Proceedings of the Fifth National Convention, March 30–April 2, 1927, pp. 98–99.

18. Amsden, "Political Dictatorship in Women's Clubs." See also "Women Dictators versus Women Voters," *Woman Patriot,* September 1, 1925, pp. 133–34.

19. Martin, "American Women and Paternalism"; Randolph, *Parallels for Thinking Men and Women.*

20. "What Every Woman Should Know," Boston: MPIL, 1927, Bailie Papers, box 1, folder—Publications, MPIL; Margaret C. Robinson, "The Responsibility of Being Led," an address before the Women's Patriotic Conference on National Defense, February 10, 1927, Catt-LOC Papers, container 27, folder 5; Randolph, *Parallels for Thinking Men and Women.*

21. Evans, *Born for Liberty,* pp. 150, 168; Muncy, *Creating a Female Dominion,* pp. 40, 104; Cott, *The Grounding of Modern Feminism,* p. 94; Lemons, *The Woman Citizen,* p. 221.

22. Cott, *The Grounding of Modern Feminism,* pp. 248–49, 258; Lemons, *The Woman Citizen,* p. 123.

23. C. C. Ousley to Mrs. Arthur C. Watkins, September 19, 1922, Tilton Papers, box 9, folder 245; Scott, *The Southern Lady,* p. 208; Annie A. Halleck to Florence Kelley, April 17, 1924, Nicholas Kelley Papers. Membership numbers come from "Honors of Martyrdom," *New York Times,* July 20, 1927, p. 22.

24. Thomas D. Clark, "George Madden Martin," *Notable American Women, 1607–1950: A Biographical Dictionary* (Boston: Radcliffe College, 1971), pp. 502–4. Other members include Mrs. James Breckenridge Speed, Mrs. Thurston Ballard, Mrs. William Belknap, Mrs. Hoyt Gamble, Mrs. Henry Burnett, Mrs. Shackelford Miller, Mrs. Robert Judge, Mrs. Henry W. Blanc, and Margaret H. (Mrs. J. C.) Engelhard, president.

25. "'Clubs' Rights' Up as Women's Issue," *New York Times,* May 25, 1926, p. 20; "Clubwomen Facing Internal Struggle," *New York Times,* May 27, 1926, p. 25; "Clubwomen Assail Movies of Crime," *New York Times,* May 31, 1926, p. 2; "Louisville Women Win Club Aid Here," *New York Times,* October 17, 1926, p. 24; Mary (Mrs. John) Marshall to Hanford MacNider, February 1, 1927, MacNider Papers, box 2, folder—American Legion Auxiliary.

26. "Honors of Martyrdom," *New York Times,* July 20, 1927, p. 22; Amsden, "Political Dictatorship in Women's Clubs"; "Women's Clubs Ask Congress Inquiry," *New York Times,* May 30, 1928, p. 1; Lemons, *Woman Citizen,* pp. 147, 221.

27. Cott, *The Grounding of Modern Feminism,* pp. 255–57.

28. Eva Perry Moore to Amy Woods, April 21, 1924, WILPF Records, reel 40, frame 633; Eva Perry Moore to Amy Woods, April 21, 1924, ibid., frame 637; Amy

Woods to Eva Perry Moore, September 16, 1924, ibid., frame 638; Lucia Ames Mead to Hannah Clothier Hull, September 16, 1924, Hull Papers, NCW folder; Eva Perry Moore to Amy Woods, September 20, 1924, WILPF Records, reel 40, frame 640; Hannah Clothier Hull to Eva Perry Moore, November 16, 1924, Records of the National Council of Women of the United States, Inc., 1888–ca. 1970 (Ann Arbor, MI: University Microfilms, 1988), letters following Board of Directors Meeting, October 16–18, 1924 (hereafter NCW Records); Eva Perry Moore to Members of the Executive Committee, November 20, 1924, ibid.; Eva Perry Moore to Hannah Clothier Hull, December 6, 1924, WILPF Records, reel 40, frame 645; Jane Addams to Hannah Clothier Hull, December 10, 1924, Hull Papers; Hannah Clothier Hull to Eva Perry Moore, December 16, 1924, NCW Records; letters following Board of Directors Meeting, October 16–18, 1924, ibid.; Hannah Clothier Hull to Jane Addams, ca. December 16, 1924, Addams Papers, series 1, Swarthmore College Collection; Jane Addams to Hannah Clothier Hull, December 31, 1924, Hull Papers, NCW folder; Hannah Clothier Hull to Jane Addams, January 21, 1925, plus enclosures, Addams Papers; Alice Hamilton to Jane Addams, December 1924, Addams Papers; Foster, *Woman and the Warriors*, pp. 53–54.

The NCW clearly backed down when faced with an angry contingent of women's organizations in which antipacifist sentiment prevailed. Despite that, the organization's executive committee did try a feeble protest. In October 1924, the committee passed a resolution expressing its "disapproval and censure" of Haviland Lund for "promoting distrust" among member organizations and requested that the American Lovers of Music, of which she was a former vice-president, not send her as delegate to future NCW meetings. Executive Committee Meeting, October 16–18, 1924, NCW Records.

29. "New Attack Is Made by Women Critics on World Council," *New York Times*, May 3, 1925, pp. 1, 2; "Heated Discussion of League Foreseen for Quinquennial," *Washington Post*, May 3, 1925, p. 2; "U.S. Women Oppose Resolution Data as League Propaganda," *Washington Post*, May 4, 1925, p. 1; "Women Convene World Council," *New York Times*, May 5, 1925, p. 20; "Negro Singers Quit Women's Concert," *New York Times*, May 6, 1925, p. 5; "Quinquennial Tea Guests' Exclusion Disturbs Morale," *Washington Post*, May 7, 1925, p. 1; "Council of Women Lauded by Dr. Rowe," *Washington Post*, May 8, 1925, p. 5; "Threatens to Leave Council of Women," *New York Times*, May 9, 1925, p. 3; "World Peace Issue Threatens Discord in Women's Council," *Washington Post*, May 9, 1925, p. 1; "Women Urge Study of Home in College," *New York Times*, May 12, 1925, p. 3; *New York Times*, May 13, 1925, p. 3; "Defends Loyalty of World Council," *New York Times*, May 14, 1925, p. 3.

The NPC was founded in 1924 by Potts, who also presided over the D.C. branch of the Daughters of 1812. She became a public figure when she interrupted the 1924 convention of the WILPF, questioning whether the women attendees upheld the U.S. Constitution. The NPC never numbered over 200 but included representatives of the Woman Patriots, the Sentinels of the Republic, the American Legion, the DAR, and several military officials, including Brigadier-General Amos Fries of the War Department. Potts always went by the name Mrs. Noble Newport Potts. I thank Francesca Morgan for helping me find her first name.

Hapgood, *Professional Patriots*, pp. 167–68; Gibbs, *The DAR*, p. 107; "Patriotic Societies Cooperate," *Woman Patriot*, July 15, 1924, pp. 7–8; "News Release," April 1924,

WILPF Records, reel 39, frame 44; "Patriotic Council Scores International," ibid., May 13, 1925, p. 3. Potts also testified in 1928 hearings before the House Naval Committee. See "Agreement in Sight on 15 Cruisers," *New York Times*, February 18, 1928, pp. 1, 3.

30. Lemons, *The Woman Citizen*, pp. 123–24; Strayer, *The D.A.R.*, p. 121; Gibbs, *The DAR*, pp. 108–12; Mrs. Anthony Wayne Cook to Ralph Easley, National Civic Federation, May 24, 1924, National Civic Federation Papers, New York Public Library, Rare Books and Manuscript Division, box 27, general correspondence files; Craig, "Red-baiting, Pacifism, and Free Speech."

31. Marion Parkhurst to Florence Kelley, August 7, 1927, Nicholas Kelley Papers.

32. Fred R. Marvin, *The Common Enemy*, n.d., Catt-LOC Papers, container 27, folder 6.

33. Peck, *Carrie Chapman Catt*, pp. 422–30; Van Voris, *Carrie Chapman Catt*, pp. 194–97; Strayer, *The D.A.R.*, pp. 134–35.

34. Carrie Chapman Catt to Jane Addams, May 26, 1927, Addams Papers, series 1, Swarthmore College Collection; Jane Addams to Carrie Chapman Catt, May 31, 1927, ibid.; Carrie Chapman Catt to Jane Addams, June 11, 1927, ibid.; Carrie Chapman Catt to Florence Kelley, May 27, 1927, Catt-LOC Papers; Carrie Chapman Catt to Florence Kelley, June 3, 1927, ibid.; Florence Kelley to Carrie Chapman Catt, June 4, 1927, NAWSA Papers, general correspondence—Florence Kelley.

35. Carrie Chapman Catt, "Lies-at-Large," *Woman Citizen*, June 1927, pp. 10–11, 41.

36. Carrie Chapman Catt, "An Open Letter to the DAR," *Woman Citizen*, July 1927, pp. 10–12, 41–42.

37. "Mrs. Catt Assails D.A.R. 'Red Hunt,'" *New York Times*, July 1, 1924, p. 24; "Says D.A.R. Literature Is Slander," *Des Moines Register*, July 3, 1927, p. 2L; "Mrs. Catt's Attacks," *Iowa Legionaire*, August 5, 1927, p. 5; Peck, *Carrie Chapman Catt*, p. 427; Van Voris, *Carrie Chapman Catt*, p. 194.

38. "Won't Reply to Mrs. Catt," *New York Times*, July 2, 1927, p. 21; "D.A.R. Head Answers Mrs. Catt's Criticism," *New York Times*, July 14, 1927, p. 14; "National Defense Work of DAR Upheld," *DAR Magazine* 61 (1927): 576.

39. *Daily Data Sheet*, July 5, 1927; *National Bulletin of the Military Order of the World War*, typewritten copy in Park Papers, folder 231. See also *Daily Data Sheet*, July 7, 1927; July 12, 1927; July 27, 1927; and December 8, 1927.

40. Hermine Schwed, "The Strange Case of Mrs. Carrie Chapman Catt," August 1927, Bailie Papers, Catt folder. Schwed was also a periodic speaker for both the Better America Federation and the DAR. See Marguerite Wells to Gladys Harrison, November 7, 1927, and attachments, LWV Papers, part 3, series A, reel 9, frames 884–89.

41. "Hurting Their Own Cause," *New York Times*, July 24, 1927.

42. "Concerning the D.A.R.," *Woman Citizen*, August 1927, p. 20; Carrie Chapman Catt to Florence Kelley, September 2, 1927, Nicholas Kelley Papers.

43. Cook, *Eleanor Roosevelt*, p. 243; "With Our Readers," *Woman Citizen*, September 1927, p. 41.

44. Gibbs, *The DAR*, pp. 118–34; Strayer, *The D.A.R.*, pp. 135–44.

45. Bailie was married to William Bailie, a manufacturer who owned a willow and wicker goods store in Boston. Originally from Belfast, Ireland, William Bailie had been affiliated with the Socialist League in London. He contributed to journals and magazines, occasionally lectured upon economic subjects, and in 1906 published a

biography of Josiah Warren. William Bailie, *Who Was Who in America,* vol. 4 (Chicago: Marquis Who's Who, 1968), p. 48.

46. March 22, April 6, May 15, and May 26, 1927, diary entries, Bailie Papers.

47. Helen Tufts Bailie to Carrie Chapman Catt, December 21, 1927, Catt-LOC Papers. See also Catt's replies: Carrie Chapman Catt to Helen Tufts Bailie, December 29, 1927, ibid.; Carrie Chapman Catt to Helen Tufts Bailie, January 4, 1928 (but dated 1927), ibid. H. M. Haldeman was father of Watergate figure H. R. Haldeman.

48. Helen Tufts Bailie to Carrie Chapman Catt, January 9, 1928, Catt-LOC Papers; Helen Tufts Bailie to Jane Addams, February 19, 1928, WILPF Records; February 19, February 21, 1928, diary entries, Bailie Papers.

49. February 25, 1928, diary entry, Bailie Papers.

50. Grace L. Brosseau to Helen Tufts Bailie, February 20, 1928, Bailie Papers, box 2, folder—Correspondence, Brosseau; Helen Tufts Bailie to Mrs. Elliott, February 23, 1928, WILPF Records, series C, box 5; Jane Addams to Helen Tufts Bailie, May 9, 1928, Addams Papers, Sophia Smith Collection, Smith College; Helen Tufts Bailie to Carrie Chapman Catt, June 14, 1928, Catt-LOC Papers; Helen Tufts Bailie to Julia Lathrop, June 14, 1928, Lathrop Papers, folder—Correspondence 1928, January–June; Julia Lathrop to Josepha Whitney, June 24, 1928, ibid.; Julia Lathrop to Helen Tufts Bailie, June 24, 1928, ibid.; Helen Tufts Bailie to Julia Lathrop, June 27, 1928, ibid.; Eleanor St. Omer Roy to Mrs. Mattie Vaughn Boone, March 14, 1928, WILPF Records, reel 47, series C, box 8, folder 26; Eleanor St. Omer Roy to Mrs. Blanche O. Curtis, March 26, 1928, ibid.

51. March 11, 1928, diary entry, Bailie Papers.

52. Clippings in Bailie Papers, box 1, clippings folder; S. Ralph Harlow to Eleanor Roy, April 21, 1928, WILPF Records, reel 47, frames 917–18.

53. Helen Tufts Bailie, "Our Threatened Heritage," April 1928, enclosure in Nellie Fender to Jane Addams, May 2, 1928, Addams Papers, series 1, Swarthmore College Collection.

54. "D.A.R. Drops Mrs. Bailie, Accused of Injuring Good Name of Body in Black-list Charges," *New York Times,* June 23, 1928, p. 1. See also "Seeks Reinstating by D.A.R. Congress," *New York Times,* April 14, 1929, sec. 2, p. 4; "Mrs. Bailie Takes Case to Delegates," *New York Times,* April 14, 1929, p. 52; "Good Calls on D.A.R. to Uphold Law," *New York Times,* April 16, 1929, p. 4; "DAR Reaffirms Bailie Ouster," *New York Times,* April 17, 1929, p. 12; April 17, June 8, June 28, 1928, diary entries, Bailie Papers; "Bailie Is Expelled from Ranks of the DAR," *Boston Herald,* June 23, 1928; "Withhold Bailie 'Trial' Verdict," *Boston Herald,* June 22, 1928, p. 1; "My Appeal," April 15, 1929, Bailie Papers, box 1, folder—publications, HTB.

55. Eleanor St. Omer Roy to Mrs. Alfred J. Brosseau, February 24, 1928, WILPF Records, reel 47, series C, box 8, folder 26; Eleanor St. Omer Roy to Friends at the Molly Foster Berry DAR Chapter, March 2, 1928, ibid.; Eleanor St. Omer Roy to Friends at the Molly Foster Berry DAR Chapter, April 1928, ibid.; Eleanor St. Omer Roy to Mrs. Gertrude Shewell, March 13, 1928, ibid.; Mrs. Alfred J. Brosseau to Mrs. Roy, March 3, 1928, ibid.; Sadie F. Earle, Recording Secretary General, National Society DAR to Mrs. Eleanor St. Omer Roy, April 28, 1928, ibid.; Mrs. Alfred J. Brosseau to Mrs. Roy, June 6, 1928, ibid.; Eleanor St. Omer Roy to Mrs. Alfred J. Brosseau, June 9, 1928, ibid.

56. "Charges D.A.R. Heads Back Oil 'Whitewash,'" *New York Times,* April 4, 1928, p. 3; "Lists 28 Societies on DAR Blacklist," *New York Times,* September 30, 1928, sec. 2, p. 1; "DAR Expels Jersey Critic of Blacklist," *New York Times,* November 11, 1928, p. 1; *Boston Herald,* November 12, 1928, clipping in Park Papers, folder 250. MacFarland's pamphlets are *To Members of the Daughters of the American Revolution,* March 1928, Addams Papers, series 14, box 6, folder DAR, 1927–1928, Swarthmore College Collection; *Achray,* September 1928, ibid.

57. March 3, 1928, diary entry, Bailie Papers; H. Ralph Burton, "A Statement with Regard to the National Society, Daughters of the American Revolution, and Mrs. Helen Tufts Bailie," 1928, p. 5, State Historical Society of Wisconsin. See also "Denies He Supplied D.A.R. Blacklist," *New York Times,* April 10, 1928, p. 9.

In 1926, in a move indicating that Marvin may have had some sort of blacklist, the MID went to the *New York Commercial* for a list of over 200 organizations "directly or indirectly" connected with socialists and communists. Lt. Col. Mark Brooks to Lt. Col. Joseph A. Marmon, January 14, 1926, RG 165, 10110–2515/7.

58. Margaret C. Robinson, "Defends 'Blacklist,'" *Boston Herald,* March 18, 1928, clipping in Bailie Papers, box 1, clippings folder. See also Bailie, "Our Threatened Heritage"; Oswald Garrison Villard, "What the Blue Menace Means," *Harper's Magazine* 157 (October 1928): 538.

59. "D.A.R. Blacklist Was Born in Hub," *Boston Daily Advertiser,* April 5, 1928, pp. 4–5.

60. Though this never came up in discussion of the DAR blacklist, lists of undesirables were also compiled and released by the American Legion. Garland Powell of the American Legion's Americanism Commission told his colleagues in 1928, "I am perfectly willing to admit that the American Legion had what we called, not a blacklist, but a list of men who were revolutionaries." Pencak, *For God and for Country,* p. 11.

61. *Washington Post,* April 21 and April 22, 1928.

62. See "Whose Blacklist?" *Woman's Journal,* June 1928, p. 22; "The Blue Menace," *Nation* 126 (April 18, 1928): 422; "The D.A.R. Upholds the Black List," *Outlook* 149 (May 2, 1928): 14; "The 'Black List' Fight Goes On," *Outlook* 149 (July 1928): 369–70; "The D.A.R. Black List," *Outlook* 148 (April 18, 1928): 615; "The Dear Old D.A.R.," *New Republic* 55 (June 6, 1928): 64–66; Villard, "What the Blue Menace Means," pp. 529–40; "What Is behind the DAR Blacklists?" *Literary Digest* 97 (April 14, 1928): 1–2; "More Light on the D.A.R. Blacklists," *Literary Digest* 97 (April 21, 1928): 9; Edwin Mead, "The 'Daughters' and the Fathers," *Zion's Herald,* March 28, 1928, pp. 395–97.

For defenses of the DAR, see Margaret Cobb, "The Soviet of Lady Patriots," *American Mercury* 15 (September 1928): 94–102; "DAR Blacklist," *Iowa Legionaire,* April 20, 1928, p. 5.

63. "Sees Klan's Hand in D.A.R. Blacklist," *New York Times,* April 6, 1928, p. 20.

64. "The Blacklist Party," *Nation* 126 (May 23, 1928): 580–581; Eleanor Roy to *Nation,* May 8, 1928, WILPF Records, reel 47, frame 935; "Blacklist Party Invites Coolidge," *New York Times,* May 4, 1928, p. 30; "Blacklist Party Draws 1,000 Persons," *New York Times,* May 10, 1928, p. 30.

Mary Anderson, director of the Women's Bureau of the Department of Labor and a name on the blacklist, reported that a few weeks after the publicity surrounding the blacklists began, she met Brosseau at a Washington reception. A friend introduced

Anderson, saying, "Here are the ladies you think are subversive." Anderson wrote, "We were all most polite but Mrs. Brosseau was flustered." Mary Anderson and Mary N. Winslow, *Woman at Work*, p. 191.

65. Catt, "Open Letter to the DAR," p. 42; Bailie, "Our Threatened Heritage," p. 17; "D.A.R. Expels Jersey Critic," p. 1.

66. "Summary of Report of Special Committee," p. 2, WJCC Records, Library of Congress, reel 6, frames 248–60.

67. For various discussions of the fate of feminism in the 1920s, see O'Neill, *Everyone Was Brave;* Chafe, *The American Woman;* Lemons, *The Woman Citizen;* Freedman, "Separatism as Strategy"; Penn, "Discontented Black Feminists"; Joan M. Jensen, "All Pink Sisters"; Kessler-Harris, "Problems of Coalition-Building"; Cott, *The Grounding of Modern Feminism.*

CONCLUSION

1. "Rebels in Retirement," *Colliers,* January 25, 1925, pp. 17, 42; "Sweetened Reds and Rebels of Yesteryear," *Literary Digest,* January 31, 1925, pp. 36, 38, 40. These were major magazines. In 1920, *Colliers* and *Literary Digest* ranked sixth and seventh in national circulation; in 1930, they ranked sixth and eighth. Filene, *Americans and the Soviet Experiment,* p. 289.

2. For example, see Carrie Chapman Catt to Florence Kelley, September 2, 1927, Nicholas Kelley Papers; Carrie Chapman Catt to Jane Addams, June 11, 1927, Catt-LOC Papers, reel 2, frame 348; Florence Kelley to Jane Addams, July 20, 1927, Jane Addams Papers, Rockford College Archives; Dorothy Kenyon to Mary Garrett Hay, July 27, 1927, Park Papers, folder 231.

3. For a discussion of "facts" in the ERA debate, see DeHart and Matthews, *Sex, Gender.*

4. For samples of exposés, see Hapgood, *Professional Patriots;* Carrie Chapman Catt, "Poison Propaganda," *Woman Citizen,* May 31, 1924; Carrie Chapman Catt, "The Lie Factory," *Woman Citizen,* September 20, 1924; Carrie Chapman Catt, "Polluted Sources," *Woman Citizen,* October 4, 1924; "Three Super States," *Woman Citizen,* October 18, 1924; "The 'Red Menace,'" *Woman Citizen,* November 1, 1924; Carrie Chapman Catt, "Conspiracy or Slander," *Woman Citizen,* November 15, 1924; "Conspiracy vs. Conspiracy," *Woman Citizen,* November 29, 1924; Carrie Chapman Catt, "Much Ado about Nothing," *Woman Citizen,* May 30, 1925; Carrie Chapman Catt, "The Communist Question," *Woman Citizen,* January 1926; Leonard Cline, "Others Carry on War Department's Attack on Women," *New York World,* June 8, 1924, pp. 1, 10, 11; Leonard Cline, "'Spider-Web' Orator's Charges Aren't Supported by 'Informants,'" *New York World,* June 9, 1924, pp. 13, 14; Leonard Cline, "Army Fights Women's Societies because They're in War on War," *New York World,* June 10, 1924, p. 15; Leonard Cline, "The War on the Peace Seekers," *New Republic,* July 2, 1924, pp. 149–50; Leonard Cline, "The War on the Peace Seekers, II," *New Republic,* July 9, 1924, pp. 184–85; Will Irwin, "Patriotism That Pays," *Nation,* November 12, 1924, pp. 513–16; Sidney Howard, "Ralph Easley: Dean of the Prodigy," *New Republic,* August 20, 1924; "Patriotic Perils," *New Republic,* September 3, 1924; "Sweeping Up the Crumbs," *New Republic,* September 10, 1924; "The Patriots and the Peace Seekers," *New Republic,* September 17, 1924; "The New

Crusade," *New Republic*, September 24, 1924; "Bigger and Better Americans," *New Republic*, October 1, 1924; "Better Americans in California," *New Republic*, October 8, 1924; "The Constitution Worshippers," *New Republic*, October 15, 1924; Vance Armentrout, "The Red Brand," a series of articles originally from the Louisville *Courier-Journal*, March 24–31, 1929, WILPF Records, series A5, box 1, folder 4; Elizabeth McCausland, "The Blue Menace," a series of articles originally from the *Springfield Republican*, March 19–27, 1928, Hull Papers, attacks folder; Emily Greene Balch, *Statement of Facts Concerning the WIL in Regard to Certain Misrepresentations* (Washington, D.C.: WILPF, 1927), NAWSA Papers, General Correspondence—Emily Balch.

5. Diamond, *Not by Politics Alone*, p. 127.

6. Cott, *The Grounding of Modern Feminism*, p. 261. For additional information on the National Woman's Party, see Cott, "Feminist Politics in the 1920s," p. 62; Lunardini, *From Equal Suffrage;* Becker, *Origins.*

7. Kristi Anderson, *After Suffrage.*

8. Green, "From Antisuffragism to Anti-Communism"; Erickson, "'I Have Not Had One Fact Disproven.'"

Bibliography

PERSONAL MANUSCRIPT COLLECTIONS

Papers of Edith and Grace Abbott. University of Chicago, Department of Special Collections.

Jane Addams Papers. Ann Arbor, Michigan: University Microfilms International, 1985. Editor, Mary Lynn McCree Bryan.

Jane Addams Papers. Rockford College, Illinois. Rockford College Archives.

Mary Anderson. Papers of the Women's Trade Union League and Its Principal Leaders, Schlesinger Library, Radcliffe College, microfilm edition.

Helen Tufts Bailie Papers, 1896–1960. Sophia Smith Collection, Smith College.

Emily Green Balch Papers. Swarthmore College Peace Collection. Microfilm Edition.

Alice Stone Blackwell, Papers of the Blackwell Family. Library of Congress.

Dorothy Kirchwey Brown Papers, 1920–1956. Schlesinger Library, Radcliffe College.

Carrie Chapman Catt Papers, 1887–1947. New York Public Library.

The Papers of Carrie Chapman Catt. Library of Congress.

Elizabeth Gurley Flynn Collection, 1917–1923. State Historical Society of Wisconsin.

Amos A. Fries Papers, 1903–1952. University of Oregon, Special Collections.

Edith Fischel Gellhorn Papers, 1919–1960. Schlesinger Library, Radcliffe College.

Alice Hamilton Papers, 1909–1965. Schlesinger Library, Radcliffe College.

Hannah Clothier Hull Papers, 1889–1958. Swarthmore College Peace Collection. Microfilm edition: Scholarly Resources, Inc.

Rossiter Johnson Papers. Manuscripts and Archives Division. The New York Public Library. Astor, Lenox and Tilden Foundations.

Nicholas Kelley Papers. New York Public Library.

Paul Kellogg Papers. Social Welfare History Archives, University of Minnesota.

Julia Lathrop Papers. Rockford College.

Alexander Lincoln Papers, 1919–1940. Schlesinger Library, Radcliffe College.

Hanford MacNider Papers. Herbert Hoover Presidential Library.

Papers of Edwin D. and Lucia Ames Mead, 1876–1936, Swarthmore College Peace Collection, Scholarly Resources microfilm edition.

Maud Wood Park Papers, Papers in the Women's Rights Collection, 1870–1960, Schlesinger Library, Radcliffe College.

Elizabeth Lowell Putnam, 1887–1935. Schlesinger Library, Radcliffe College.

Margaret Dreier Robins Papers. Papers of the Women's Trade Union League and Its Principal Leaders, Schlesinger Library, Radcliffe College, microfilm edition.

Benjamin Lincoln Robinson Faculty File. Harvard University Archives.

Elizabeth (Hewes) Tilton Papers, 1914–1949. Schlesinger Library, Radcliffe College.

Alice Hay Wadsworth, Wadsworth Family Papers. Library of Congress.

Lillian Wald Papers. New York Public Library.

Everett P. Wheeler Papers, 1840–1925. New York Public Library.

ORGANIZATIONAL MANUSCRIPT COLLECTIONS

American Civil Liberties Union, Papers, 1912–1926. Princeton University Library. Microfilm edition, State Historical Society of Wisconsin.

Papers of the Boston Women's Trade Union League. Papers of the Women's Trade Union League and Its Principal Leaders, Schlesinger Library, Radcliffe College, microfilm edition.

Investigative Case Files of the Bureau of Investigation, 1908–1922. Record Ground 65, National Archives.

Records of the Children's Bureau. National Archives.

Daughters of the American Revolution Papers, 1909–1968. State Historical Society of Iowa.

General Federation of Women's Clubs Archives. Washington, D.C.

Iowa American Legion Correspondence, 1919–1963, State Historical Society of Iowa.

Iowa League of Women Voters. Iowa Women's Archives, University of Iowa.

Papers of the League of Women Voters, 1918–1974. Frederick, MD: University Publications of America, Inc. Part I: Minutes of the Board of Directors and the Executive Committees, 1918–1974; Part II: Transcripts and Records of National Conventions and of General Councils; Part III: Series A, National Office Subject Files, 1920–1932.

Papers of the National American Woman Suffrage Association. Library of Congress.

Papers of the National American Woman Suffrage Association. New York Public Library.

National Civic Federation Records, 1834–1949. New York Public Library.

Records of the National Consumers League, 1882–1973. Library of Congress.

Records of the National Council of Women of the United States, Inc., 1888–ca. 1970. Ann Arbor, Michigan: University Microfilms Incorporated, 1988. New York Public Library.

Records of the New York Women's Trade Union League. Papers of the Women's Trade Union League and Its Principal Leaders, Schlesinger Library, Radcliffe College, microfilm edition.

War Department General Staff, Military Intelligence Division, 1917–1941. Record Group 165, National Archives.

Records of the Women's International League for Peace and Freedom United States Section, 191–1959, Swarthmore College Peace Collection, Scholarly Resources microfilm edition.

Records of the Women's Joint Congressional Committee. Library of Congress.

Papers of the Women's Trade Union League. Papers of the Women's Trade Union League and Its Principal Leaders, Schlesinger Library, Radcliffe College, microfilm edition.

PRIMARY AND SECONDARY SOURCES

Abbott, Grace. *The Child and the State.* Chicago: University of Chicago Press, 1938.

Addams, Jane. *Twenty Years at Hull House.* New York: MacMillan, 1923.

———. *The Second Twenty Years at Hull House.* New York: Macmillan, 1930.

Allen, Frederick Lewis. *Only Yesterday: An Informal History of the Nineteen-Twenties.* New York: Harper and Row, 1931.

Alonso, Harriet Hyman. "Nobel Peace Laureates, Jane Addams and Emily Greene Balch: Two Women of the Women's International League for Peace and Freedom." *Journal of Women's History* 7 (Summer 1995): 6–26.

———. *Peace as a Women's Issue: A History of the U.S. Movement for World Peace and Women's Rights.* Syracuse, N.Y.: Syracuse University Press, 1993.

Anderson, Kristi. *After Suffrage: Women in Partisan and Electoral Politics before the New Deal.* Chicago: University of Chicago Press, 1997.

Anderson, Mary, and Mary N. Winslow. *Woman at Work: The Autobiography of Mary Anderson.* Minneapolis: University of Minnesota Press, 1951.

Anderson, Peggy. *The Daughters: An Unconventional Look at America's Fan Club—the DAR.* New York: St. Martin's Press, 1974.

Ariouat, Jacqueline Fellague. "The Dearborn Independent: A Mirror of the 1920s." *Michigan History* 80 (September/October 1996): 41–47.

Auslander, Leora. *Taste and Power: Furnishing Modern France.* Berkeley: University of California Press, 1996.

Baker, Paula. "The Domestication of Politics: Women and American Political Society, 1780–1920." *American Historical Review* 89 (June 1984): 620–47.

Barrett, James. "Americanization from the Bottom Up: Immigration and the Remaking of the Working Class in the United States, 1880–1930." *Journal of American History* 79 (December 1992): 996–1020.

Beatty, Jack. *The Rascal King: The Life and Times of James Michael Curley.* Reading, Mass.: Addison-Wesley Publishing, 1992.

Becker, Susan D. *The Origins of the Equal Rights Amendment: American Feminism between the Wars.* Westport, Conn.: Greenwood Press, 1981.

Bederman, Gail. *Manliness and Civilization: A Cultural History of Gender and Race in the United States, 1880–1917.* Chicago: University of Chicago Press, 1995.

Bell, Daniel, ed. *The New American Right.* New York: Criterion Books, 1955.

Bennett, David H. *The Party of Fear: From Nativist Movements to the New Right in American History.* New York: Vintage Books, 1988.

Bennett, Judith M. "Feminism and History." *Gender and History* 1 (Autumn 1989): 251–72.

Blee, Kathleen M. "Women in the 1920s' Ku Klux Klan Movement." *Feminist Studies* 17 (Spring 1991): 57–77.

———. *Women of the Klan: Racism and Gender in the 1920s.* Berkeley: University of California Press, 1991.

Bonnett, Clarence E. *Employer's Associations in the United States.* New York: Macmillan, 1922.

Boris, Eileen. "What about the Working of the Working Mother?" *Journal of Women's History* 5 (Fall 1993): 104–9.

Boris, Eileen, and Peter Bargadlio. "The Transformation of Patriarchy: The Historic Role of the State." In *Families, Politics, and Public Policy: A Feminist Dialogue on Women and the State,* edited by Irene Diamond. New York: Longman Press, 1983.

Breckinridge, Sophonisba P. *Women in the Twentieth Century: A Study of Their Political, Social and Economic Activities.* New York: McGraw-Hill, 1933.

Brinkley, Alan. "The Problem of American Conservatism." *American Historical Review* 99 (April 1994): 409–29.

Brody, David. *Labor in Crisis: The Steel Strike of 1919.* Philadelphia: J. B. Lippincott, 1965.

Brown, Elsa Barkley. "Womanist Consciousness: Maggie Lena Walker and the Independent Order of Saint Luke." In *Unequal Sisters: A Multi-Cultural Reader in U.S. Women's History,* edited by Vicki L. Ruiz and Ellen Carol DuBois, pp. 268–83. New York: Routledge, 1994.

Brush, Lisa D. "Love, Toil, and Trouble: Motherhood and Feminist Politics." *Signs* 21 (Winter 1996): 429–43.

Buckingham, Peter H. *America Sees Red: Anti-Communism in America, 1870s to 1980s, a Guide to Issues and References.* Claremont, Calif.: Regina Books, 1988.

Burgchardt, Carl R. *Robert M. La Follette, Sr.: The Voice of Conscience.* New York: Greenwood Press, 1992.

Burton, Shirley J. "The Espionage and Sedition Acts of 1917 and 1918: Sectional Interpretations in the United States District Court of Illinois." *Illinois Historical Journal* 87 (Spring 1994): 41–50.

Bussey, Gertrude, and Margaret Tims. *Pioneers for Peace: Women's International League for Peace and Freedom, 1915–1965.* London: Women's International League for Peace and Freedom, British Section, 1980.

Cahn, Susan K. *Coming on Strong: Gender and Sexuality in Twentieth-Century Women's Sport.* Cambridge, Mass.: Harvard University Press, 1995.

Camhi, Jane Jerome. "Women against Women: American Anti-Suffragism, 1880–1920." Ph.D. diss., Tufts University, 1973.

———. *Women against Women: American Anti-Suffragism, 1880–1920.* Brooklyn, N.Y.: Carlson Publishing, 1994.

Campbell, Ballard C. *The Growth of American Government: Governance from the Cleveland Era to the Present.* Bloomington: Indiana University Press, 1995.

Cayleff, Susan E. *Babe: The Life and Legend of Babe Didrikson Zaharias.* Urbana: University of Illinois Press, 1995.

Chafe, William. *The American Woman: Her Changing Social, Economic and Politics Roles, 1920–1970.* New York: Oxford University Press, 1972.

———. "Women's History and Political History: Some Thoughts on Progressivism and the New Deal." In *Visible Women: New Essays on American Activism,* edited by

Nancy A. Hewitt and Suzanne Lebsock, pp. 101–18. Urbana: University of Illinois Press, 1993.

Chafetz, Janet Saltzman, and Anthony Gary Dworkin. "In the Face of Threat: Organized Antifeminism in Comparative Perspective." *Gender and Society* 1 (March 1987): 33–60.

Chambers, Clarke A. *Seedtime of Reform: American Social Service and Social Action, 1918–1933.* Minneapolis: University of Minnesota Press, 1963.

Chauncey, George. *Gay New York: Gender, Urban Culture, and the Making of the Gay Male World, 1890–1940.* New York: Basic Books, 1994.

Chepaitis, Joseph B. "The First Federal Social Welfare Measure: The Sheppard-Towner Maternity and Infancy Act, 1918–1932." Ph.D. diss., Georgetown University, 1968.

Chrislock, Carl H. *Watchdog of Loyalty: The Minnesota Commission of Public Safety during World War I.* St. Paul: Minnesota Historical Society, 1992.

Coben, Stanley. *A. Mitchell Palmer: Politician.* New York: Columbia University Press, 1963.

———. "A Study in Nativism: The American Red Scare of 1919–1920." *Political Science Quarterly* 79 (March 1964): 52–75.

Cook, Blanche Wiesen. "The Impact of Anti-Communism in American Life." *Science and Society* 53 (Winter 1989): 470–75.

———. *Eleanor Roosevelt.* Vol. 1. New York: Penguin Books, 1992.

Cook, Bonnie. "Antifeminists and Women's Liberation: A Case Study of a Paradox." *Women and Politics* 3 (Spring 1983): 21–38.

Copeland, Tom. *The Centralia Tragedy of 1919: Elmer Smith and the Wobblies.* Seattle: University of Washington Press, 1993.

Costin, Lela B. *Two Sisters for Social Justice: A Biography of Grace and Edith Abbott.* Urbana: University of Illinois Press, 1983.

Cott, Nancy. "Feminist Politics in the 1920s: The National Woman's Party." *Journal of American History* 71 (1984): 43–68.

———. *The Grounding of Modern Feminism.* New Haven, Conn.: Yale University Press, 1987.

———. "What's in a Name? The Limits of 'Social Feminism'; or, Expanding the Vocabulary of Women's History." *Journal of American History* 76 (December 1989): 809–29.

Craig, John M. "Redbaiting, Pacifism, and Free Speech: Lucia Ames Mead and Her 1926 Lecture Tour in Atlanta and the Southeast." *Georgia Historical Quarterly* 71 (Winter 1987): 601–22.

Cubberly, Ellwood. *Public Education in the United States.* Boston: Riverside Press, 1934.

Cumberland, William H. "The Davenport Socialists of 1920." *Annal of Iowa* 47 (Summer 1984): 451–74.

Curtis, Verna Posever, and Stanley Mallach. *Photography and Reform: Lewis Hine and the National Child Labor Committee.* Milwaukee, Wis.: Milwaukee Art Museum, 1984.

Daniels, Doris Groshen. *Always a Sister: The Feminism of Lillian D. Wald.* New York: Feminist Press, 1989.

Davis, Allen F. *American Heroine: The Life and Legend of Jane Addams.* New York: Oxford University Press, 1973.

Davis, David Brion, ed. *The Fear of Conspiracy: Images of Un-American Subversion from the Revolution to the Present.* Ithaca, N.Y.: Cornell University Press, 1971.

Dawley, Alan. *Struggles for Justice: Social Responsibility and the Liberal State.* Cambridge, Mass.: Belknap Press of Harvard, 1991.

DeBenedetti, Charles. *Origins of the Modern American Peace Movement, 1915–1929.* New York: Kto Press, 1978.

Degler, Carl. *At Odds: Women and the Family in America from the Revolution to the Present.* New York: Oxford University Press, 1980.

———. *In Search of Human Nature: The Decline and Revival of Darwinism in American Social Thought.* New York: Oxford University Press, 1991.

DeHart, Jane Sherron. "Gender on the Right: Meanings behind the Existential Scream." *Gender and History* 3 (Autumn 1991): 246–67.

DeHart, Jane Sherron, and Donald G. Matthews. *Sex, Gender, and the Politics of ERA.* New York: Oxford University Press, 1990.

D'Emilio, John, and Estelle B. Freedman. *Intimate Matters: A History of Sexuality in America.* New York: Perennial Library, 1989.

Diamond, Sara. *Not by Politics Alone: The Enduring Influence of the Christian Right.* New York: Guilford Press, 1998.

Douglas, Ann. *Terrible Honesty: Mongrel Manhattan in the 1920s.* New York: Farrar Straus Giroux, 1995.

Duffield, Marcus. *King Legion.* New York: Jonathan Cape and Harrison Smith, 1931.

Dumenil, Lynn. "'The Insatiable Maw of Bureaucracy': Antistatism and Education Reform in the 1920s." *Journal of American History* 77 (September 1990): 499–524.

———. *The Modern Temper: American Culture and Society in the 1920s.* New York: Hill and Wang, 1995.

Dunn, Charles W., and J. David Woodard. *American Conservatism from Burke to Bush: An Introduction.* Lanham, Md.: Madison Books, 1991.

Dye, Nancy Schrom. *As Equals and as Sisters: Feminism, the Labor Movement, and the Women's Trade Union League of New York.* Columbia: University of Missouri Press, 1980.

Early, Frances H. "Feminism, Peace, and Civil Liberties: Women's Role in the Origins of the World War I Civil Liberties Movement." *Women's Studies* 18 (1990): 99–115.

Edwards, John Carver. *Patriots in Pinstripe: Men of the National Security League.* Washington, D.C.: University Press of America, 1982.

Ellis, Mark. "J. Edgar Hoover and the 'Red Summer' of 1919." *Journal of American Studies* 28 (April 1994): 39–59.

Erickson, Christine. "'I Have Not Had One Fact Disproven': Elizabeth Dilling's Crusade against Communism." Unpublished paper.

Evans, Sara M. *Born for Liberty: A History of American Women.* New York: Basic Books, 1989.

Falk, Candace. *Love, Anarchy, and Emma Goldman: A Biography.* New Brunswick, N.J.: Rutgers University Press, 1990.

Faragher, John Mack. *Daniel Boone: The Life and Legend of an American Pioneer.* New York: Henry Holt, 1992.

Felsenthal, Carol. *Sweetheart of the Silent Majority: The Biography of Phyllis Schlafly.* Garden City, N.Y.: Doubleday, 1981.

Fernald, M. L. *Biographical Memoir of Benjamin Lincoln Robinson, 1864–1935.* Washington, D.C.: National Academy of Sciences, 1937.

Filene, Peter Gabriel. *Americans and the Soviet Experiment, 1917–1933.* Cambridge, Mass.: Harvard University Press, 1967.

———. "In Time of War." In *The American Man,* edited by Elizabeth H. Pleck and Joseph H. Pleck, pp. 321–35. Englewood Cliffs, N.J.: Prentice Hall, 1980.

Fine, Lisa M. "'Our Big Factory Family': Masculinity and Paternalism at the Reo Motor Car Company of Lansing, Michigan." *Labor History* 34 (Spring–Summer 1993): 274–91.

Foglesong, David S. *America's Secret War against Bolshevism: U.S. Intervention in the Russian Civil War, 1917–1920.* Chapel Hill: University of North Carolina Press, 1995.

Foster, Carrie A. *The Women and the Warriors: The U.S. Section of the Women's International League for Peace and Freedom, 1915–1946.* Syracuse, N.Y.: Syracuse University Press, 1995.

Foster, Catherine. *Women for All Seasons: The Story of the Women's International League for Peace and Freedom.* Athens: University of Georgia Press, 1989.

Fowler, Robert Booth. "The Feminist and Antifeminist Debate within Protestant Evangelicalism." *Women and Politics* 5 (Summer/Fall 1985): 7–39.

Frank, Dana. *Purchasing Power: Consumer Organizing, Gender, and the Seattle Labor Movement, 1919–1929.* New York: Cambridge University Press, 1994.

Fraser, Nancy. *Unruly Practices: Power, Discourse, and Gender in Contemporary Social Theory.* Minneapolis: University of Minnesota Press, 1989.

Fraser, Nancy, and Linda Gordon. "Contract versus Charity: Why Is There No Social Citizenship in the United States?" *Socialist Review* (1992): 45–67.

Freedman, Estelle. "Separatism as Strategy: Female Institution Building and American Feminism, 1870–1930." *Feminist Studies* 5 (Fall 1979): 512–29.

Friedheim, Robert L. *The Seattle General Strike.* Seattle: University of Washington Press, 1964.

Fuller, Raymond G. *Child Labor in Massachusetts.* Boston: Massachusetts Child Labor Committee, 1926.

Gibbs, Margaret. *The DAR.* New York: Holt, Rinehart and Winston, 1969.

Giddings, Paula. *When and Where I Enter: The Impact of Black Women on Race and Sex in America.* New York: Bantam Books, 1984.

Gilmore, Glenda. *Women and the Politics of White Supremacy in North Carolina, 1896–1920.* Chapel Hill: University of North Carolina Press, 1996.

Ginsburg, Faye D. *Contested Lives: The Abortion Debate in an American Community.* Berkeley: University of California Press, 1990.

Goldman, Ralph Morris. *The National Party Chairmen and Committees: Factionalism at the Top.* New York: M. E. Sharpe, 1990.

Goldmark, Josephine. *Impatient Crusader: Florence Kelley's Life Story.* Urbana: University Press of Illinois, 1953.

Goldstein, Robert Justin. *Political Repression in Modern America: From 1870 to the Present.* New York: Schenkman Publishing, 1978.

Gordon, Linda. *Woman's Body, Woman's Right: A Social History of Birth Control in America.* New York: Penguin Books, 1974.

————. *Heroes of Their Own Lives: The Politics and History of Family Violence.* New York: Penguin Books, 1988.

————. "Family Violence, Feminism, and Social Control." In *Women, the State, and Welfare,* edited by Linda Gordon, pp. 178–99. Madison: University of Wisconsin Press, 1990.

————. "Black and White Visions of Welfare: Women's Welfare Activism, 1890–1945." *Journal of American History* 78 (September 1991): 559–90.

————. *Pitied but Not Entitled: Single Mothers and the History of Welfare, 1890–1935.* New York: Free Press, 1994.

————. "Putting Children First: Women, Maternalism, and Welfare in the Early Twentieth Century." In *U.S. History as Women's History: New Feminist Essays,* edited by Linda Kerber, Alice Kessler-Harris, and Kathryn Kish Sklar, pp. 63–86. Chapel Hill: University of North Carolina Press, 1995.

Graham, Sara Hunter. *Woman Suffrage and the New Democracy.* New Haven, Conn.: Yale University Press, 1996.

Green, Elna C. *Southern Strategies: Southern Women and the Woman Suffrage Question.* Chapel Hill: University of North Carolina Press, 1997.

————. "From Antisuffragism to Anti-Communism: The Conservative Career of Ida M. Darden." *Journal of Southern History* 65 (May 1999): 287–316.

Griswold, Robert L. *Fatherhood in America: A History.* New York: Basic Books, 1993.

Gruber, Carol S. *Mars and Minerva: World War I and the Uses of Higher Learning in America.* Baton Rouge: Louisiana State University Press, 1975.

Hall, Jacquelyn Dowd. *Revolt against Chivalry: Jessie Daniel Ames and the Women's Campaign against Lynching.* New York: Columbia University Press, 1974.

Hanson, Ole. *Americanism versus Bolshevism.* New York: Doubleday, 1920.

Hapgood, Norman, ed. *Professional Patriots.* New York: Albert and Charles Boni, 1927.

Haraway, Donna. *Primate Visions: Gender, Race, and Nature in the World of Modern Science.* New York: Routledge, 1989.

Harper, Charles A. *Development of the Teachers College in the United States.* Bloomington, Ill.: McKnight and McKnight, 1935.

Hawley, Ellis W. *The Great War and the Search for a Modern Order: A History of the American People and Their Institutions, 1917–1933.* New York: St. Martin's Press, 1979.

Heale, M. J. *American Anticommunism: Combating the Enemy Within, 1830–1970.* Baltimore: Johns Hopkins University Press, 1990.

Hendricks, Luther V. *James Harvey Robinson: Teacher of History.* New York: King's Crown Press, 1946.

Hicks, John D. *Republican Ascendancy, 1923 to 1933.* New York: Harper and Row, 1960.

Higgenbotham, Evelyn Brooks. "In Politics to Stay: Black Women Leaders and Party Politics in the 1920s." In *Women, Politics, and Change,* edited by Louise A. Tilly and Patricia Gurin, pp. 199–220. New York: Russell Sage Foundation, 1990.

Higham, John. *Strangers in the Land: Patterns of American Nativism, 1860–1925.* Various editions. New Brunswick, N.J.: Rutgers University Press, 1955, 1988, 1994.

Himmelstein, Jerome L. *To the Right: The Transformation of American Conservatism.* Berkeley: University of California Press, 1990.

Hine, Darlene Clark. "The Housewives' League of Detroit: Black Women and Economic Nationalism." In *Visible Women: New Essays on American Activism,* edited by

Nancy A. Hewitt and Suzanne Lebsock, pp. 222–41. Urbana: University of Illinois Press, 1993.

Hine, Darlene Clark, and Kathleen Thompson. *A Shining Thread of Hope: The History of Black Women in America.* New York: Broadway Books, 1998.

Hixson, William B., Jr. *Search for the American Right Wing: An Analysis of the Social Science Record, 1955–1987.* Princeton, N.J.: Princeton University Press, 1992.

Hodgson, Godfrey. *The World Turned Upside Down: A History of the Conservative Ascendancy in America.* Boston: Houghton Mifflin, 1996.

Hofstadter, Richard. *The Paranoid Style in American Politics and Other Essays.* New York: Alfred A. Knopf, 1965.

Hornaday, William T. *The Lying Lure of Bolshevism.* New York: American Defense Society, 1919.

Hubbard, Benjamin. *Socialism, Feminism, and Suffragism: The Terrible Triplets.* Chicago: American Publishing, 1915.

Huthmacher, J. Joseph. *Massachusetts People and Politics, 1919–1933.* New York: Atheneum Press, 1969.

Jablonsky, Thomas James. "Duty, Nature, and Stability: The Female Anti-Suffragists in the United States, 1894–1920." Ph.D. diss., University of Southern California, 1978.

———. *The Home, Heaven, and Mother Party: Female Anti-Suffragists in the United States, 1868–1920.* Brooklyn, N.Y.: Carlson Publishing, 1994.

Jaffe, Julian J. *Crusade against Radicalism: New York during the Red Scare, 1914–1924.* Port Washington, N.Y.: Kennikat Press, 1972.

Jeansonne, Glen. *Women of the Far Right: The Mothers' Movement and World War II.* Chicago: University of Chicago Press, 1996.

Jensen, Joan M. *The Price of Vigilance.* Chicago: Rand McNally, 1968.

———. "All Pink Sisters: The War Department and the Feminist Movement in the 1920s." In *Decades of Discontent: The Women's Movement, 1920–1940,* edited by Lois Scarf and Joan M. Jensen. Boston: Northeastern University Press, 1983.

———. *Army Surveillance in America, 1775–1980.* New Haven, Conn.: Yale University Press, 1991.

Jensen, Kimberly. "Minerva on the Fields of Mars: American Women, Citizenship, and Military Service in the First World War." Ph.D. diss., University of Iowa, 1992.

Johnson, Donald. *The Challenge to American Freedoms: World War I and the Rise of the American Civil Liberties Union.* Louisville: University of Kentucky Press, 1963.

Kann, Mark E. *On the Man Question: Gender and Civic Virtue in America.* Philadelphia: Temple University Press, 1991.

Kazin, Michael. "The Grass-Roots Right: New Histories of U.S. Conservatism in the Twentieth-Century." *American Historical Review* 97 (February 1992): 136–55.

Kenneally, James. "The Opposition to Woman Suffrage in Massachusetts, 1868–1920." Ph.D. diss., Boston College, 1963.

———. "Women Divided: The Catholic Struggle for an Equal Rights Amendment, 1923–1945." *Catholic Historical Review* 75, no. 2 (1989): 249–63.

Kennedy, David M. *Over Here: The First World War and American Society.* New York: Oxford University Press, 1980.

Kennedy, Kathleen. *Disloyal Mothers and Scurrilous Citizens: Women and Subversion during World War I.* Bloomington: Indiana University Press, 1999.

Kent, Susan Kingsley. *Making Peace: The Reconstruction of Gender in Interwar Britain.* Princeton, N.J.: Princeton University Press, 1993.

Kerber, Linda K. *No Constitutional Right to Be Ladies: Women and the Obligations of Citizenship.* New York: Hill and Wang, 1998.

Kessler-Harris, Alice. "Problems of Coalition-Building: Women and Trade Unions in the 1920s." In *Women, Work and Protest: A Century of U.S. Women's Labor History,* edited by Ruth Milkman. Boston: Routledge and Kegan Paul, 1985.

Kirk, Russell. *The Conservative Mind from Burke to Santayana.* Chicago: Regnery Press, 1953.

Klatch, Rebecca. *Women of the New Right.* Philadelphia: Temple University Press, 1987.

Kornbluh, Felicia A. "The New Literature on Gender and the Welfare State: The U.S. Case." *Feminist Studies* 22 (Spring 1996): 171–97.

Kovel, Joel. *Red Hunting in the Promised Land: Anticommunism and the Making of America.* New York: Basic Books, 1994.

Koven, Seth, and Sonya Michel. "Womanly Duties: Maternalist Politics and the Origins of Welfare States in France, Germany, Great Britain, and the United States, 1880–1920." *American Historical Review* 95 (1990): 1076–108.

Kraditor, Aileen S. *The Ideas of the Woman Suffrage Movement, 1890–1920.* New York: W. W. Norton, 1981.

Lackie, Shirley A. *Elizabeth Bacon Custer and the Making of a Myth.* Oklahoma City: University of Oklahoma Press, 1993.

Ladd-Taylor, Molly. "Hull House Goes to Washington: Women and the Children's Bureau." In *Gender, Class, Race, and Reform in the Progressive Era,* edited by Noralee Frankel and Nancy Dye, pp. 110–26. Louisville: University Press of Kentucky, 1991.

———. "Federal Help for Mothers: The Rise and Fall of the Sheppard-Towner Act in the 1920s." In *Gendered Domains: Rethinking Public and Private in Women's History,* edited by Dorothy Helly and Susan Reverby, pp. 217–27. Ithaca, N.Y.: Cornell University Press, 1992.

———. "'My Work Came out of Agony and Grief': Mothers and the Making of the Sheppard-Towner Act." In *Mothers of a New World: Maternalist Politics and the Origins of Welfare States,* edited by Seth Koren and Sonya Michel, pp. 321–42. New York: Routledge Press, 1993.

———. "Toward Defining Maternalism in U.S. History." *Journal of Women's History* 5 (Fall 1993): 110–13.

———. *Mother-Work: Women, Child Welfare, and the State, 1890–1930.* Urbana: University of Illinois Press, 1994.

Landsman, Gail H. "The 'Other' as Political Symbol: Images of Indians in the Woman Suffrage Movement." *Ethnohistory* 39 (Summer 1992): 247–84.

Langum, David. *Crossing over the Line: Legislating Morality and the Mann Act.* Chicago: University of Chicago Press, 1994.

Lasch, Christopher. *The American Liberals and the Russian Revolution.* New York: Columbia University Press, 1962.

Lasser, Carol. "Party, Propriety, Politics and Woman Suffrage in the 1870s: National Developments and Ohio Perspectives." In *New Viewpoints in Women's History: Working Papers from the Schlesinger Library 50th Anniversary Conference,* edited by Susan Ware, pp. 134–57. Cambridge, Mass.: Schlesinger Library, 1994.

Layton, Edwin. "The Better America Federation: A Case Study of Superpatriotism." *Pacific Historical Review* 30 (May 1961): 137–47.

Lea, Arden J. "Cotton Textiles and the Federal Child Labor Act of 1916." *Labor History* 16 (Fall 1975): 485–94.

Lebsock, Suzanne. "Woman Suffrage and White Supremacy: A Virginia Case Study." In *Visible Women: New Essays on American Activism,* edited by Nancy A. Hewitt and Suzanne Lebsock, pp. 62–100. Urbana: University of Illinois Press, 1993.

Leed, Eric J. *No Man's Land: Combat and Identity in World War I.* New York: Cambridge University Press, 1979.

Leiren, Terje I. "Ole and the Reds: The 'Americanism' of Seattle Mayor Ole Hanson." *Norwegian-American Studies* 30 (1985): 75–95.

Lemons, Stanley. "Sheppard-Towner Act: Progressivism in the 1920s." *Journal of American History* 55 (March 1969): 776–86.

———. *The Woman Citizen: Social Feminism in the 1920s.* Urbana: University of Illinois Press, 1973.

Lescohier, Don D., and Elizabeth Brandeis. *History of Labor in the United States, 1896–1932.* Vol. 3. New York: Macmillan, 1935.

LeSueur, Meridel. *Crusaders: The Radical Legacy of Marian and Arthur LeSueur.* St. Paul: Minnesota Historical Society Press, 1984.

Leuchtenberg, William E. *The Perils of Prosperity, 1914–1932.* Chicago: University of Chicago Press, 1958.

Levin, Murray B. *Political Hysteria in America: The Democratic Capacity for Repression.* New York: Basic Books, 1971.

Levin, N. Gordon, Jr. *Woodrow Wilson and World Politics: America's Response to War and Revolution.* New York: Oxford University Press, 1968.

Lindenmeyer, Kriste. *"A Right to Childhood": The U.S. Children's Bureau and Child Welfare, 1912–1946.* Urbana: University of Illinois Press, 1997.

Link, Arthur S. "What Happened to the Progressive Movement in the 1920s?" *American Historical Review* 64 (July 1959): 833–51.

Luker, Kristin. *Abortion and the Politics of Motherhood.* Berkeley: University of California Press, 1984.

Lunardini, Christine A. *From Equal Suffrage to Equal Rights: Alice Paul and the National Woman's Party, 1910–1928.* New York: New York University Press, 1986.

McClelland, John, Jr. *Wobbly War: The Centralia Story.* Tacoma: Washington State Historical Society, 1987.

McDougall, William. *Is America Safe for Democracy?* New York: Charles Scribner's Sons, 1921.

McEnaney, Laura. "He-Men and Christian Mothers: The America First Movement and the Gendered Meanings of Patriotism and Isolationism." *Diplomatic History* 18 (Winter 1994): 47–57.

MacKay, Kenneth Campbell. *The Progressive Movement of 1924.* New York: Octagon Books, 1966.

MacLean, Nancy. "White Women and Klan Violence in the 1920s: Agency, Complicity and the Politics of Women's History." *Gender and History* 3 (Autumn 1991): 285–303.

———. *Behind the Mask of Chivalry: The Making of the Second Ku Klux Klan.* New York: Oxford University Press, 1993.

McMann, Carole R. *Birth Control Politics in the United States, 1916–1945.* Ithaca, N.Y.: Cornell University Press, 1994.

McMurry, Linda O. *To Keep the Waters Troubled: The Life of Ida B. Wells.* New York: Oxford University Press, 1998.

McQuade, Rev. Vincent A. *The American Catholic Attitude on Child Labor since 1891: A Study of the Formation and Development of a Catholic Attitude on a Specific Question.* Washington, D.C.: Catholic University of America, 1938.

Marshall, Susan. "In Defense of Separate Spheres: Class and Status Politics in the Antisuffrage Movement." *Social Forces* 65 (December 1986): 327–51.

———. "Keep Up on a Pedestal: Women against Feminism in Twentieth-Century America." In *Women: A Feminist Perspective,* 3rd ed., edited by Jo Freeman, pp. 568–81. Palo Alto, Calif.: Mayfield Publishing, 1989.

———. "Who Speaks for American Women? The Future of Antifeminism." *Annals of the American Academy of Political Science* 515 (May 1991): 50–62.

———. *Splintered Sisterhood: Gender and Class in the Campaign against Female Suffrage.* Madison: University of Wisconsin, 1997.

May, Elaine Tyler. *Homeward Bound: American Families in the Cold War Era.* New York: Basic Books, 1988.

May, Henry F. "Shifting Perspectives on the 1920's." *Mississippi Valley Historical Review* (December 1956): 405–27.

Michel, Sonya. "The Limits of Maternalism: Policies toward American Wage-Earning Mothers during the Progressive Era." In *Mothers of a New World: Maternalist Politics and the Origins of Welfare States,* edited by Seth Koven and Sonya Michel, pp. 277–320. New York: Routledge Press, 1993.

Michel, Sonya, and Robyn Rosen. "The Paradox of Maternalism: Elizabeth Lowell Putnam and the American Welfare State." *Gender and History* 4 (Autumn 1992): 364–86.

Mink, Gwendolyn. *The Wages of Motherhood: Inequality in the Welfare State, 1917–1942.* Ithaca, N.Y.: Cornell University Press, 1995.

Montgomery, David. "Nationalism, American Patriotism, and Class Consciousness among Immigrant Workers in the United States in the Epoch of World War I." In *"Struggle a Hard Battle": Essays on Working-Class Immigrants,* edited by Dirk Hoerder, pp. 327–51. DeKalb: Northern Illinois University Press, 1986.

———. *The Fall of the House of Labor: The Workplace, the State, and American Labor Activism, 1865–1925.* New York: Cambridge University Press, 1987.

———. "Thinking about American Workers in the 1920s." *International Labor and Working Class History* 32 (Fall 1987): 4–24.

Moore, Leonard J. "Good Old-Fashioned New Social History and the Twentieth-Century American Right." *Reviews in American History* 24 (1996): 555–73.

Morgan, Francesca. "'Regions Remote from Revolutionary Scenes': Regionalism, Nationalism, and the Iowa Daughters of the American Revolution, 1890–1930." *Annals of Iowa* 56 (Winter/Spring 1997): 46–79.

———. "'Home and Country': Women, Nation, and the Daughters of the American Revolution, 1890–1930." Ph.D. diss., Columbia University, 1998.

Morlan, Robert L. *Political Prairie Fire: The Nonpartisan League, 1915–1922.* Minneapolis: Minnesota Historical Society Press, 1955, 1985.

Morone, James A. *The Democratic Wish: Popular Participation and the Limits of American Government.* New York: Basic Books, 1990.

Mosse, George L. *Nationalism and Sexuality: Middle-Class Morality and Sexual Norms in Modern Europe.* Madison: University of Wisconsin Press, 1985.

Muncy, Robyn. *Creating a Female Dominion in American Reform, 1890–1935.* New York: Oxford University Press, 1991.

Munger, Frank J., and Richard F. Fenno, Jr. *National Politics and Federal Aid to Education.* Syracuse, N.Y.: Syracuse University Press, 1962.

Murphy, Paul L. "Sources and Nature of Intolerance in the 1920s." *Journal of American History* 51, no. 1 (1964): 60–76.

———. "Normalcy, Intolerance, and the American Character." *Virginia Quarterly Review* 40 (1964): 445–59.

———. *The Meaning of Freedom of Speech: First Amendment Freedoms from Wilson to FDR.* Westport, Conn.: Greenwood Publishing, 1972.

———. *World War I and the Origin of Civil Liberties in the United States.* New York: W. W. Norton, 1979.

Murray, Robert K. *Red Scare: A Study in National Hysteria, 1919–1920.* Minneapolis: University of Minnesota Press, 1955.

———. "Ole Hanson." *Dictionary of American Biography,* vol. 22, suppl. 2. New York: Charles Scribner's Sons, 1958.

Nash, George H. *The Conservative Intellectual Movement since 1945.* New York: Basic Books, 1976.

Neather, Andrew E. "Popular Republicanism, Americanism, and the Roots of Anti-Communism, 1890–1925." Ph.D. diss., Duke University, 1993.

Nielsen, Kim E. "'We Are All Leaguers by Our House': Women, Suffrage, and Red-Baiting in the National Nonpartisan League." *Journal of Women's History* 6 (Spring 1994): 31–50.

———. "The Security of the Nation: Anti-Radicalism and Gender in the Red Scare of 1918–1928." Ph.D. diss., University of Iowa, 1996.

———. "Dangerous Iowa Women: Pacifism, Patriotism, and the Woman-Citizen in Sioux City, 1920–1927." *Annals of Iowa* 56 (Winter/Spring 1997): 80–98.

Noggle, Burl. "The Twenties: A New Historiographical Frontier." *Journal of American History* 53 (1966): 299–314.

Norton, Mary Beth. *Founding Mothers and Fathers: Gendered Power and the Forming of American Society.* New York: Alfred A. Knopf, 1996.

Ocko, Stephanie. "Victoria Woodhull's Siege of New York." *American History Illustrated* 16 (1981): 32–37.

Odem, Mary. *Delinquent Daughters: Protecting and Policing Adolescent Female Sexuality in the United States, 1885–1920.* Chapel Hill: University of North Carolina, 1995.

O'Neill, William. *Everyone Was Brave: The Rise and Fall of Feminism in America.* Chicago: Quadrangle Books, 1969.

Parenti, Michael. *The Anti-Communist Impulse.* New York: Random House, 1969.

Parrish, Michael E. *Anxious Decades: American in Prosperity and Depression, 1920–1941.* New York: W. W. Norton, 1992.

Peck, Mary Gray. *Carrie Chapman Catt: A Biography.* New York: H. W. Wilson, 1944.

Peiss, Kathy. *Cheap Amusements: Working Women and Leisure in Turn-of-the-Century New York.* Philadelphia: Temple University Press, 1986.

Pencak, William. *For God and Country: The American Legion, 1919–1941.* Boston: Northeastern University Press, 1989.

Penn, Rosalyn Terborg. "Discontented Black Feminists: Prelude and Postscript to the Passage of the Nineteenth Amendment." In *Decades of Discontent: The Women's Movement, 1920–1940,* edited by Lois Scarf and Joan M. Jensen, pp. 261–78. Boston: Northeastern University Press, 1987.

Perlmann, Joel. *Ethnic Differences: Schooling and Social Structure among the Irish, Jews, and Blacks in an American City, 1880–1935.* New York: Cambridge University Press, 1988.

Petcheskey, Rosalind. "Antiabortion, Antifeminists, and the Rise of the New Right." *Feminist Studies* 7 (Summer 1981): 206–46.

Pohli, Carol Virginia. "Church Closets and Back Doors: A Feminist View of Moral Majority Women." *Feminist Studies* 9 (Fall 1983): 529–58.

Pounds, Diana. "Suffragists, Free Love, and the Woman Question." *Palimpsest* 72 (1991): 2–15.

Powers, Richard Gid. *Not without Honor: The History of American Anticommunism.* New York: Free Press, 1995.

Preston, William. *Aliens and Dissenters: Federal Suppression of Radicals, 1903–1933.* Cambridge, Mass.: Harvard University Press, 1963.

Quadagno, Jill. *The Color of Welfare: How Racism Undermined the War on Poverty.* New York: Oxford University Press, 1994.

Rapp, Rayna, and Ellen Ross, "The Twenties' Backlash: Compulsory Heterosexuality, the Consumer Family, and the Waning of Feminism." In *Class, Race, and Sex: The Dynamics of Control,* edited by Amy Swerdlow and Hanna Messinger, pp. 93–107. Boston: G. K. Hall, 1983.

Remele, Larry. "The North Dakota State Library Scandal of 1919." *North Dakota History* 44 (Winter 1977): 21–29.

Ribuffo, Leo P. "Why Is There So Much Conservatism in the United States and Why Do So Few Historians Know Anything about It?" *American Historical Review* 99 (April 1994): 438–49.

Riley, Denise. *"Am I That Name?" Feminism and the Category of 'Women' in History.* Minneapolis: University of Minnesota Press, 1988.

Roberts, Mary Louise. *Civilization without Sexes: Reconstructing Gender in Postwar France, 1917–1927.* Chicago: University of Chicago Press, 1994.

Roosevelt, Theodore. *The Works of Theodore Roosevelt.* Vol. 19. New York: Scribner's Sons, 1926.

Rosen, Robyn Lisa. "Federal Responsibility or Governmental Tyranny? The Reproductive Reform Impulse and the Welfare State, 1917–1940." Ph.D. diss., State University of New York–Binghamton, 1992.

Rosenberg, Rosalind. *Beyond Separate Spheres: Intellectual Roots of Modern Feminism.* New Haven, Conn.: Yale University Press, 1982.

Ross, William G. *Forging New Freedoms: Nativism, Education, and the Constitution, 1917–1927.* Lincoln: University of Nebraska Press, 1994.

Rossiter, Clinton. *Conservatism in America.* New York: Knopf, 1954, 1966, 1982.

Rouse, Jacqueline Anne, *Lugenia Burns Hope: Black Southern Reformer.* Athens: University of Georgia Press, 1989.

Rumer, Thomas A. *The American Legion: An Official History, 1919–1989.* New York: M. Evans, 1990.

Russell, Francis. *A City in Terror: 1919, the Boston Police Strike.* New York: Viking Press, 1975.

Schlesinger, Arthur M., Jr. *The Age of Roosevelt: The Crisis of the Old Order.* Boston: Houghton Mifflin, 1957.

Schott, Linda. "'Middle-of-the-Road' Activists: Carrie Chapman Catt and the National Committee on the Cause and Cure of War." *Peace and Change* 21 (January 1996): 1–21.

———. *Reconstructing Women's Thoughts: The Women's International League for Peace and Freedom before World War II.* Stanford, Calif.: Stanford University Press, 1997.

Scott, Anne Firor. *The Southern Lady: From Pedestal to Politics, 1830–1930.* Chicago: University of Chicago Press, 1970.

———. "On Seeing and Not Seeing: A Case of Historical Invisibility." *Journal of American History* 71 (June 1984): 7–21.

———. *Natural Allies: Women's Associations in American History.* Urbana: University of Illinois Press, 1991.

Scott, Anne Firor, and Andrew MacKay Scott. *One Half the People: The Fight for Woman Suffrage.* Urbana: University of Illinois Press, 1975.

Sherman, Richard B. "The Rejection of the Child Labor Amendment." *Mid-America* 45 (January 1963): 3–17.

Sicherman, Barbara. *Alice Hamilton: A Life In Letters.* Cambridge, Mass.: Harvard University Press, 1984.

Sims, Anastatia. "Beyond the Ballot: The Radical Vision of the Antisuffragists." In *Votes for Women! The Woman Suffrage Movement in Tennessee, the South, and the Nation,* edited by Marjorie Spruill Wheeler, pp. 105–28. Knoxville: University of Tennessee Press, 1995.

Sklar, Kathryn Kish. "The Historical Foundations of Women's Power in the Creation of the American Welfare State, 1830–1930." In *Mothers of a New World: Maternalist Politics and the Origins of Welfare States,* edited by Seth Koven and Sonya Michel, pp. 321–342. New York: Routledge Press, 1993.

———. *Florence Kelley and the Nation's Work: The Rise of Women's Political Culture, 1830–1900.* New Haven, Conn.: Yale University Press, 1995.

———. "Two Political Cultures in the Progressive Era: The National Consumers' League and the American Association for Labor Legislation." In *U.S. History as Women's History: New Feminist Essays,* edited by Linda Kerber, Alice Kessler-Harris, and Kathryn Kish Sklar, pp. 36–62. Chapel Hill: University of North Carolina Press, 1995.

Skocpol, Theda. *Protecting Soldiers and Mothers: The Political Origins of Social Policy in the United States.* Cambridge, Mass.: Harvard University Press, 1992.

Solomon, Barbara Miller. *In the Company of Educated Women: A History of Higher Education in America.* New Haven, Conn.: Yale University Press, 1985.

Stevenson, Louise L. "Women Anti-Suffragists in the 1915 Massachusetts Campaign." *New England Quarterly* 52, no. 1 (1979): 80–91.

Strayer, Martha. *The D.A.R.: An Informal History.* Washington, D.C.: Public Affairs Press, 1958.

Strong, Anna Louise. *I Change Worlds: The Remaking of an American.* 1935. Seattle: Seal Press, 1979.

Swerdlow, Amy. *Women Strike for Peace: Traditional Motherhood and Radical Politics in the 1960s.* Chicago: University of Chicago Press, 1993.

Taub, Nadine, and Elizabeth Schneider. "Perspectives on Women's Subordination and the Role of Law." In *The Politics of Law: A Progressive Critique,* edited by David Kairys, pp. 117–39. New York: Pantheon Books, 1982.

Testi, Arnaldo. "The Gender of Reform Politics: Theodore Roosevelt and the Culture of Masculinity." *Journal of American History* 81 (March 1995): 1509–33.

Thompson, Mildred I. *Ida B. Wells-Barnett: An Exploratory Study of an American Black Woman, 1893–1930.* Brooklyn, N.Y.: Carlson Publishing, 1990.

Thurner, Manuela. "'Better Citizens without the Ballot': American Anti-Suffrage Women and Their Rationale during the Progressive Era." *Journal of Women's History* 5 (Spring 1993): 33–60.

Tone, Andrea. *The Business of Benevolence: Industrial Paternalism in Progressive America.* Ithaca, N.Y.: Cornell University Press, 1997.

Trattner, William I. *Crusade for the Children: A History of the National Child Labor Committee and Child Labor Reform in America.* Chicago: Quadrangle Books, 1970.

Tuttle, William M. *Race Riot: Chicago in the Red Summer of 1919.* New York: Atheneum Press, 1970.

Tweton, D. Jerome. "The Anti-League Movement: The IVA." In *The North Dakota Political Tradition,* edited by Thomas E. Howard, pp. 93–122. Ames: Iowa State University Press, 1981.

Ullmann, Sharon. *Sex Seen: The Emergence of Modern Sexuality in America.* Berkeley: University of California Press, 1997.

Van Voris, Jacqueline. *Carrie Chapman Catt: A Public Life.* New York: City University Press, 1987.

Waller, Altina L. *Reverend Beecher and Mrs. Tilton: Sex and Class in Victorian America.* Amherst: University of Massachusetts Press, 1982.

Ward, Robert D. "Against the Tide: The Preparedness Movement of 1923–1924." *Military Affairs* 38 (April 1974): 59–61.

Ware, Susan. *Still Missing: Amelia Earhart and the Search for Modern Feminism.* New York: W. W. Norton, 1993.

Ware, Vron. *Beyond the Pale: White Women, Racism and History.* London: Verso Books, 1992.

Weigand, Kate. "The Red Menace, the Feminine Mystique, and the Ohio Un-American Activities Commission: Gender and Anti-Communism in Ohio, 1951–1954." *Journal of Women's History* 3 (Winter 1992): 70–94.

Wenger, Beth S. "Radical Politics in a Reactionary Age: The Unmaking of Rosika Schwimmer, 1914–1930." *Journal of Women's History* 2 (Fall 1990): 66–99.

Westbrook, Robert B. "Fighting for the American Family: Private Interests and Political Obligation in World War II." In *The Power of Culture: Critical Essays in American History,* edited by Richard Wightman Fox and T. J. Jackson Lears, pp. 194–221. Chicago: University of Chicago Press, 1993.

Wexler, Alice. *Emma Goldman in America.* Boston: Beacon Press, 1984.

White, Deborah Gray. "The Slippery Slope of Class in Black America: The National Council of Negro Women and the International Ladies' Auxiliary to the Brotherhood of Sleeping Car Porters." In *New Viewpoints in Women's History: Working Papers from the Schlesinger Library 50th Anniversary Conference,* edited by Susan Ware, pp. 180–95. Cambridge, Mass.: Schlesinger Library, 1994.

Whitney, Richard Merrill. *Peace at Any Old Price.* New York: Beckwith Press, 1923.

———. *La Follette, Socialism, Communism.* New York: Beckwith Press, 1924.

Wingo, Patricia Wesson. "Clayton R. Lusk: A Study of Patriotism in New York Politics, 1919–1923." Ph.D. diss., University of Georgia, 1966.

Yohn, Susan M. "Will the Real Conservative Please Stand Up? or, The Pitfalls Involved in Examining Ideological Sympathies: A Comment on Alan Brinkley's 'Problem of American Conservatism.'" *American Historical Review* 99 (April 1994): 430–37.

Young, Louise M. *In the Public Interest: The League of Women Voters, 1920–1970.* New York: Greenwood Press, 1989.

Zeiger, Susan. "Finding a Cure for War: Women's Politics and the Peace Movement in the 1920s." *Journal of Social History* 24 (Fall 1990): 69–86.

———. "She Didn't Raise Her Boy to Be a Slacker: Motherhood, Conscription, and the Culture of the First World War." *Feminist Studies* 22 (Spring 1996): 7–39.

Zelizer, Viviana A. *Pricing the Priceless Child: The Changing Social Value of Children.* New York: Basic Books, 1985.

Index